AIR POWER
and
Emerging Technologies

AIR POWER
and
Emerging Technologies

Edited by

Air Vice Marshal Anil Golani (Retd) | Group Captain Vijay Shankar Rana

Introduction by

Air Marshal Anil Chopra PVSM AVSM VM VSM (Retd)

Centre for Air Power Studies
New Delhi

in association with

KW Publishers Pvt Ltd
New Delhi

Second Reprint February 2024

The Centre for Air Power Studies is an independent, non-profit, academic research institution established in 2002 under a registered Trust to undertake and promote policy-related research, study and discussion on the trends and developments in defence and military issues, especially air power and the aerospace arena, for civil and military purposes. Its publications seek to expand and deepen the understanding of defence, military power, air power and aerospace issues without necessarily reflecting the views of any institution or individuals except those of the authors.

Centre for Air Power Studies
P-284, Arjan Path
Subroto Park
New Delhi 110010

Tele: (91-11) 25699131

E-mail: capsnetdroff@gmail.com
website: www.capsindia.org

ISBN 978-93-91490-97-3 Hardback
ISBN 978-93-94915-00-8 ebook

Published in India by Kalpana Shukla

KW Publishers Pvt Ltd
4676/21, First Floor, Ansari Road
Daryaganj, New Delhi 110002
Phone: +91 11 43528107
Marketing: kw@kwpub.in
Editorial: production@kwpub.in
Website: www.kwpub.in

Printed and bound in India

CENTRE FOR AIR POWER STUDIES

VISION

To be an independent centre of excellence on national security contributing informed and considered research and analyses on relevant issues.

MISSION

To encourage independent and informed research and analyses on issues of relevance to national security and to create a pool of domain experts to provide considered inputs to decision-makers. Also, to foster informed public debate and opinion on relevant issues and to engage with other think-tanks and stakeholders within India and abroad to provide an Indian perspective.

Contents

Introduction

By end of the 1960s, it had become clear that the one who controls aerospace will control planet earth. The United States and Soviet Union initially led the new aircraft and space associated technologies. Supersonic aircraft, long-range aerial missiles, aircraft agility and range, and precision weapons, all made air the great enabler of military power. As humans moved into space, some of the tasks performed earlier with aerial platforms, being the ultimate vantage point for Intelligence, Surveillance, and Reconnaissance (ISR), moved there. Space also enabled communications, navigation, and much more. But the thin line between the atmosphere and space is fast disappearing with many crafts routinely transiting between the two domains to take advantage of each.

In the changing geopolitical landscape, the world kept witnessing asymmetric threats and technological disruptions. The change was significant in air and space. *Air Power and Emerging Technologies* is a book meant to look at the existing aviation technologies and crystal gaze into the future. Predictions are invariably complex. A 15-year horizon is realistic, but a 30-50-year horizon is what air power dreams are made of.

Advances in technology are bringing about a revolution in military affairs for air power. Military aircraft now travel global distances. Aerial sensors and weapons have moved air combat hundreds of kilometres apart. Unlike in the past, there is no place to hide in the air now. The proliferation of Unmanned Aerial Systems (UAS) and even very cheap armed quad-copters have introduced asymmetric risks. Surface-based air defence weapons have become accurate and lethal, and can take on even small projectiles. With large ranges they can sanitise huge air defence bubbles. Directed Energy Weapons (DEWs), including high powered lasers and microwaves, are revolutionising the ways to handle threats. They also eliminate the need for a large inventory of costly weapons.

Networked sensors and weapons allow very quick decision-making and reaction, but they are susceptible to cross-domain cyber attack threats. Cyber tools have also been used to steal sensitive data and platform designs by some countries to bridge technology gaps. Data transfer across platforms and operations centres will be at 5G and faster rates. Telecom technologies and high-speed wireless data-links will be crucial. Supply chains of micro-chips will be important for higher serviceability and mission accomplishment. Stealth continues to be an expensive but desirable feature. Aircraft will require a greater power source for DEWs and the cockpits will become control centres with geospatial tools. The air and space domains will have to work in close unison, and more air forces are exercising control over both. With successes in hypersonic flight, the interest in space-planes has got revived.

The concepts of air supremacy or superiority have not been tested for long because most recent wars were in less contested conflict environments. With capability to perform all aerial tasks by unmanned platforms, the Manned Unmanned Teaming (MUMT) will become important for both aerial strike and area access denial missions. Machine Learning (ML) and Artificial Intelligence (AI) will allow this with much higher efficiency, and autonomy. Notwithstanding the high degree of autonomy, the aerial platforms on the design boards for the next four decades are still having a pilot in the cockpit, and are at best optionally manned. The warriors of the future will leap-frog wearing jet-packs.

The revolution in airframe design will include aerodynamic elastic wings, and self-healing structures and systems. Structural Health Monitoring (SHM), advanced materials to take on hypersonic flight forces, smart automation and block-chain technologies for logistics and maintenance, additive manufacturing (3D printing), are some of the areas of the future. The aircraft maintainability will increase with failure prediction and data-linked transmission, maintenance and repairs. Utilising the Internet of Things (IoT) to anticipate maintenance will help. Using robots for turn-around-servicing and major maintenance will ensure greater reliability and save time. Aircraft aero-engines will be much more efficient and reliable. Electric or hybrid propulsion will soon be a reality. There is big potential for beamed power propulsion. There is talk of aneutronic fusion for power systems with the potential for dramatic cost reductions by converting energy directly to electricity. There could even be a nuclear powered, large aircraft soon enough. The private sector start-ups will keep throwing up disruptive technologies that will impact air power employment. The best air power estimates come from a net assessment of relative numbers, technology and training. The Chinese approach has been not so much to win an air war, as to make the prospect of war too costly for the opponent through a shadow war. They have used their critical technology supply chains to make things difficult.

This book looks at the basic tenets of air power. Undoubtedly, the classic roles of air power will endure. Air superiority in time and space will be crucial for all kinds of air and surface operations. The means to achieve this will be technology driven. The space domain will see an exponential increase in platforms and applications. It will drive and influence all civil and military activities on the planet. It will be important to have space domain awareness, and for militaries to evolve concepts to match technologies or drive them.

Electronic Warfare (EW) will make a sizeable impact on situational awareness, command and control and weapon system degradation. EW systems and employment techniques will have to be contemporary and state-of-the-art. Aerial weapons are already seeing major technological changes in sensors, guidance technologies, and warhead design and lethality. Hypersonic weapons will alter the status quo. Some of the larger slow moving platforms like aircraft carriers and battleships will be severely threatened. Air defence weapons to neutralise these will have to evolve.

All newer technologies will need a relook at their employability and human resource development and training. Technologies come through years of research and funding. They remain guarded and cost huge sums to acquire. Often no one shares them. China has been investing heavily in all aerospace technologies, including stealth aircraft and aircraft carriers. It has two fifth-generation aircraft projects, large transport aircraft, amphibious aircraft, airborne early warning platforms, stealth bombers, a variety of helicopters and Unmanned Aerial Vehicles (UAVs), and civil airliner projects. Similarly, it is important for India to invest in aerial defence research and development. Alternatively, to take a collaborative approach.

This book looks at all this and much more. All the authors have great domain knowledge and years of experience in aerospace. It should make interesting reading for practitioners of air power, students and researchers of military aviation, and for technologists, strategists, and policy-makers.

Air Marshal **Anil Chopra**
Director-General
Centre for Air Power Studies

1. Air Power

Anil Golani

Introduction

The evolution of air power, a little over a century ago, has seen it transform from being an adjunct of land or maritime forces, to an inalienable instrument of military power. The increasing salience of the air or aerospace domain in all modern conflicts since the World Wars during the last century has only increased the investment, time and effort of all nations to ensure that their inherent security is not threatened through this domain. No modern nation can ensure the sanctity of its airspace and thereby its sovereignty without a credible air force. There is a lot that has changed in the last century in terms of technology and the usage of the aerospace domain, which has become increasingly contested and congested with the plethora of users and applications, making it more complex by the day. The application of air power as an instrument of national military power serves the twin purposes of coercion and deterrence. When employed in the offensive role, the destruction and the violence unleashed may at times be counter-productive to the gains that are sought to be achieved in the first place. The doctrinal precepts of air power, ascribed to Douhet, Trenchard and Mitchell, have stood the test of time. There have since been many theorists, from Colin Gray to John Warden and Philip Mellinger, the latter propounding the Ten Propositions Regarding Air Power. There is a need to examine the applicability of air power as an important tool for the nation in the Indian context.

Air Power: Capacity and Capability

Many diverse factors would determine the capacity required by a nation in terms of its air power resources. The size of the country, its geopolitics, threats, alliances, economy, quantum of airspace that needs to be defended and its role as a net security provider in the region are some of the factors that would determine its air power capacity. Capacity inherently would be platform-and technology-centric, apart from the nation's indigenous design, development and production capability to generate these resources nationally, within its boundaries. Strategic partnerships leading to transfer of technology, with production capacity to meet the nation's requirements, as well as export options should be the way ahead instead of series production, which is the model hitherto being used for fighter aircraft, radars and missiles. With the space domain merging seamlessly into the air domain, and air power transforming into aerospace power, the challenges and opportunities have only grown in the recent past. The threats have also morphed from the traditionally kinetic, counter-force to non-kinetic options that could paralyse the enemy's air power without the firing of a single shot. The capacity and capability of a nation's aerospace power, therefore, would have to be measured not only by the tangible assets that the nation has, but also by its human capital resource and its investment in research and development, leading to innovation and assimilation of cutting edge technologies.

Ten Propositions Regarding Air Power

The ten propositions regarding air power, as enumerated by Colonel Phillip S. Mellinger, United States Air Force (USAF), are as follows:[1]

1. Whoever controls the air generally controls the surface.
2. Air power is an inherently strategic force.
3. Air power is primarily an offensive weapon.
4. In essence, air power is targeting, targeting is intelligence, and intelligence is analysing the effects of air operations.
5. Air power produces physical and psychological shock by dominating the fourth dimension: time.
6. Air power can conduct parallel operations at all levels of war, simultaneously.
7. Precision air weapons have redefined the meaning of mass.
8. Air power's unique characteristics necessitate that it be controlled centrally by airmen.
9. Technology and air power are integrally and synergistically related.

10. Air power includes not only military assets, but an aerospace industry and commercial aviation.

Whoever Controls the Air Generally Controls the Surface

While this remains true to a large extent, there have been exceptions that have in the past demonstrated the frailty of air power with respect to the political objectives that were sought to have been accomplished with this all important military tool. Operation Allied Force by the North Atlantic Treaty Organisation (NATO) was conducted with the aim of preventing human rights abuses by Slobodan Milosevic in Serbia against the ethnic Albanians. The reluctance of the Allied forces to use ground troops due to a lack of unanimity and a lack of understanding of the ground realities led to a protracted air campaign which was forced to operate at medium levels due to the scattered and well camouflaged air defence weapon systems. This effort resulted in a lot of collateral damage and also enabled Milosevic to continue with his ethnic cleansing in the interim, the very objective against which the entire operation was launched. Though Milosevic capitulated and surrendered eventually, the most important lesson that could be learned from this campaign was that however capable air forces may have become, they can never be more effective than the strategy that they intend supporting.[2]

On October 7, 2001, the United States launched Operation Enduring Freedom, a joint and combined war against the Al Qaeda and Taliban, a little over three weeks after the World Trade Centre twin towers had been hit by a terror strike on September 11, 2001. The conflict was led by the United States, with an unprecedented international coalition to wipe out the terror infrastructure by destroying Al Qaeda's grip over the Taliban, disrupting its global operations and terror financing networks, and destroying the terrorist training camps. The campaign was led by air power, which was instrumental in waging the war, logistics, deployment of the International Security Assistance Force (ISAF) and eventually eliminating Osama bin Laden through Operation Neptune Spear. The Global War on Terror (GWOT) lasted almost two decades and ended abruptly with the United States pulling out of Afghanistan in August 2021, leading to the return of the Taliban, While the goalposts and strategy kept shifting during the two decades that the American and Allied forces were there, in the end, the jury is still out on whether air power was successful or effective in achieving what was set out to be done. The 1971 Indo-Pak War, leading to the liberation of Bangladesh, is a classic example of control of the air in the Eastern Theatre by the Indian Air Force (IAF) that enabled the surface forces to march on to Dacca, ensuring its capitulation.

While the requirement of control of the air is necessary and inescapable in a conventional conflict, it cannot be treated as an end in itself. When the belligerents indulge in unconventional or irregular warfare and remain intransigent, the effort and effects become questionable. This gets further compounded when the political will or objectives are not clearly defined as can be seen by the air campaigns in Operation Allied Force and Operation Enduring Freedom.

Air Power is an Inherently Strategic Force

With the advent of the third dimension, air power did not have to fight contact battles like the surface forces, thereby taking the fight deep into the enemy territory. With the advancement of technology, avionics and weapon systems, the ability of air power to operate 24×7, notwithstanding weather and terrain constraints, further strengthened its role as an inherently strategic force as compared to the surface forces. The utilisation and employment of air power, therefore, has to be planned and executed at the strategic level. Operation Desert Storm during the 1991 Gulf War demonstrated this, when the 100-hour air campaign decimated the centralised Iraqi air defence command and control system, forcing it to fight tactical battles and rendering it incapable of operating at the strategic level. The requirement of airlift, from force projection to humanitarian assistance has only magnified over the years. Due to its reach, speed and mobility, the soft power or non-kinetic utilisation of air power is more often than not the first responder in any Humanitarian Assistance and Disaster Relief (HADR) mission and its utilisation as a strategic force is often understated. This capability of the Indian Air Force has been amply demonstrated in the recent past, getting accolades from countries far and wide, and enabling it to become a net security provider in the region.

Air Power is Primarily an Offensive Weapon

While launching an offensive, surface forces talk in terms of ratios and numbers, which vary from 1:3 to 1:7, while carrying out attacks on targets ranging from the plains to the mountains. This is because the enemy in its own territory is well entrenched and fortified, close to its lines of communication, and the flanks from where the attacker is likely to emerge may be limited due to terrain or geography. This creates a feeling of invincibility in the mind of the defender. While this may be true to a large extent, wars cannot be won by defending one's territory. To win a war, it has to be taken to the enemy and this makes air power the instrument of choice. Air power is not constrained by corridors of attack, geography, terrain or weather and can emerge from space as well to surprise and shock the enemy. The advancement of technology, including stealth, electronic counter-measures and the advent of hypersonic weapons and capability, have made detection and interception difficult and complex, if not impossible. Unlike the defender on the ground, the defender in the air does not have any inherent advantage of taking cover with passive measures. Moreover, in an aerial campaign, the defender would need to spread his resources to cover all his Vital Areas (VAs) and Vital Points (VPs). Conversely, a fighter aircraft cannot dig in and be present 24×7 as a defender. The old adage that the bomber will always get through holds true even today. The bomber may be manned or unmanned, but the destruction of the target or the enemy in any conventional war can best be achieved by utilising air power as an offensive weapon. Pearl Harbour, the 1967 Arab Israeli War and Operation Desert Storm and the 1991 Gulf War have amply demonstrated the efficacy of air power as a decisive offensive weapon of choice. In any aerial conflict, the converse of force ratios as compared to the surface forces holds true, as the defenders have to be available in larger numbers to thwart any aerial attack. The Balakot strikes by the IAF carrying out punitive strikes on a non-military target, with no collateral damage, demonstrated the offensive capability of the IAF.

Air Power: Intelligence and Targeting

Air power theorists from Billy Mitchell to Douhet and John Warden have all advocated the importance and significance of selecting the correct targets or centres of gravity. Billy Mitchell considered the enemy's army to be the primary target, while John Warden proposed the enemy leadership as the centre of gravity. The results have been mixed, as can be seen from past conflicts: the capitulation of Slobodan Milosevic after a protracted air war, the fall of Saddam Hussein in Iraq, and the capture and assassination of Osama bin Laden in Pakistan. However, whether peace has returned to Iraq and Afghanistan after the fall of their leadership remains unanswered. As the study of air power and targeting progressed, the concept of Effects-Based Operations or EBOs came into being. This analysed the critical and crucial vulnerabilities of a target system which had to be neutralised with minimal effort and precision weapons, such that the entire system would collapse like a house of cards. For example, to make the Air Defence (AD) system of the enemy redundant, instead of neutralising all the sensors and the AD weapon systems, the AD network could be rendered ineffective by attacking the command and control system or the communication network. In order to conduct an EBO, careful study and analysis of the target system are essential which can only be done with detailed intelligence. Intelligence is crucial to targeting and, more importantly, intelligence especially geared towards air warfare. Accurate and timely intelligence is a strategic asset and it requires hours of painstaking effort and analysis during peace-time for it to be successful and decisive in the eventuality of a conflict. Post targeting, the efficacy of an air attack, conventionally carried out through Battle Damage Assessment or BDA has its limitations in modern warfare. The availability of precision weapons and the non-linear or intangible effects of an aerial strike that may take time to manifest into results have their own challenges. Intelligence, targeting and its effects are important cogs in the aerial warfare chain that cannot be ignored if the campaign has to succeed. Accurate intelligence would, in turn, lead to precision strikes, which, aided by precision weapons, would avoid collateral damage, thereby legitimising the use of force on targets of importance. The Osirak nuclear reactor strike, and the Balakot strikes are classic examples that underscore the importance of intelligence and targeting while using air power as the instrument of choice.

Air Power: Physical and Psychological Shock

As armies evolved and their mobility increased from cavalry to armoured formations, shock and awe became synonymous with mechanised formations. Physical shock is due to the concentration of firepower in a given time and space. Air power can produce physical shock by the amount of weapons that any modern fighter aircraft can drop, with precision, over a small area. A single Rafale can carry more than nine tonnes of payload. The speed with which modern air forces can deliver payload, thousands of miles away over an unsuspecting enemy can cause psychological shock, disrupting his Observe, Orient, Decide, Act (OODA) cycle, apart from the physical shock of weapons raining over him. The destruction of Carthage by the Romans took more than two decades while the destruction at Hiroshima by an American B-29 bomber dropping nuclear weapons took a couple of seconds only. This factor of time causes tremendous psychological shock, apart from the physical destruction, which may take decades to fade or recover from. For any protracted war or conflict like guerrilla warfare, fought against an asymmetrical enemy, the effects of air power may be counter-productive, as happened during the Vietnam War. The physical and psychological shock caused by aerial warfare in a compressed timeframe, therefore, has to be carefully planned and orchestrated. The attack on the Governor's House in Dacca on December 4, 1971, turned out to be the last straw that broke the camel's back causing physical and psychological shock, which prompted Pakistan to accept the instrument of surrender. Operation Neptune Spear, carried out by the US Navy Seals, because of its secrecy and the manner of its execution, could be termed as another fine example of physical and psychological shock for Al Qaeda and Pakistan.

Air Power and Parallel Operations

The ability of air power to conduct operations at the tactical, operational and strategic levels is intrinsic and unique. While armies fight counter-force battles based on numbers, air power is governed more by its capacity and capability, irrespective of the size of the force. Air forces may be termed as tactical or strategic; armies, however, are never referred to in these terms. The Indian Air Force has today evolved from being a tactical air force just after independence, to a widely acclaimed and acknowledged strategic air force. Air power can concurrently conduct battles across the entire spectrum of warfare and it does not have to disengage from one conflict to get into another. In addition, due to its speed and reach, it can conduct warfare across the length and breadth of countries and continents, simultaneously, when called upon to do so. Parallel operations can induce several crises in a country, making it difficult for it to respond. Command and control centres, industrial targets, communication networks, airfields and logistics nodes can all be targeted simultaneously, paralysing the enemy. Saturating the enemy with attacks on multiple fronts would make even the most resilient of forces capitulate against an onslaught which can only be inflicted by air power alone.

Importance of Precision Air Weapons

From the bombing raids carried out by the Allied forces over Germany during World War II to the present times, there has been a quantum change in the methodology and its implications. Earlier, hundreds of aircraft were required to drop thousands of tonnes of bombs over multiple raids to destroy a target system. With the advent of precision weapons, during the Vietnam War, these numbers reduced drastically. The 1991 Gulf War was the first war in which large scale use of precision weapons was made. It was also the first war which enabled people to view what was happening from their homes on television channels. These developments have had far-reaching implications on the manner in which aerial attacks are being carried out today. The air commander of today would be watched and judged by an increasingly penetrative media that moulds public opinion and any collateral damage would be detrimental for the nation, apart from his career. The importance of precision weapons, therefore, that minimise collateral damage and ensure that precise attacks are carried out, cannot be undermined in today's scenario. In fact, the quest for non-lethal weapons continues, because air power, by its very nature of being precise and discriminate, is ideally suited for the same. The use of air power in the offensive role requires careful and deliberate planning, with accurate intelligence, and the element of surprise in its execution. This has been facilitated today, with precision weapons, as was demonstrated during the Balakot strikes carried out by the IAF in February 2019.

Centralised Control of Air Power

There is no denying the fact that it takes years of training to hone the skills of a professional soldier, sailor or air warrior. Advancements in technology, battlespace management and communications have impacted the nature of warfare universally. The surface forces commander's immediate concern, however, is still with the fire that rages around him, because that is what is going to impinge upon his success or failure. The air force commander, on the other hand, has a broader and overall view of the entire theatre as his resources are engaged in the conflict across the theatre. Having been trained and equipped to fight the battle in parallel, simultaneously at all the levels of war, the air warrior is best suited to command the air power resources, which can be switched rapidly from one theatre to another, as the conflict unfolds, depending upon the requirement. If these resources were to be carved out to different surface forces commanders, it would be virtually impossible to shift or reallocate them for the emerging requirements of the conflict. Tough decisions regarding allocation of scarce air power resources can best be made by a commander who understands their utilisation and implications. Unity of command through a centralised control of air power is, therefore, non-negotiable and essential for any conflict to be successful.

Technology and Air Power

The impact of technology on air power is most profound, and pales in comparison to that over the surface forces. While the importance of the man behind the machine cannot be undermined in any duel, the advent of the aeroplane was facilitated by technology, which has since then been interminably linked with it. Soldiers even today are likely to get into situations that involve hand-to-hand contact warfare, as happened during the Kargil conflict. Air power, which saw its evolution as a result of technology, has been intrinsically linked to it and the advancements in metallurgy, stealth, avionics, weapon control and guidance systems, hypersonics, space, artificial intelligence and aerodynamics, etc. have only cemented the bond between technology and air power, where the latter cannot survive without the former. The effect of technology in the advancement of land power from machine guns to tanks, artillery and other autonomous systems pales in comparison to the aircraft, from the piston engine aircraft with guns to supersonic stealth fighters with long range standoff weapons to satellites in space. Advancements in technology invariably resulted in high costs for air power resources thereby forcing nations to reduce their inventory of aircraft, depending upon the threat and the economy of the respective nations. Modern aircraft, by virtue of their capability to undertake many roles simultaneously, have facilitated this reduction, leading to leaner and meaner forces the world over.

Air Power is All Encompassing

Like the earliest theorists of air power like Billy Mitchell, who advocated "air mindedness" as an essential prerequisite towards the growth of the air power of any nation, it is necessary to understand its implications. Mere collection of military aircraft does not constitute air power. Due to its capital and technology intensive attributes, traditionally, governments or states had to invest in the infrastructure to manufacture and sustain the aerospace industry. This industry is all encompassing, including airlines and cargo aircraft, aircraft operated by other users in the country, the industrial infrastructure to manufacture and the personnel trained to produce, maintain and sustain these assets. Unlike the soldiers qualified to operate land systems, skilled personnel in the aerospace industry can seamlessly move from the civil to the military domain with little training. Air power in its 'soft power' *avataar* has been instrumental in uniting the world and making it a global village. The important and often underacknowledged, non-kinetic employment of air power in HADR has played a very significant role in alleviating human suffering. Cargo aircraft have been used for bombing missions in the past and aircraft from the civil aviation industry could be requisitioned for military logistics as and when the need arose. The interdependence between the civil and military aviation sectors, in the form of radars and air traffic controllers, aircraft technicians, pilots and navigators is peculiar and specific to the air power domain. It would be a fallacy, therefore, to assume that air power comprises military aircraft only. With the advent of the space domain, the utilisation of which through satellites could again shift from military to non-military applications, this relationship has become even more symbiotic.

Conclusion

The growth of air power in the last century has changed the manner in which wars have been planned and waged. This very important third dimension of war, which had been synonymous with speed, precision, flexibility, physical and psychological shock, strategic effect, and offensive operations, has transcended to the fourth and fifth dimensions of space and cyber. The enduring precepts of air power as propounded by its earliest theorists hold true to a large extent even today. However, we must inculcate the knowledge and wisdom to continuously review and challenge them with the march of technology and circumstances, as applicable in the present context. The capability and the capacity to build upon this very important tool of military and national power will empower us with the ability to utilise it as the instrument of choice when the need arises. The utility of air power as an effective coercive and deterrent tool has been demonstrated time and again in the Indian scenario. The effort towards self-reliance in the aerospace domain and the use of air and space in the non-kinetic domain would only enhance India's standing in the region and the world community as a net security provider. Premeditated and carefully planned and calibrated employment of air power during the Kargil conflict and the Balakot strikes have debunked the myth that the use of air power is escalatory in nature. The expanded spectrum of conflict, regional challenges and inimical forces, all contribute in goading the nation to ensure that the capability and capacity of air power to deliver at the time is not found wanting.

Notes

1. Colonel Phillip S. Mellinger, "10 Propositions Regarding Air Power", USAF, School of Advanced Air Power Studies, Air Force History and Museums Programme, 1995, pp. 6-7. https://media.defense.gov/2010/May/25/2001330281/-1/-1/0/AFD-100525-026.pdf. Accessed on January 3, 2022.
2. Benjamin S. Lambeth, *Operation Allied Force: Lessons for the Future* (Santa Monica, CA: RAND Corporation, 2001). https://www.rand.org/pubs/research_briefs/RB75.html. Accessed on January 5, 2022.

2. Future Aircraft Technologies

Anil Chopra

The Balakot strikes by the Indian Air Force's (IAF) and the engagement that followed during the riposte by the Pakistan Air Force (PAF) on March 27, 2019, once again rekindled interest in fighter aircraft technologies and air combat capabilities. Combat aviation, which has become the most preferred means of the prosecution of war, has seen the fastest growth of technology. The aircraft's special features were agility (speed, manoeuvrability), accurate weapon delivery, capability to operate in all kind of weather and at night, and be secure from enemy air and surface threats. As technology grew, the pilot was not just flying the aircraft accurately and safely, but was also a weapon systems manager and operator. With the increase in the aircraft and systems performance, technological advances helped the pilot reduce the workload to be able to take on more tasks. After the advent of the jet age, the aviation community started classifying jet fighters by "generations". Today, most air forces operate fourth generation aircraft. There are a few fifth generation aircraft flying, and sixth generation aircraft are on the drawing boards, and technologies are evolving.

Evolving Trends in Aerial Combat

For long, combat requirements were driving the kind of technologies that were needed to be developed. In the last three decades, the technologies started evolving at an exponential rate and, in a way, started driving the air combat options. Also, space became the ultimate enabler for most forms of warfare and it greatly supported air operations. Dr. John Stillion conducted a detailed analysis of air-to-air combat, using a database of over 1,450 air-to-air victories in different conflicts, from 1965 to 2015.[1] He found that advanced sensors and weapons and other technologies had changed the air combat approach and concepts. The need for combat manoeuvring with high rates of turn may become less consequential. To attain air superiority in the future, airborne platforms will require sensors that can detect farther, aerial weapons with longer reach and ability to operate in an intense electronic warfare environment. Thus, stealth, integrated sensors, secure data-linked communications, and electronic warfare suites would be more important.

Aerospace Dominance

The one who controls air and space, will control all operations in the air, on surface and sub-surface. Space-based platforms will support Intelligence, Surveillance, and Reconnaissance (ISR) and provide both early warning and control. Air and space-based kinetic and Directed Energy Weapons (DEWs) will be used for all forms of offensive and defensive actions. Multi-domain operations require the system-of-systems approach to engineering and integration.[2] The US Air Force (USAF) is already conceptualising networks of integrated systems spread across multiple platforms. All major powers are investing in hypersonic platforms and weapons, cyber warfare capabilities, and Artificial Intelligence (AI) to increase operational capabilities to outdo their adversaries.

Next Generation Fighters

The future fighter aircraft will have to adapt to newer technologies for air-to-air capability, survivability in a contested, well defended environment, and yet deliver arsenal for effect-based results. They must have the flexibility to undertake mixed manned and unmanned missions, and simultaneously integrate with a host of data-linked sensors across domains and terra-firma. Intelligent usable data, without information overload, often termed "data-to-decision" (D2D)[3] capability will be crucial. This will greatly enhance situational awareness, operational reach and survivability. The aim is to have the capability to counter the next generation adversary platforms using electronic measures through own integrated next generation capabilities.

Typical design characteristics would include high data handling and processing capability, and processing over secure networks with high-bandwidth. AI will support multiple data assessment and high speed decision-making. The situational awareness will be greatly enhanced through advanced human and systems integration. Helmet-mounted or even eye-retina displays will endeavour to give the pilot and systems operator an all hemisphere picture, allowing more complete threat assessment and attack/response options.

The new aircraft will feature next generation avionics, more efficient thrust-vectoring engines with in-built super-cruise, advanced stealth features, conformal weapon bays with extended long-range weapons with a high degree of post-launch autonomy; greater use of lasers and other forms of DEWs; improved on-board power generation and capacity to support powerful electronic warfare systems and DEWs. All the systems will talk to each other. The aircraft will have a powerful health monitoring and diagnostics suite and self-healing options. At the design board stage itself, the airframe shaping, composite materials, emissions absorbing paints, engine inlets, and all emitters will support low Radar Cross-Section (RCS) over cross-section of all frequencies without trading any flight performance.

Plug-and-play interchangeable hardware will have appropriate software; 3D tools will be used for both design and manufacture processes. The sixth generation fighters would have self-healing structures, breakthroughs in propulsion, materials, power generation and weapon technology.

Large Platform Concept

The next generation fighter may be large, more like a bomber. Such aircraft will have a larger weapon and sensor real estate. Flexibility for sensors will increase detection capabilities. The ability to carry much bigger missiles with longer ranges and other heavy weapons will make the platform more potent. More power generation for lasers and DEWs makes sense. These aircraft will have greater range and on-station time. Stealth in large aircraft would be required for tankers, transports, and bombers. The new stealth bomber design could be used for the stealth tanker.

Long Range Missiles and Counters

Future aerial engagements will necessitate sensors with long range detection capability. The Raytheon AIM-120D, and the AIM-260 Joint Advanced Tactical Missile (JATM), Russian Novator K-100, Chinese PL-15, MBDA Meteor, and India's Astra Mk-2, are some of the modern missiles. High-energy laser weapon pods for fighters are being designed to protect from missiles. The US Air Force Research Laboratory (AFRL) is developing a fibre laser system called the Self-protect High Energy Laser Demonstrator, or SHiELD.[4] The system will be in a pod containing a laser weapon. There will be a beam controller for the crew. It could take on incoming missiles or even daze or burn the electronics of other airborne platforms. It would be a giant leap for directed energy systems and self-protection.

Unmanned Aerial Systems (UAS)

Drones and unmanned systems are already flying in large numbers and more action in these is unfolding. Dual use (optionally manned) aircraft are evolving. Unmanned American F-4s and F-16s aircraft have been tested. Other programmes include the French Mirage-2000, multi-nation nEUROn Unmanned Combat Aerial Vehicle (UCAV) demonstrator,[5] BAE 'Taranis'[6] of the UK, and the French and British joint Future Combat Air System.[7] UAS are operating from aircraft carriers. The Boeing MQ-25 become the first unmanned aircraft to refuel another aircraft.[8] Lockheed Martin has chosen the flying wing design for its next generation UCAV which will be used for both strike and refuelling roles. Boeing's design is based on its Phantom Ray stealth UAV demonstrator.[9] The USA's hypersonic SR-72 bomber is likely to be unmanned.[10] Autonomous delivery drones are already revolutionising military logistics. By the mid-2040s, it is envisaged that every aerial mission could be flown unmanned.

Drone Swarms and Counters

Aerial drones operating in mutual coordination, flying synchronously, and performing operational tasks have been repeatedly demonstrated, including by Indian manufacturers. Swarms of drones display collective intelligence and perform collective tasks. Even very small drones can cause devastating effect if armed with weapons, and flown as a large swarm. Very small drones are difficult to detect, and cannot be easily engaged using conventional weapons. The swarm could overwhelm the defences by numbers. Yet, drone swarms have some weaknesses and limitations. Well known drone counters include both "hard kill" and "soft kill" capabilities.[11] These could be small arms fire, electro-optical weapons such as lasers, data-link jamming, electronic or cyber attack, and directed energy weapons like microwaves. A drone swarm may also be engaged by a counter-drone swarm.

Evolving Future Weaponry

As part of its conventional "Prompt Global Strike and Long-Range Ballistic Missile" programme, the US is developing hypersonic weapons that would manoeuvre to improve accuracy or evade defences as they approach their targets.[12] Russian Defence Minister Sergei Shoigu announced[13] that the "Avangard hypersonic glide vehicle entered service on 27 December 2019". In August 2021, China launched a Long March rocket carrying a Hypersonic Glide Vehicle (HGV) into Low Earth Orbit (LEO), which will give China new capability.[14] Could it be a "Fractional Orbit Bombardment System?" Earlier China had showcased the Dongfeng-ZF/DF-17 HGV.[15] DEWs will be used in both offensive and defensive roles in the future. The US Air Force, along with Raytheon, is working on a mini-missile that an aircraft could use to shoot down incoming air-to-air and surface-to-air missiles as part of the Miniature Self-Defence Munition (MSDM) programme.[16] New turret systems are being designed to allow high-energy lasers to engage enemy aircraft and missiles above, below and behind the aircraft.[17]

Future Pilot Support Systems

Many new technologies have improved pilot endurance for long flights. On-board oxygen generation (OBOX) now obviates the need to have oxygen cylinders, and increases endurance. Smart drugs and hybrid supplements increase endurance, stamina, physical strength, and alertness levels, and regulate the sleep and waking hours—pilots could keep awake for days. Modified genes will convert fat into energy so as to last for long flights. A trans-dermal nutrient delivery system will provide just enough nourishment to keep the body going. The pilot's physical and mental state will be monitored by sensors to check overload, physiological stress and the same transmitted to the ground controller. Light-weight helmets with visor displays will provide integrated information from all sensors for weapon cueing and shoot command. Fire-resistant bullet-proof clothing is in use. Voice activated commands will be used for multiple aircraft functions.

Secure data-links aided commands will allow radio silence. Also evolving is information display directly on the contact lens. There would even be helmets with sensors that can generate telepathic signals. Next generation helmets will pick up vibrations from the skull and transmit sound directly into the head instead of using the traditional microphone-earpiece combine. To fit the body contours, flexible display screens would be of easy to bend synthetic material, other than glass. Bone conduction[18] technology can transmit sound through the bones of the skull, allowing audio content bypassing the inner ear.

Airframe Design Materials

The design of any aircraft takes into consideration many factors such as aerodynamic efficiency, flight safety, crew and passenger comfort, reliability, and reparability. The world has come a long way from using wood and fabric to build aircraft structures. Newer, lighter materials and structural designs are stronger, and yet have elasticity and tensile strength, and resistance to corrosion and wear and tear in extremes of flight and weather conditions. Each part of the aircraft has a different functional structural requirement. High strength-to-weight ratio is highly desirable, and this is more relevant in the direction of the likely applied load.

Most parts in the aircraft are now made of metal such as steel, aluminium, titanium and their alloys. Aluminium alloys have lower density and are better at corrosion resistance. Steel alloys have a greater tensile strength, as well as a higher elastic modulus.[19] Steel is used in landing gears because of the need for strength. Titanium is a lighter, yet strong and corrosion resistant metal. It is great for engine parts, including turbine blades, where heat resistant nickel-based super titanium alloys may be used.

There is a very high use of composite materials nowadays. They are also strong, light weight and have corrosion resistance. Composites are made using different materials with different structural properties. Fibres are used in a resin matrix. The fibre layout orientation in a specific direction before lamination gives strength and stiffness in the desired direction. Composites are divided into three main types. Polymer matrix composites, famously known as Fibre Reinforced Polymers (FRPs); natural fibre, carbon, glass are used as reinforcements for polymer-based resins; metal matrix composites, mostly used in the automobile industry, are made of fibre and silicon carbides; and the ceramic matrix composites are used in high temperature zones.

Boron reinforced epoxy composites started being used in American fighters such as the F-14, and F-15 in the 1970s.[20] Toughened carbon fibre epoxy could weigh nearly 15-22 per cent less and also be resistant to rusting. The Boeing 777 uses glass and carbon fibres in the wing to body fairings. India's own Tejas Light Combat Aircraft (LCA) uses Chlorofluorocarbon (CFC) material for up to 47 per cent of its frame, including in the doors and skin, wings, etc., one of the highest by any contemporary aircraft.[21] The LCA also uses glass and Kevlar composites. Similarly, India's Light Combat Helicopter (LCH) has carbon-glass rotor blades, Kevlar for large parts of the airframe structure, and glass and carbon at various other parts, including the tail rotor.

The wings comprise a critical part of the aircraft. They also have moving parts such as ailerons, flaps and slats which operate under high loads. The wings also house large quantities of fuel within the spars, skin and ribs. Mostly steel and aluminium alloys are used for the ribs, and composites for the wing skin and the control surfaces.

New materials are continuously being developed. Flexible aerofoil or flexfoil wings is a concept evolved by jointly by the National Aeronautics and Space Administration (NASA), the Air Force Research Laboratory (AFRL) and the US-based company FlexSys.[22] Essential to the concept is to be able to change the profile of the wing during flight by rotating the flexible edges. The traditional aircraft flaps are being replaced by a torsional wing surface that could make large twisting movements to alter the lift and drag for take-off and landing. The natural elasticity of aviation-grade materials is used. Actuators and sensors are used to create computed wing deformations. The wing does not require the traditional control surfaces. The wing literally operates like that of the birds. FlexSys has claimed that the gains could be 12 per cent in fuel efficiency, and also involve considerable noise reduction during the take-off and landing phases. Science and technology will ensure that aircraft materials will keep evolving further. However, due to stringent safety requirements, innovative technologies take a long time to get flight worthiness approvals.

Modern Airborne Radars

Modern airborne radars are mostly multi-mode. They have air-to-air features including look-up and look-down modes for detection and tracking. Air-to-ground operations include ground ranging, and mapping. For multi-mode operations, the radars use different (low, medium and high) Pulse Repetition Frequency (PRF) and different waveforms. The radar search mode involves fast sweeping beams covering a large volume of airspace ahead. In the tracking mode, the radar uses a narrow pencil beam in the target direction for increasing the probability of detection. The tracking could be for a single or multiple targets. Radars allow raid assessment. Fixed and rotary wing targets can be differentiated by analysing the doppler spectrum of the echoes. Even the returns from the jet engine compressors can be analysed to identify the target aircraft using the "micro-doppler" (m-D) effect. In addition to ground target ranging, the ground echo returns are used for ground mapping and terrain-following data and image. Airborne radars are also used for weather mapping. Radars assist in guiding aerial missiles, and in rendezvous for air refuelling. Modern radar pictures can be transmitted to buddy fighters that could attack in radar-silence mode. In a hostile environment, the radar should be able to defend against Electronic Counter-Measures (ECMs).

Then there are side looking Synthetic Aperture Radars (SARs). For this, a large antenna is mounted on the side wall of the aircraft. The radar beam is transmitted perpendicular to the flight line. The SAR simulates a real aperture by integrating the pulse echoes into a composite signal. The doppler effect due to the motion is compensated. The challenge for a designer is to manage so many modes with effectiveness within constraints of size and weight.

Earlier, radars had mechanically scanning antennae to sweep the beam sideways or in the vertical plane. Modern radars have an Active Electronically Scanned Array (AESA) controlled by high performance computer steering beams electronically, without moving the antenna. The antenna is made up of small solid-state Transmit/Receive (TR) modules. This architecture and technology allows multiple beams radiated at multiple frequencies simultaneously. This increases power, range, and flexibility, and makes them more resistant to jamming. The Americans were the first to have AESA radars. The AN/APG-77 on the F-22 Raptor; the AN/APG-80 on the F-16E/F Desert Falcon; and the AN/APG-81 on the F-35 Lightning II are all AESA radars. Many countries today make AESA radars, and these are now the baseline in all state-of-the-art combat aircraft. China's Chengdu J-20 reportedly uses the Type 1475 radar. Rafale has the RBE2-AESA, and the Elta EL/M-2052 is the interim radar for the Hindustan Aeronautics Limited's (HAL's) Tejas (LCA) till the Defence Research and Development Organisation's (DRDO's) Uttam AESA is developed. The electronic steering limit for a flat array is currently 120 degrees, but the same can be increased by part mechanical steering.

In order to reduce the size, weight, power and cost of AESA radars, small computer-controlled solid-state Transmit/Receive Modules (TRMs) are put together in an array, using the Multiple-Input Multiple-Output (MIMO) technology.[23] AESA brings beam forming and beam steering agility, thus, permitting better tracking of very fast supersonic cruise missiles and aircraft.[24] The antenna can also take on multiple tasks at the same time. Failure of a few TRMs, at worst, degrades the performance by a small amount. To avoid the spectrum congestion at lower microwave frequencies, many applications have moved beyond 20 GHz. Millimetre wave radars can give much better resolution because of ultra wide bandwidths, and lower ground clutter, and they also give the benefit of smaller size.[25] They are very effective even in dust and fog conditions, and can detect and identify ground targets such as vehicles. Radar components are nowadays 3D printed. Modern AESAs use Gallium Nitride, or GaN power transistors that are able to operate at higher power levels and higher frequencies, more efficiently.[26] GaN allows 15 per cent better thermal conductivity and efficiency than silicon substrates. There are also significant advancements in the materials used to manufacture polymer capacitors.

Infrared Search and Track

The Infrared Search and Track (IRST) systems detect and track objects by sensing infrared radiations emitted by aircraft and helicopters. Forward Looking Infrared (FLIR) systems are also IRST systems, albeit for search and situational awareness. Unlike radars, these systems are passive, and do not radiate, and, as such, don't expose own location. Since the system is dependent on energy emitted by the target, the detection range is not as high as that of a radar. These systems also face attenuation due to weather. The IRST systems first came on fighter aircraft in the 1960s. By the 1980s, the infrared sensor sensitivities improved, resulting in better angular resolution and larger detection ranges. For long, the MiG-29 has had the S-31E2 KOLS IRST on the nose.[27] It was claimed to be the world's first Optical Laser System (OLS).

Mostly, the sensors are mounted in a glass dome on top or below the nose for better front hemisphere coverage. The detection performance depends on many factors, such as the sensor sensitivity, clouds, target and own altitude, outside air temperature, etc. Infrared (IR) detection is better at high altitudes. Lower temperature at high altitude also increases temperature contrast for easier detection. A target using the afterburner also emits higher IR energy, and, thus, increases the detection range. Lack of very high accuracy of range at long distances for weapon firing solutions needs to be factored in or supplemented with other sensors. Alternatively, the weapon firing may be done at conservatively closer ranges.

Current technology typically allows detection ranges of as high as 100 km. It could have a laser rangefinder with around 40 km range. The Rafale has the Optronique secteur frontal IRST sensor located on top of the nose, next to the refuelling probe.[28] The Passive Infrared Airborne Track Equipment (PIRATE) is the FLIR/IRST on the Eurofighter Typhoon.[29] The more modern F-35 uses the AN/AAQ-37 Distributed Aperture System[30] (DAS) with around the aircraft coverage using six IR sensors. This also doubles as the missile approach warning system. The system is currently under an update. The Chinese J-20 and FC-31 also have the IRST, with 360 degree coverage. In the J-20 aircraft, the IRST is called the EORD-31. It remains conformal, and on an as required basis; it protrudes out upwards from the nose.[31] IRST systems are also operational on China's Chengdu J-10B, and Shenyang J-11/15/16. The Saab JAS 39 Gripen E/F has the Leonardo Skyward-G.[32] Most Russian aircraft of the Su-27/30/35 Flanker family, the Mikoyan MiG-31, and the Sukhoi Su-57 have the IRST. All American fighters since the Grumman F-14 Tomcat have had the IRST.

In all aircraft, the IRST is connected on the data sharing bus, and sensor data can be shared with other sensors on-board the aircraft or with external platforms or the ground control.

Northrop Grumman has developed an open architecture pod called the OpenPod (TM).[33] It is a sort of universal pod that allows changing, integrating or upgrading sensors on a military aircraft. It gives flexibility to match the sensors to the mission quickly. Any Litening family of the advanced targeting pod can be converted to an OpenPod(TM). The U.S. Air Force and Lockheed Martin have further evolved the Legion Pod. It could carry the IRST system, or other sensors, and all these would be data-linked with on-board systems.[34] The US Air Force is pushing to get the system for its F-15C/D Eagle and other jets.[35]

Aircraft Diagnostics and Repair

Aircraft airworthiness requirements are very stringent. Therefore, the aircraft and its parts and sub-assemblies are subjected to defect rectification, routine inspections, replacements, overhaul, and modifications and upgrades.

Aircraft health monitoring is a crucial activity. It is required to increase aircraft safety, efficiency, and operational effectiveness. Modern systems use real-time data from multiple sensors that are fully integrated. They are further connected to the fleet data bases trough plug-in devices or remote data-links such as wi-fi or satellite communications. The systems are combined with machine learning, Internet of Things (IoT)-enabled sensor technologies, and other sophisticated data processing systems.[36] They incorporate the fault diagnostics system, artificial intelligence, wireless sensor network, high-speed communication, etc. Technology will allow predictive maintenance solutions after automatically acquiring and analysing data from IoT-enabled aircraft health monitoring sensors.

Engine analysis is now being done in real-time. This allows instant data collection and evaluation for early corrective responses and actions. The IoT allows such processing. Similarly, the flight parameters are also continuously being analysed by on-board computers and could suggest alterations to the flight plan for shortening the flight time to the destination or for better fuel efficiency. Online real-time engine monitoring would reduce turnaround maintenance time, and improve the aircraft utilisation rate. It could, in the long run, reduce the 'life cycle cost', and profitability.

Fault diagnostics requires an information database and man-machine interface. Artificial Intelligence (AI) helps interpretation in real-time, and suggests repair solutions and timelines. AI also supports predictions. Modern techniques would result in reduction of maintenance, repair, and overhaul. In the future, data diagnostics could end unscheduled aircraft grounding. The maintenance programme and associated manuals could also become dynamic documents. With the emerging electric engines, diagnostics and repair will change further. Robots and drones are likely to play a greater role in maintenance in the future.[37] Camera and imaging systems equipped drones are greatly supporting aircraft/engine inspection, and, in turn, maintenance. Inspecting the airframe surface of large airliners for cracks or damage, or reaching into otherwise less accessible places, including engines, could be done by drones. There will be no need to open up the engine. Also it will reduce inspection time from hours to minutes for large planes, greatly saving time and man-hours. After detecting, the drones could also be used for surface and other repairs.

Interestingly, Soviet designer Andrei Tupolev had created crawl spaces on the wings of the aircraft ANT-20, in 1934, so that the technicians could go across, in flight, to make changes to engine settings.[38] Things have come a long way since then. Today, there are self-healing materials that react to a situation somewhat akin to the blood clotting or adrenaline rise in the human body, and repair the damaged areas.[39] With greater usage of composites, it is possible to use healing agents.[40] Self-healing is based on the biological structure and nanotechnology. A pocket of epoxy resin and a hardener could be installed near pre-assessed vulnerable parts of the aircraft airframe. At the time of damage, the contents of the pocket could be automatically or manually released to fix the crack or damaged portion, and at least allow a safe flight to some landing ground. Polymer materials are best suited for self-healing currently. Since aircraft wings, fins and control surfaces make extensive use of composites, they make better contenders for self-healing applications. Studies are also on for self-healing of engine parts, albeit that will be more complex. Exposed wires are now fixable in flight. Special dispensers could be strategically located near wire bundle nodes, and these could spray appropriate sealing chemicals.

Artificial Intelligence and Machine Learning Applications

Artificial Intelligence (AI) and Machine Learning (ML) in aviation can increase decision speed, efficiency, and safety, and reduce workload. The ability to collect, collate and store large amounts of data, combined with huge computing power, and supported by powerful algorithms and architectures have made AI and ML great tools. AI supports autonomous operations, and intelligent navigation and helps in high speed multi-tasking. It supports weapon selection and firing solutions. AI enhances flight safety. But there are issues that need resolving for greater AI usage.[41] These include ethical guidelines and accountability, robustness and safety, oversight mechanism, privacy and data governance and safety risk mitigation. While neural nets hold a lot of benefits, AI programmes do not always follow explicit programming, and can sometimes self-learn and behave in unexpected ways.

AI would help enhance multi-layer capabilities for handling many undefined combat situations in a hostile environment.[42] AI will allow rapid decision-making in a dynamic information dense or sparse environment, and, thus, hastening the OODA (Observe-Orient-Decide-Act) loop. AI also supports multiple aircraft/drone swarms and this has, to a significant extent, changed the mechanics of air combat.[43] AI will help the system take over many crew chores in intense combat engagements while they take on multiple adversaries, including keeping track of the evolving threat. Human-AI teaming is a reality now. AI will support integrated decision-making for fighter transport and helicopter operations and also for Airborne Warning and Control Systems (AWACS) and flight refuellers. It will support air traffic and radar controllers.

Robotics and Automation

Automation in the aviation industry has been going on for some time. Uninhabited aerial platforms have been flying for long. More and more optionally manned platforms are evolving. Even in commercial aircraft, many chores are being handled by computers. With advances in AI, more piloting tasks are being given to automated systems. In most airliners, the autopilot does around 90 per cent of the flying.[44] Mostly, the pilot has to only take-off and thereafter take charge when things go wrong. Automation has greatly reduced aircraft accidents. Actions are already on-hand to make more foolproof "autoland" systems. Technology will soon make it possible to have pilotless airliners, though the same may not go through because sceptical passengers are still not prepared for such a scenario. Till then, the pilot would remain in a supervisory role.

Robots in aviation are taking many seats, including those of the co-pilot, tester and inspector. Collaborative robots are bringing much-needed automation. Robots are also supporting aircraft manufacturers, albeit because of the low production scale, they are not as involved as in the automobile industry. Robots will maximise efficiency, reduce errors and greatly improve reliability and safety.[45] They will take over many house-keeping chores for passenger services handling at airports related to check-in, baggage handling; ground handling of aircraft; and aircraft maintenance tasks. Robots would handle multiple languages, and identify potential security risks. Wearable robots (exoskeletons) will improve physical performance and precision handling of employees and help them move and lift heavy loads or perform taxing work like riveting.[46] Robots have been performing cockpit control panel testing and reducing a few hours of human labour, including checking the switches, lights, and the LED brightness. Boeing is already testing the UR3 collaborative robot arm to perform the job of, and act as, a robotic co-pilot.[47] Sensors, processors, and specially created software combine to make the Aircrew Labour In-Cockpit Automation System (ALIAS).[48] The aim of such automation is to have the pilot performing at peak capacity. The reassignment of cockpit jobs would be required to increase the efficiency. ALIAS also ensures that the pilot is not bored or overtaxed. Another design goal is to reduce the training time of the pilot on new aircraft.

Jet Engine Technology

Very high engine rotation speeds and very high turbine temperatures when combined with high altitude, make an aircraft engine a very complex machine. Civil aerospace industry is primarily being influenced by environmental issues and the cost of operations. Top engine-makers are unveiling new technologies to cut Carbon Dioxide (CO2) emissions, and yet boost the performance of aircraft engines. The measure of an aircraft engine's efficiency is the Specific Fuel Consumption[49] (SFC) which is essentially the amount of fuel consumed for each unit of power output. Modern engines must have low SFC. The other critical issue is the need for lower discharged emissions and noise levels. Among the means to achieve these include improving fuel combustion efficiency and looking at possible electric and hybrid engines. As more and more unmanned aircraft or drones begin flying for air transportation within towns, engine noise levels will become a serious issue. Future engine technologies must support a reduced development cycle, evolve means to reduce engine weight, improve engine propulsive efficiency and better SFC, improve reliability and maintainability, and reduce life cycle costs.

The turbofan engine market is dominated by a handful of, mostly Western, players. With globalisation, air travel is increasing exponentially. Also much more cargo moves by air. The demand for aircraft engines is on the rise. Many large companies have large portfolios of engines for different uses. Pratt & Whitney, Rolls Royce, GE Aviation, and Safran are the leading engine manufacturers. Many large manufacturers have created joint ventures so as to get better access to different markets. The USA's GE joined up with Safran of France to create CFM International. Similarly Pratt & Whitney has combined with Germany's MTU Aero Engines, and Japan's Aero Engine Corporation to form International Aero Engines. Engine Alliance is a joint venture between GE and Pratt & Whitney. Honeywell Aerospace and some Russian and Chinese companies are also significant engine players. As per the report released by the global business data platform "Statista" in August 2021,[50] CFM International had 39 per cent market share of the commercial aircraft engines in 2020; Pratt & Whitney had 35 per cent; GE Aviation had 14 per cent; and Rolls Royce had 12 per cent.

Engine Technology Methodology

For some time now, gas turbine engine technologists have been working on measures such as increasing compressor pressure and engine bypass ratios to improve pressure recovery. One method was to improve the fan and nacelle performance. Capability to increase turbine inlet temperature would mean better energy recovery and more complete combustion. All this will be possible through better engine-airframe integration. New materials would be lighter and withstand higher temperatures. Better turbines machining would also reduce weight and blade balance. Computational Fluid Dynamics (CFD)[51] will support engine design. The carbon-fibre blades allowed developing high-bypass jet engines for efficient long-haul jets like the Boeing 777 to be certified and cleared with just two engines instead of four. Full computer controlled "smart engines" and use of magnetic bearings will also improve engine operations. Additive 3D manufacture will reduce production time and cost. It will also reduce maintenance time.

Greener Engine Approach

High efficiency turbines, better airframe engine design interface and other noise attenuation, advanced high speed turbine design, aggressive mid-turbine inter-duct; and even a low emission combustion chamber for next generation rotary-craft engine are being evolved. Ceramic Matrix Composites (CMCs),[52] are much lighter than steel and yet can withstand very high temperatures, much higher than even the melting point of other metallic super-alloys, thus, improving the engine's thermal efficiency. 3D-printed components, hybrid-electric systems, advanced heat-transfer circuits are other breakthrough technologies.

Various other design considerations are being looked at. These include refined wing-body blending and ultra-high bypass turbofans. Unducted fans, or open rotor engines will deliver the speed and performance of a turbofan, and the fuel efficiency of a turboprop. Sustainable alternative fuels such as biofuels will reduce greenhouse gas emissions. Better interface with the airframe or location at alternative places may reduce noise both inside and outside the aircraft. Electrically powered aircraft will be much greener. Till now, the engine and airframe have been looked at as separate entities for the purpose of design. Evolving the aircraft design as a whole and taking into account the shaping of all aircraft surfaces, including controls and other protrusions, along with engine interface, would a better overall solution. More aircraft engines are being designed by using power from solar cell arrays and very efficient lithium polymer batteries. These could fly round the clock without the need for conventional fuel. NASA's Pathfinder[53] solar-electric-powered, remotely piloted aircraft is already a reality and under flight testing.

Engine Heat Recovery Concept

The heat energy at the engine exhaust normally goes waste. If the same is tapped, recovered and then converted into electric or mechanical energy, it would increase efficiency, save fuel, and, in turn, reduce emissions. If a heat exchanger could convert the heat recovered from the hot exhaust into electricity, that could be used to power on-board systems. This would also reduce emissions. The combustor chambers are being modified into heat exchangers. The excess heat is exchanged between the Combined Cycle Gas Turbine (CCGT) and Partitioned Combined Cycle Turbine (PCGT).[54] The multi-fuel hybrid engine is also evolving. It would involve the use of more than one type of fuel. This hybrid engine would have much less climate impact.

ADVENT, AETD and ACE Technologies

Many engine technology development programmes are being run by the major manufacturers. There are three programmes of significance: GE's Adaptive Cycle Engine[55] (ACE), the US Department of Defence's Adaptive Versatile Engine Technology (ADVENT) and the Adaptive Engine Technology Development (AETD). Unlike the traditional fixed airflow engine, the variable cycle engine is so programmed that it selects the high-thrust mode when maximum power is required, such as during take-off or fast acceleration, and high-efficiency mode during cruise for fuel savings and best range. GE's XA100, a fighter jet engine, adapts for fuel efficiency during long patrols and increased thrust in combat conditions. The AETD is expected to improve fuel efficiency, durability, and thrust performance. The ACE[56] is a variable cycle engine equipped with an extra bypass (3rd bypass) stream. The engine varies the bypass ratio and fan pressure ratio, thus, improving efficiency, and dissipates surplus heat. Typically, such an engine could increase thrust by 20 per cent, and improve fuel efficiency by 25 per cent. It would translate into extended radius of action.

Power Efficiency: GE9X Engine

As per the GE press release of September 2020, the GE9X engine had been certified[57] by the US Federal Aviation Administration (FAA), thus, clearing the way for it to power the new twin-engine Boeing 777X aircraft series. The engine is designed to achieve 10 per cent better SFC than the GE90-115B and 5 percent lower SFC than any other engine in its class. At 110,000 lbf (490 kN) rated thrust, it is less than the GE90-115, despite the very wide 134-inch-diameter front fan. However, it will be the company's most fuel-efficient engine. There is a significant use of Ceramic Matrix Composites (CMCs) in it.

Smart Engines

In the Full Authority Digital Engine Control (FADEC), a computer manages the aircraft ignition and engine control system to control all aspects of engine performance digitally. The engines are backed by significant computational power. These engines use data from various aircraft sensors such as engine temperatures and pressure, fuel flow, air density, and then act on pilot inputs, and automatically adjust engine settings to optimise performance. They ensure automatic engine protection against out-of-tolerance, prevent compressor surge or stall, and also monitor system redundancy to prevent failures. Smart engines do their own health monitoring till the component level, using the feedback loop. Modern engines use magnetic bearings that support a load using magnetic levitation, thus, the moving part makes no or little physical contact. This greatly eliminates friction and vibrations, and reduces mechanical wear and tear, and the need for lubrication.

Aircraft Electric Power and Propulsion

The future will see an increased use of electrical power for aircraft propulsion and various sub-systems. Hybrid-electric aircraft are already being developed. More electric-driven systems are being experimented with in modern aircraft and airliners. Ultimately, there may one day be all-electric aircraft. Such aircraft may be powered using renewable resources such as fuel cells. Powerful electric motors, more efficient power electronics and control systems, and newer battery systems for power generation will be required. Many of the current tasks being done using hydraulic fluids and compressed air to move control system actuators, etc. are being shifted to directly connected electric motors, thus, greatly freeing critical aircraft real estate and reducing weight. Redundancy and reliability are being in-built. This would require larger on-board power generation. Typically, the Boeing 787 produces around 1,000 kVA to operate many systems electrically. Modern aircraft batteries are smaller and lighter, and have much higher rating and longer uncharged life, thus, allowing higher on board power storage.

There could be various sources of power. It could be using a gas turbine. It could be hybrid where storage batteries alone are used for some phase of the flight. The aircraft propulsion itself could be from an electricity driven fan. The power requirement will be dictated by the phase of flight. It will be much higher during take-off and the initial climb, and much less during cruise. Electric aircraft will greatly reduce emissions.

Airbus and Rolls-Royce are working on a hybrid E-Fan X demonstrator. They are supported by Siemens. Initially, they plan to replace one of the four aircraft engines in the test aircraft by a 2MW electric motor. Boeing had begun greater use of electric power with the 787, which generates greater electricity, using six generators, with two on each engine and two on the Auxiliary Power Unit (APU). On the ground, the APU battery starts the APU generators, which start the APU to power the engine generators, which then start the engines. Boeing and JetBlue Airways Corp. have invested in a start-up to develop a small 10-seat electric-powered aircraft for short-haul flights. Hybrid planes carrying around 100 people could be flying commercially by 2029.[58] A 100-seat electric plane will be ready by 2027, according to the Los Angeles start-up Wright Electric.[59] "We expect to reach significantly higher energy densities of more than 400 Wh per kg and near 1,000 Wh/l, which is significantly more than what can be achieved today in lithium-ion cells," says Doug Campbell,[60] co-founder and Chief Executive Officer (CEO) of Solid Power, an industry-leading producer of all-solid-state batteries for electric vehicles.

Additive Manufacturing

GE Aviation, a leading jet engines manufacturer recently produced its 100,000th 3D printed fuel nozzle tip for its CFM International's Leading Edge Aviation Propulsion (LEAP) engine. Technologies are being upscaled and maintaining production quality. Maintenance, Repair and Overhaul (MRO) organisations will also benefit from the additive manufacturing revolution. Spares on demand will save from costly inventories of spare parts. However, the capital costs to set up such a capability still remain an issue.

Major Manufacturers

Pratt & Whitney's,[61] GTF engine, with its revolutionary geared fan technology, powers the Airbus A220, the Airbus A320neo family and Embraer E190-E2. The PW4000 series has replaced the JT9D engines on many airliners. It is certified for 180-minute Extended Twin Operations (ETOPS) when used in twinjets. The military aircraft engines by Pratt & Whitney include the F-15 Eagle (P&W F100), F-119 (F-22 Raptor), and F135 (F-35 Lightning II).

For long, GE had the CF6 engine for large jets. The GE90 has been used only on the Boeing 777. The GenX was developed next. The GE9X is the most powerful engine in the world as of now. The engine is already testing on the latest Boeing 777X. GE's F110 powers the F-16, and the F404 and F414 engines are on the F-18 variants. The F404 powers India's LCA 'Tejas', and the F414 will be used on the LCA Mk 2.

The GE90 that powers the Boeing 777 is the world's most powerful turbofan. GE has now successfully completed phase 1 testing on the second XA100 adaptive cycle engine.[62] Rolls-Royce is most known for the RB211 (high-bypass turbofans) and Trent series. The very powerful Rolls-Royce Trent 970s engines powered the initial Airbus A380. The AE 3007N,[63] a variant of the F137 turbofan engine, powers many American High Altitude, High Endurance (HALE) Unmanned Aerial Vehicles (UAVs). The RB-199 powered the Panavia Tornado. The Pegasus thrust vectoring engine variants were the primary power plant of the Harrier "Jump Jet" and its derivatives.

CFM International's very successful CFM56 series, derived from GE's CF6 and Snecma's M56, flew on many airliners. The LEAP[64] (Leading Edge Aviation Propulsion) engine entered service in 2016. The LEAP engines are much more fuel efficient than the CFM56. They are also less maintenance intensive and have lower life-cycle costs. LEAP engine variants are on the Airbus A320neo, Boeing 737 MAX, and COMAC C919. The latest CFM RISE (Revolutionary Innovation for Sustainable Engines) engines will incorporate the latest technologies and are slated to enter service around the mid-2030s. They would be hybrid electric, and use 100 percent sustainable aviation fuel, and hydrogen capability. Engine Alliance's GP7200 series engine powers an estimated 60 per cent of the Airbus A380. International Aero Engines' collaboration produced the V2500 which powers many airliners.

Honeywell Aerospace is also a significant manufacturer of aircraft engines and Auxiliary Power Units (APUs). The Honeywell/ITEC F124 series engines are used in military jets. The HTF7000 series are flying on business jets. International Turbine Engine Co. is a partnership between Honeywell and China's state-owned Industrial Development Corporation. The US-based Williams International makes small gas turbine engines for cruise missiles and for smaller jets. These are in the range of between 1,000 and 3,600 pounds of thrust.

Russia's Aviadvigatel manufactures aircraft engines. The PS-90 engines power the large Ilyushin and Tupolev aircraft. The new Aviadvigatel PD-14 engine will power the new Russian MS-21 airliner. Ukraine's Ivchenko-Progressis makes D-436 engine variants for many Antonov and Yakovlev aircraft, and also the Beriev Be-200. The Progress D-18T engines are on-board the very large Antonov An-124 and Antonov An-225. Russia's NPO Saturn engines include the Lyulka AL-31, Lyulka (Su-27 and J-10 fighters), and NPO Saturn AL-55 (HAL HJT-36 Sitara). Russia's Klimov manufactures the Klimov RD-33 (MiG 29, JF-17) turbofan engines. The multi-nation engine consortium EuroJet Turbo GmbH makes the EJ200 turbofan engine for the Eurofighter Typhoon.

For long, China was producing Russian engines under licensed production agreements. There were allegations of the Chinese reverse engineering some European and Russian turbofans. The WS-10, WS-13 and WS-15 are the indigenous Chinese turbofan engines. China's J-20 aircraft was initially powered with the Russian Saturn AL-31 variant. It was replaced with the Chinese WS-10 in 2019. The thrust vectoring WS-15 is planned to eventually power the J-20. India's Gas Turbine Research Establishment's (GTRE's) GTX-35VS Kaveri turbofan engine was to originally power the HAL LCA Tejas. The development of the same will now continue for the Advanced Medium Combat Aircraft (AMCA). The dry variant of the same may go on-board the "Ghatak" UCAV.

Evolution of Aircraft Cockpits

Closed cockpits began evolving around the mid-1920s. Perspex canopies came around 1933. Canopies soon started getting anti-reflective coating, and an internal heating element to melt ice. Except for some helicopters, the captain or pilot in command sits in the left seat. The pilot's control column or joystick is mostly located centrally. A few aircraft have a side-stick located on the right hand side. Some modern airliners have side-sticks for both crew members. Ergonomics and human factors decide the cockpit design, positioning and function of cockpit displays and controls. The aim is to support high situational awareness for the aircrew. Cockpits must support a cross-section of crew physical sizes, from low percentile female pilots to high percentile males. Piloting instrument locations have got universally refined, called the "Basic Six" (later the "Basic T") pattern to optimise pilot instrument scanning.

Modern Cockpit Concepts

The traditional "knobs and dials" have been replaced in modern cockpits by electronic displays, and are often referred to as glass cockpits. The display screens are reconfigurable for crew convenience and stage of flight. While some hard-wired switches are still there for safety, most traditional controls have been replaced by multi-function "soft keys". The stick and throttle now have many controls, and are termed the "Hands on Throttle and Stick" or HOTAS controls. They reduce the pilot's hand interactions at the critical stage of flight such as the combat and attack phases. The pilot could, thus, keep his attention on out of cockpit tasks. Modern cockpits also have the helmet mounted sighting system and the Direct Voice Input (DVI) to reduce the pilot's head-down work.

Over the years, the layout of control panels in modern airliners has almost got standardised. Selections for automatic flight controls such as the autopilot are normally placed for access during critical phases without having to look inside the cockpit. For better human-machine visual interface, all workstations are built around the user Design Eye Position (DEP). Similarly, for military aircraft, cockpit displays are appropriately angled so that displays can be seen without distortions. Pilots need to adjust the seat height to be at the DEP. This is yet another reason why rudder pedals are kept adjustable. Modern Head-Up Display (HUD) systems use a scanning laser to display images or videos on a transparent medium. Newer micro-display imaging technologies are evolving. Some airliners are even getting HUDs which help in reduced-visibility take-offs, and landings. Virtual Retinal Displays

(VRDs) are also being developed. Conventional looking glasses are used for retinal projection via a vertical-cavity surface-emitting laser.

Flight Instruments

Modern cockpits have electronic flight instruments. The main Multi-Function Display (MFD) is located centrally in front. It may also have a selection to engage or disengage both the autopilot and autothrottle in large aircraft. The Primary Flight Display (PFD) is usually located either centrally or on either side of the cockpit. It normally has both analogue and digitised presentation of important piloting parameters. The navigation display may be adjacent to the PFD. The Electronic Centralised Aircraft Monitor (ECAM) and the flight management system/control unit would also be upfront.

New Human-Machine Interface Technologies

A lot of research is going on for new cockpit Human-Machine Interface (HMI) technologies. The key areas are support to the crew for improving situational awareness, crew seniority gradient matrix and decision-making, workload sharing analysis, display designs and human interface, and automation failure states and management. Touchscreens allow direct interaction, and result in savings in the use of cockpit real-estate. Touchscreens too have positioning issues. They can cause elbow or eyesight fatigue. Effective touch-based interaction under conditions of turbulence or vibration could be of concern. There remains a need for an indirect device as a back-up. New input devices like the "Trackball", a ball held in a socket and rolled using the hand or fingers, have evolved. It has advantages over the computer mouse, in terms of great freedom of movement and actions. Touchpads are another possibility.

The Direct Voice Input (DVI) would open up many opportunities in future cockpits, and it will be possible to activate many cockpit tasks, but there are hurdles that need to be crossed. These include managing vocabulary and accent adaptation of a wide variety of people from different ethnic backgrounds. Suppressing background noise in a multi-speaker environment is also an issue.

The use of eyes out displays and appropriate symbology is considered to be a key enabler. Due to operational differences, the fixed-wing civil aircraft prefer the Head-Up Display (HUD) solutions, whereas the rotary-wing aircraft prefer the Head Mounted Display (HMD). These displays include both primary flight information and relevant operational symbols.

Current HUDs have a limited field of view, and require the pilot to maintain the head position within a very small zone near the DEP. This can be obviated to some extent by canopy displays and helmet mounted displays. Advanced displays would increase situational awareness and safety in reference to airborne obstacles and navigation hazards.

Cockpit Automation and Safety

Automation in modern cockpits supports many flight assist features. The automated flight path control will allow flights in much lower weather visibility conditions. Automation will support multiple systems monitoring and failure alerts and remedial pilot actions. Automation will also assist system health diagnostics. Automation will also relieve pilots from boring repetitive tasks and allow crucial parameter monitoring.

Automation also has its disadvantages. While a pilot may master the system monitoring role, his own flying skills may decline for want of regular control handling. This may require dedicated additional sorties or practice by disengaging selective automation. Automatic system disengagement due to a failure state may be missed by the aircrew and have adverse consequences. Attending to automation can distract the flight/crew pilots from monitoring the flight path. Short notice changes by the Air Traffic Controller (ATC) may require reprogramming and add intense workload. Diagnostic systems have limitations for dealing with multiple failures and there may be situations that may require deviations from pre-fed Standard Operating Procedures (SOPs). Unanticipated situations requiring manual override of automation can induce peaks of workload and stress. Data entry errors may have critical consequences, and need sufficient cross-checks. Uncommanded automatic disengagements or automation failure may add workload. Automation dependency, inadequate systems knowledge and lack of manual flying and aircraft management competence comprise a deadly combination. Automation failure may also take the aircraft to a flight state from where it will become more complex for the pilot to recover. Many pilots get so used to automation, that they may become reluctant to take over manually.

A 2013 report by the Federal Aviation Administration (FAA) found that more than 60 per cent of 26 accidents over a decade involved pilots making errors after automated systems abruptly shut down or behaved in unexpected ways.[65] The Air France Flight 447,[66] an Airbus A330, a scheduled international passenger flight from Rio de Janeiro to Paris on June 1, 2009, had a case of autopilot disengagement, probably because the pitot tubes had icing, and the aircraft transitioned to standby flight law. The auto-thrust of the engines also disengaged. The pilots took control manually, but were unable to manage the now complex situation that had got created by the automation cut-off. The sensitivity of controls had increased in the standby control laws. It led to a complex "error chain" that ended in a crash and the loss of 228 lives.

In another case, a Boeing 737 MAX flying the Lion Air Flight 610 from Jakarta to Pangkal Pinang on October 29, 2018, crashed into the Java Sea 13 minutes after take-off, killing all 189 on board. Investigations indicated serious flight control problems, related to a design flaw involving the Manoeuvring Characteristics Augmentation System (MCAS) of the MAX series, resulting in worldwide grounding of all MAX aircraft. Clearly the automated systems have to be made more resilient and reliable.

At the same time, the advantages of automation cannot be ignored. The day is not far when a single pilot would fly an airliner, with the co-pilot monitoring from the ground. He could take over the controls remotely, if required. The pilot on the ground could simultaneously act as a co-pilot to several aircraft.

Single Pilot and Autonomous Plane Issues

Both Boeing and Airbus have been looking at single pilot operations in commercial jetliners. That will also open the path for unpiloted operations. The path is similar to what is happening in surface transportation like cars and ships. Artificial intelligence will make it possible. As is happening in military UAVs. A single pilot adds to the risk of a suicide crash. It will also take a long time for passengers, and also aircraft insurers to be ready for it. The single crew airliner is still probably 20 years away but the single pilot cargo aircraft may be closer to becoming a reality. Of course, legal and procedural issues would have to resolved, and pilot incapacitation fully factored in.

To Summarise

Militaries have driven many technologies over the years. The defence of a nation brings funding into research. Most military technologies in the long run find applications to improve the quality of life of ordinary citizens. Aerospace has particularly led from the front. The radar, internet, militarised electronics, space exploration, satellite navigation, precision electronics, miniaturisation, data-links, multifunction displays, HUDs, unmanned mobility, electro-optical systems, advanced cyber applications, among many others, all first evolved for military use.

Technologies continue to evolve further and will support more wireless, wearable systems. Robotics and AI will make a huge difference in the times to come. Self-driving robots drones are permeating all daily requirements and future warfare will be mostly through uninhabited systems. Wheel chairs and luggage will become self-driven. Full-body wearable exoskeletons will enhance human capability. Autonomous cars and other vehicles are being inducted at airfields and airports in larger numbers.

Unmanned systems will greatly support flight testing of newer technologies and platforms. Lighter, longer lasting batteries will greatly support automation. Tele-presence will support single-pilot operations, and along with AI, it will keep enhancing decision-making. AI will also support actions to prevent catastrophic events or accidents. 360-degree virtual-reality systems will help improve situational awareness. 5G technologies are already bringing data at nearly 100 times faster than 4G. Further generations will make things even faster, which will be crucial for the large volume of data exchange. Biometrics technologies will evolve further, and their usage increase. Personal and data security will see more developments. Voice and hearing technologies will change things further in cockpits and in operations rooms and airports. There will be much improved cloud-based voice "Alexa" type services. Increasing urban air mobility will seek navigation and traffic safety solutions.

Miniaturisation will continue in more areas. Sensors and weapon ranges will be important. Weapon precision will increase further. The costs will also increase. Maintainability, and systems upgrades to keep up with technology will get more attention. The change from fossil fuels and more efficient greener systems will evolve.

The one who leads in technology will lead the world. First movers will have the advantage. More and more start-ups will evolve disruptive technologies. Technology would, thus, be the new form of deterrence.

Notes

1. John Stillion, "Trends in Air-to-Air Combat: Implications for Future Air Superiority," Centre for Strategic and Budgetary Assessments," April 14, 2015. https://csbaonline.org/research/publications/trends-in-air-to-air-combat-implications-for-future-air-superiority. Accessed on December 21, 2021.
2. Steve Jameson, "Multi-Domain Operations Require System-of-Systems Approach to Engineering and Integration," Federal News Network, November 23, 2021. https://federalnewsnetwork.com/commentary/2021/11/multi-domain-operations-require-system-of-systems-approach-to-engineering-and-integration/. Accessed on December 21, 2021.
3. Erik P. Blasch, Stephen Russell, Guna Seetharaman, "Joint Data Management for MOVINT - Data-to-Decision Making," Paper presented at 14th International Conference on Information Fusion, Chicago, July 5-8, 2011, p. 176. https://www.researchgate.net/publication/252027507_Joint_data_management_for_MOVINT_data-to-decision_making. Accessed on December 21, 2021.
4. Inder Singh Bisht, "US Air Force SHiELD Laser System to Receive Critical Component," *The Defence Post*, February 26, 2021. https://www.thedefensepost.com/2021/02/26/usaf-shield-laser-system-critical-component/. Accessed on December 21, 2021.
5. Dassault Aviation Official Website https://www.dassault-aviation.com/en/defense/neuron/introduction/. Accessed on December 22, 2021.
6. "Taranis Unmanned Combat Air Vehicle (UCAV) Demonstrator," *Air Force Technology*. https://www.airforce-technology.com/projects/tanaris/. Accessed on December 22, 2021.
7. BAE Website, "The Future of Air Combat, July 15, 2021." https://www.baesystems.com/en/the-future-of-combat-air. Accessed on December 22, 2021.
8. "Boeing MQ-25 Becomes First Unmanned Aircraft to Refuel Another Aircraft," You Tube, June 7, 2021. https://www.youtube.com/watch?v=q2uGkF2J1Y0. Accessed on December 22, 2021.
9. The "Race to be the US Navy's First Carrier-Based Drone is Heating up," *Business Insider*, April 6, 2018. https://www.businessinsider.in/slideshows/miscellaneous/the-race-to-be-the-us-navys-first-carrier-based-drone-is-heating-up/slidelist/63634907.cms#slideid=63634910. Accessed on December 22, 2021.

10. Sebastian Roblin, "SR-72: The US Air Force's Secret Plan For a Mach 6 Bomber? 1945," December 19, 2021. https://www.19fortyfive.com/2021/12/sr-72-the-us-air-forces-secret-plan-for-a-mach-6-bomber/. Accessed on December 22, 2021.
11. Hercules Reyes, "India to Procure Drone 'Swarms,' Anti-Drone Systems," *The Defense Post*, September 6, 2021. https://www.thedefensepost.com/2021/09/06/india-drone-swarms-anti-drone/. Accessed on December 22, 2021.
12. From the Congressional report to Congress on Conventional Prompt Global Strike and Long-Range Ballistic Missiles, dated July 16, 2021, USNI News, July 20, 2021. https://news.usni.org/2021/07/20/report-to-congress-on-conventional-prompt-global-strike-and-long-range-ballistic-missiles-4. Accessed on December 22, 2021.
13. Jonathan Marcus, "Russia Deploys Avangard Hypersonic Missile System," BBC News, December 27, 2019. https://www.bbc.com/news/world-europe-50927648. Accessed on December 22, 2021.
14. Dr Sidharth Kaushal and Sam Cranny-Evans, "China's New Hypersonic Capability," RUSI, October 26, 2021. https://rusi.org/explore-our-research/publications/commentary/chinas-new-hypersonic-capability. Accessed on December 22, 2021.
15. "DF-ZF Hypersonic Glide Vehicle," Missile Defence Advocacy Alliance, March 2019. https://missiledefenseadvocacy.org/missile-threat-and-proliferation/todays-missile-threat/china/df-zf-hypersonic-glide-vehicle/. Accessed on December 22, 2021.
16. Joseph Trevithick, "Tiny Missile Interceptor To Defend Aircraft Against Enemy Missile Attacks Moves Forward," *The Drive*, July 22, 2020. https://www.thedrive.com/the-war-zone/35038/tiny-missile-interceptor-to-defend-aircraft-against-enemy-missile-attacks-moves-forward. Accessed on December 22, 2021.
17. Tyler Rogoway, "Lockheed's New Laser Super Turret Could Change Air Combat Forever," *Jalopnik*, September 16, 2014. https://jalopnik.com/lockheeds-new-laser-super-turret-could-change-air-comba-1635210849. Accessed on December 22, 2021.
18. R. Dauman, "Bone Conduction: An Explanation for this Phenomenon Comprising Complex Mechanisms," *Science Direct*, June 3, 2013. https://www.sciencedirect.com/science/article/pii/S1879729613000227#! Accessed on December 23, 2021.
19. Alessio Spampinato, "The Materials Used in the Design of Aircraft Wings," AZO Materials, June 9, 2015. https://www.azom.com/article.aspx?ArticleID=12117. Accessed on December 15, 2021.
20. Abhinav Swami, Akshay Sharma, Devesh Mahawar, Jayesh Raj Singh, Pramod Kumar Verma, "Composite Materials in Aerospace Applications," Paper presented in 15th International Conference on Engineering and Applied Sciences Management, April 1, 2018, http://data.conferenceworld.in/GIET/47.pdf. Accessed on December 15, 2021.
21. Ibid.
22. "Flexibly Engineering The 'Impossible'", The Flexsys Company Website, https://www.flxsys.com/flexfoil. Accessed on December 15, 2021.
23. Irvine Pasternack, "Radar Technology Advancements and New Applications," *Microwave Journal*, March 14, 2017. https://www.microwavejournal.com/

articles/27994-radar-technology-advancements-and-new-applications. Accessed on December 16, 2021. https://www.microwavejournal.com/articles/17992-evolution-of-aesa-radar-technology?gclid=Cj0KCQiA2ZCOBhDiARIsAMRfv9Iuz04zmzLd0ZHmOpRrOMjuOlvHa4_Wk10W3t-jw7pZupyob7qR68caAmR4EALw_wcB. Accessed on December 23, 2021.

24. Carlo Kopp, "Evolution of AESA Radar Technology," *Microwave Journal*, August 14, 2012.
25. "Ground Moving Target Detection in MIMO-SAR System," 2016 IEEE International Geoscience and Remote Sensing Symposium (IGARSS), July 10-15, 2016. https://ieeexplore.ieee.org/document/7729269. Accessed on December 16, 2021.
26. Joao Pedroso, "High-Performance Radar Systems Based on GaN Technology," *Power Systems Design*, January 4, 2021. https://www.powersystemsdesign.com/articles/high-performance-radar-systems-based-on-gan-technology/138/17644. Accessed on December 16, 2021.
27. Tai Hai Chen, "S-31E2 KOLS. World's First OLS (optical laser system), an Alternative to Radar," *Pakistan Defence*, November 2, 2018. https://defence.pk/pdf/threads/s-31e2-kols-worlds-first-ols-optical-laser-system-an-alternative-to-radar.584879/. Accessed on December 17, 2021.
28. "Thales on Board the Dassault Aviation Rafale," Thales Website, https://www.thalesgroup.com/en/thales-board-dassault-aviation-rafale?utm_medium=social&utm_source=Google_ads&utm_campaign=Rafale&gclid=Cj0KCQiA5OuNBhCRARIsACgaiqUJY5MEMrfMgm8ty8ys0Fdd1YbQ9jhKuTZs1ubHFSHh8Mrh9TLGgncaAjUWEALw_wcB. Accessed on December 17, 2021.
29. "Pirate IRST," Leonardo Company Website, https://www.leonardocompany.com/en/products/pirate_irst. Accessed on December 17, 2021.
30. Joseph Trevithick, "F-35's X-Ray Vision System Is Getting An Upgrade, But Will It Actually Save Money?" *The Drive*, June 13, 2018. https://www.thedrive.com/the-war-zone/21509/f-35s-x-ray-vision-system-is-getting-an-upgrade-but-it-will-it-actually-save-money. Accessed on December 17, 2021.
31. Tyler Rogoway, "High-Quality Shots of Unpainted Chinese J-20 Stealth Fighter Offer New Capability Insights," *The Drive*, July 31, 2018. https://www.thedrive.com/the-war-zone/22534/high-quality-shots-of-unpainted-chinese-j-20-stealth-fighter-offer-new-capability-insights. Accessed on December 17, 2021.
32. "New Lightweight Radars and IRST from Leonardo," *European Security and Defence*, September 5, 2019. https://euro-sd.com/2019/09/articles/14488/new-lightweight-radars-and-irst-from-leonardo/. Accessed on December 17, 2021.
33. News Release, "Northrop Grumman Announces OpenPod (TM), the Next Generation of Podded Sensor Systems," Northrop Company Website, June 2, 2015. https://news.northropgrumman.com/news/releases/northrop-grumman-announces-openpod-tm-the-next-generation-of-podded-sensor-systems. Accessed on December 17, 2021.

34. Thomas Newdick, "Legion Infrared Search And Track Pods Can Now Carry Their Own Datalinks For More Lethal Targeting," *The Drive*, June 8, 2021. https://www.thedrive.com/the-war-zone/40980/legion-infrared-search-and-track-pods-can-now-carry-their-own-datalinks-for-more-lethal-targeting. Accessed on December 17, 2021.
35. Tyler Rogoway, "F-15 Uses New Infrared Pod To Shoot Down Target F-16 With AIM-120 Missile," *The Drive*, August 10, 2021. https://www.thedrive.com/the-war-zone/41932/f-15-uses-new-infrared-pod-to-shoot-down-target-f-16-with-aim-120-missile. Accessed on December 17, 2021.
36. Chintan Raval, "Importance of Health Monitoring System for Aircraft", E Info Chips, March 15, 2021. https://www.einfochips.com/blog/importance-of-health-monitoring-system-for-aircraft/. Accessed on December 17, 2021.
37. Carolina Martin Berardi, "Emerging Technologies in Aircraft Maintenance: Robots and Drones," *Prescouter*, December 2019. https://www.prescouter.com/2019/12/emerging-technologies-in-aircraft-maintenance-robots-and-drones/. Accessed on December 17, 2021.
38. Tom LeCompte, "How Things Work: Self-Healing Airplanes," *Air and Space Magazine*, August 2009. https://www.airspacemag.com/flight-today/how-things-work-self-healing-airplanes-35558146/. Accessed on December 17, 2021.
39. Yusuff Adeniyi Yusuff, "Development of Self-Healing Coatings in the Aerospace Industry," Azo Materials, June 4, 2020. https://www.azom.com/article.aspx?ArticleID=19336. Accessed on December 17, 2021.
40. Suman Medibonu, "Self-Healing Materials for Aircraft Applications, Create the Future," *Tech Briefs*, April 27, 2017. https://contest.techbriefs.com/2017/entries/aerospace-and-defense/7555. Accessed on December 17, 2021.
41. Kelsey Reichmann, "How Is the Aviation Industry Enabling Innovation with Artificial Intelligence?" *Aviation Today*, December 14, 2020. https://www.aviationtoday.com/2020/12/14/aviation-industry-enabling-innovation-artificial-intelligence/. Accessed on December 17, 2021.
42. Manish Kumar Jha, Amit Das, "AI Technology In Military Will Transform Future Warfare," *Business World*, August 13, 2021. http://www.businessworld.in/article/AI-Technology-In-Military-Will-Transform-Future-Warfare/13-08-2021-400525/. Accessed on December 17, 2021.
43. Will Knight, "AI Could Enable 'Swarm Warfare' for Tomorrow's Fighter Jets, Wired," March 22, 2021. https://www.wired.com/story/ai-enable-swarm-warfare-fighter-jets/. Accessed on December 17, 2021.
44. Liv, "The Future of Automation in the Aviation Industry, Robotics and Automation," July 4, 2019. https://roboticsandautomationnews.com/2019/07/04/the-future-of-automation-in-the-aviation-industry/24321/. Accessed on December 18, 2021.
45. Hemant America, "Aviation: Flying into the Future on the Wings of Robotics," *Automation, and Cybersecurity, Mindtree*, August 16, 2019. https://www.mindtree.com/insights/blog/aviation-flying-future-wings-robotics-automation-and-cybersecurity, Accessed on December 17, 2021.

46. Robotics Online Marketing Team, "How Cobots are Automating the Aviation Industry," A3 Association for Advanced Automation, September 24, 2019. https://www.automate.org/blogs/how-cobots-are-automating-the-aviation-industry. Accessed on December 18, 2021.
47. Mikael Söderman, "Collaborative Robots in the Aviation Industry", *Omad Tech*, September 21, 2020. https://omad.tech/collaborative-robots-in-the-aviation-industry/. Accessed on December 18, 2021.
48. Eugene Demaitre, "6 Novel Applications for Collaborative Robots," *Collaborative Robotics Trends*, October 4, 2019. https://www.cobottrends.com/6-novel-applications-for-collaborative-robots/. Accessed on December 18, 2021.
49. J. Preston Layton, "Specific Fuel Consumption," *Access Science*, 2014. https://www.accessscience.com/media/EST/media/641600PV0001.pdf. Accessed on December 25, 2021.
50. Erick Burgueño Salas, "Market Share of the Leading Commercial Aircraft Engine Manufacturers Worldwide in 2020," *Statista*, August 5, 2021. https://www.statista.com/statistics/1099835/global-aircraft-engine-manufacturer-market-share/. Accessed on December 19, 2021.
51. Zhi X. Chen, Ivan Langella and Nedunchezhian Swaminathan, "The Role of CFD in Modern Jet Engine Combustor Design," *IntechOpen Book Series*, August 23, 2019. https://www.intechopen.com/chapters/68313. Accessed on December 25, 2021.
52. Jim Steibel, "Ceramic Matrix Composites Taking Flight at GE Aviation," *American Ceramic Society Bulletin*, Vol. 98, No. 3. Ceramics.Org, 2019. https://www.researchgate.net/profile/Jim-Steibel/publication/332275883_Ceramic_matrix_composites_taking_flight_at_GE_Aviation/links/5cab79a3a6fdcca26d0773c8/Ceramic-matrix-composites-taking-flight-at-GE-Aviation.pdf. Accessed on December 25, 2021.
53. Yvonne Gibbs, "NASA Armstrong Fact Sheet: Pathfinder Solar-Powered Aircraft," NASA Website, August 7, 2017. https://www.nasa.gov/centers/armstrong/news/FactSheets/FS-034-DFRC.html. Accessed on December 25, 2021.
54. Aqeel Ahmad Taimoor, Muhammad Ehtisham Siddiqui and Salem S. Abdel Aziz, "Thermodynamic Analysis of Partitioned Combined Cycle Using Simple Gases," *Applied Sciences*, MDPI, October 8, 2019. file:///C:/Users/Dell/Downloads/applsci-09-04190.pdf. Accessed on December 25, 2021.
55. Alyssa Newcomb, "The Superjet: How GE's Adaptive Cycle Jet Engine Could Supercharge Military Aviation," Ge.com, October 25, 2021. https://www.ge.com/news/reports/the-superjet-how-ges-adaptive-cycle-jet-engine-could-supercharge-military-aviation. Accessed on December 26, 2021.
56. Harin Kumar Rajendra Bhai Patel, "Parametric Cycle Analysis of Adaptive Cycle Engine," The University of Texas at Arlington, May 2016. https://rc.library.uta.edu/uta-ir/bitstream/handle/10106/25899/PATEL-THESIS-2016.pdf?sequence=1&isAllowed=y. Accessed on December 26, 2021.
57. GE Aviation Press Release, "GE9X Engine Achieves FAA Certification," skiesmag.com, September 28, 2020. https://skiesmag.com/press-releases/ge9x-engine-achieves-faa-certification/. Accessed on December 26, 2021.

58. Reuters Staff, Airbus, "Boeing Expected to Turn to Hybrid Engine Technology for New Planes-Lessor," reuters.com, November 20, 2020. https://www.reuters.com/article/us-boeing-737max-air-lse-idUSKBN28004K. Accessed on December 26, 2021.
59. Charlotte Ryan, "100-Seat Electric Plane Will Be Ready by 2027, Says L.A. Start-up," Bloomberg, November 4, 2021. https://www.bloomberg.com/news/articles/2021-11-04/hundred-seat-electric-plane-ready-by-2027-startup-wright-says. Accessed on December 26, 2021.
60. Wolfgang Bernhart, "Meet The Automotive Disrupters: Building Tomorrow's Battery Today," rolandberger.com, July 15, 2021. https://www.rolandberger.com/en/Insights/Publications/Meet-the-automotive-disrupters-Building-tomorrow's-battery-today.html. Accessed on December 26, 2021.
61. "Go Beyond," Pratt & Whitney Official Website. https://prattwhitney.com/ Accessed on December 19, 2021
62. "GE Successfully Concludes Phase 1 Testing on Second XA100 Adaptive Cycle Engine," GE Aviation Website. https://www.geaviation.com/press-release/military-engines/ge-successfully-concludes-phase-1-testing-second-xa100-adaptive. Accessed on December 19, 2021.
63. "Boeing Selects Rolls-Royce AE 3007N Engines for US Navy MQ-25 Aircraft," *Naval Technology*, September 10, 2018. https://www.naval-technology.com/news/boeing-rolls-royce-ae-3007n-engines/. Accessed on December 19, 2021.
64. "A New Standard in Reliability," CFM Website. https://www.cfmaeroengines.com/engines/leap/. Accessed on December 19, 2021.
65. Alan Levin, "Lion Air Crash Sheds Light on Cockpit Automation's Dark Side," *Live Mint*, December 1, 2018. https://www.livemint.com/Companies/N6sb841OIR17MrBLULoCaO/Lion-Air-crash-sheds-light-on-cockpit-automations-dark-side.html. Accessed on December 26, 2021.
66. Jeff Wise, "What Really Happened Aboard Air France 447," *Popular Mechanics*, June 1, 2020. https://www.popularmechanics.com/flight/a3115/what-really-happened-aboard-air-france-447-6611877/. Accessed on December 26, 2021.

3. The Disruptive Phenomenon: Military Concepts and Technologies for the Space Domain

TH Anand Rao

Armed forces all over the world are faced with the constant dilemma of a continuous process of modernisation in weapons, equipment, war-fighting tactics and organisational structures to keep pace with the rapid changes in military technologies. These technology changes are fuelled by the offence-defence spiral, leading to constant improvements and upgradations in capabilities. The utility life cycle of any useful weapon system is, thus, short-lived in today's world.

Prof. Clayton M. Christensen of the Harvard Business School has categorised new technology as being of two kinds, either enduring or destructive, in his 1997 best-selling book, *The Innovator's Dilemma*. Emerging technologies could be classified as either 'sustaining' or 'disruptive'. The incremental evolution of current technology is a sustaining technology. Disruptive technology, on the other hand, revolutionises the industry, but poses risks because it is modern, untested, and initially limited in reach.[1] Most armed forces follow the path of employing a 'sustaining technology' approach. Disruptive technologies, when applied in the defence sector, alter the symmetry of military force between adversaries which makes doctrines and strategies ineffective. It is the ability to adopt disruptive technologies selectively with a strategic vision which will make the difference in future wars.

Unmanned Aerial Systems (UAS) and autonomous drones which augmented air power were always seen to have a disruptive effect, the most recent example being seen in the conflict between Azerbaijan and Armenia. The technologies being incorporated in such systems, like artificial intelligence, machine learning, quantum computing, and 5G, will be the new disruptive phenomena. Similarly, these effects are taking shape in the way we use the space domain too for military objectives.

With emerging and potentially disruptive technologies being employed in air and space, there is a fundamental change in the outlook for deterrence and defence. The size of an adversary no longer matches with power. Embracing potentially disruptive technologies and strategies will enable a smaller size state to compete and successfully challenge a great power. The rise of disruptive technologies puts the emphasis on another Revolution in Military Affairs (RMA); this time in the space domain, much like the cyber domain, which are the emerging frontiers.

Physical, Networking and Cognitive Dimensions to Space

Space, more commonly known as outer space, has emerged as an operational domain for the armed forces. This implies that it is now a war-fighting domain and combat would happen in space. It could include space objects being targeted from the Earth, space-to-space attacks, or worse still, attacks on the Earth from space. Though none of these cases has been recorded in adversarial situations, the possibility exists. However, contrary to popular belief, space is not a domain for war-fighting in isolation. There are interdependencies with other domains, and conflict in one domain can spill over to another. The five universally accepted domains for war-fighting are land, sea, air, space and cyber space. Employment of revolutionary technologies like Artificial Intelligence (AI), robotics, directed energy and nanotechnology in weapons operating through any these domains makes them disruptive.

Operations in one domain could have dependence on another domain. For example, in the cyber domain, network servers may reside in a land-based data complex, and wireless network transmissions pass through air and space. Satellites in the space domain have ground control stations and networks in the land and cyber domains and transmissions pass through the air and space domains. Therefore, activities in space will involve activities in the physical domains like land, sea, air as well as cyberspace. Space and cyber space, however, have a unique relationship. Most space operations depend on cyberspace as an enabler and a major enabler of cyberspace is provided through the space domain. Space is the key to global connectivity for cyber operations. Both space and cyberspace are the primary enablers of Network-Centric Warfare (NCW).

This interdependence of the domains of conflict is further complicated by the presence of the cognitive dimension. This was stated by A K Cebrowski who contended that conflict in the modern battlespace encompasses the physical, information and cognitive domains, in his work on *The Implementation of Network-Centric Warfare*, in 2005.[2]

The cognitive domain, on the other hand, deals with the manner in which all the other domains are utilised. It is a new area of competition. It involves the intangibles of leadership, training, experience, situational awareness and innovativeness of strategising. The intent of the leadership, doctrine, tactics, techniques and procedures resides in the cognitive domain. Dealing with the cognitive domain is vital to outplay an adversary. When applied to space operations, the cognitive dimension enables a decision matrix to conduct deterrence operations and manage escalations.

Space as a Disruptive Domain

Outer space was once considered a *sanctuary*, where orbiting objects were considered safe and enjoyed the safety associated with a *global commons* approach. During the Cold War years, space was utilised as a *high ground.* The emergence of a control regime in space has resulted in many space control strategies being fielded in space, fuelled by the development of counter-space technologies.

Counter-space technologies are being increasingly fielded in space. There is a prominent shift towards development and testing of Directed Energy Weapons (DEWs), electronic jamming and cyber techniques which can cause temporary or permanent damage to a satellite or its payload, without destroying the satellite. Such counter-space technologies are being preferred for preventing space debris as well as for the advantages offered by the lower chances of attributability. These non-kinetic weapons are also least likely to cause escalation.

Another new phenomenon being increasingly seen is the practice of proximity operations in space. Proximity operations allow a spacecraft or satellite to get close to another object in space. Proximity approaches to other operator's satellites by China, the USA and Russia have been recorded numerous times. While this technology enables facilities like repair, servicing, inspection and refuelling of satellites, its dual nature may be exploited for damaging an adversary's satellite. DEWs and electronic interference equipment could also be fielded from spacecraft performing proximity manoeuvres. Proximity operations have, thus, given rise to a whole new concept of *manoeuvre warfare* in space. US and Chinese spacecraft are reported to have had multiple close encounters. In January 2022, the US satellite USA 270 did a manoeuvre close to two Chinese satellites—the Shiyan-12; 01 and 02—in the Geostationary Earth Orbit (GEO) belt. China's Shijian-21 satellite has exhibited multiple proximity manoeuvres in the GEO belt since its launch in October 2021, before attaching itself to a Beidou-2 satellite, which it pushed into a graveyard orbit on January 26, 2022.[3] On January 21, 2022, the US launched the space situational awareness satellites GSSAP-5&6 into GEO. These satellites have the capability to do proximity operations to inspect other satellites in the GEO belt.[4]

The emerging possibilities for military activities in space has forced the space enabled nations to expand their military infrastructure and organisation to space. The USA established a Space Force in 2018, as a separate military service to handle space operations for future wars. In 2019, the US president declared space as an operational domain, which implies the US intention to extend military operations into the space domain. In the same year, the North Atlantic Treaty Organisation (NATO) alliance members, including Japan and France, too declared their intention to have space squadrons for defending their assets in space.[5] China, on the other hand, formed the Strategic Support Force (SSF) in 2015 to control its military space assets. Since then, China's military activities in space have been on an upward trajectory.

The military developments in the space domain necessitate an evaluation of military applications of 'emerging technologies'. The race to dominate space is heating up and unless these emerging technologies are adopted, the chance to be an early bird in this race may be missed.

Vulnerability of Space Infrastructure

Although space is now a vital constituent of comprehensive national power, the degree of a nation's dependence on its space infrastructure is also a source of its vulnerability. Space infrastructure and space capabilities represent easier targets than other conventional terrestrial targets, as they have no direct implications of human casualties, and, hence, we should expect interference with them. As seen in the overwhelming US military capability, space-based infrastructure and digital interconnectivity are central to this capability. Though the land, sea and air forces will continue to fight the surface war, these missions will not succeed if not supported through space. A US Space Commission's findings have described the US as an attractive candidate for a "Space Pearl Harbour".[6] Inability or lack of vision to protect satellites, their ground infrastructure or the data-links from an enemy attack would result in total disruption of services for a considerable time as these assets cannot be replaced quickly. Each of these elements of space infrastructure has its own unique vulnerabilities, which can be targeted by distinctive methods using emerging technologies. The ground infrastructure is vulnerable to conventional attacks from the ground, air and space. The data-links can be jammed, spoofed or even hacked using electronic and cyber warfare techniques. Satellites and other space-based assets are vulnerable to a range of attacks, including Anti-Satellite (ASAT) weapons space planes, DEWs (land or space-based) like lasers and Electro-Magnetic Pulse (EMP) weapons or space-based weapons like space mines and parasite micro/nano satellites. The options are endless. Hence, the importance of *space control*, an area in which countries like the US, Russia and China have taken the lead.

Space Control

While space systems have proven to be enablers in wars of the past, the focus is now shifting to offensive and defensive activities in space for national objectives while denying freedom of space operations to the adversary. Space powers are now embarking on programmes for space control and space force projection. This can be called 'space weaponisation'. Space control is, hence, the next logical step in dominating the ultimate high ground, as space in the years to come will not be just an emerging battlefield, but a gateway to prosperity for those who have control over it.

Seemingly, the space economy is a major driver for space security. A well-established space economy and technological superiority is a precursor to space supremacy. Space control is essential to maintain space supremacy. A combination of space supremacy and space control, thus, gives a condition of '*space dominance*' (Fig 1).[7] Thus, it can be stated that the economy, technology, and security are interdependent activities and one flows from the other. They represent the economic, technological and military dimensions of national power.

Fig 1

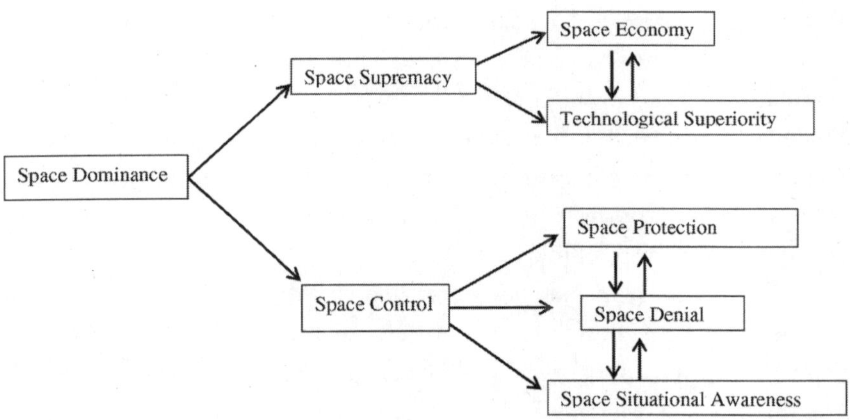

Space control essentially involves ensuring own freedom of operations in space and uninterrupted availability of space services, in peace-time as well as in war. It can be said to comprise *space protection*, *space denial* and *space situational awareness* (Fig 1). While *space protection* involves securing own space assets from disruption and damage, *space denial* means denying an enemy access to its space resources during a conflict. *Space control* and *space supremacy* together contribute towards *space dominance* which will be crucial for any nation for achieving national security objectives. The strategy for *space control* can either be defensive (protecting own space assets) or offensive (degrading/destroying the enemy's space assets). *Space situational awareness* would be a prerequisite for any space mission. While space dominance is an overwhelming superiority in space and offers unrestricted freedom of operation of space assets, space control, through space protection and space denial, will be limited in time and space, and would be more practical in a multipolar space order.

Space protection, space denial and space situational awareness are, hence, the primary drivers of military space technology development programmes.

Space Protection

Space protection techniques reduce the vulnerabilities of satellites and other space systems by defending them through various measures – passive, semi-active, and active defences– or a combination of these to minimise any adverse consequences when they are exposed to counter-space weapons. Passive measures are design features which can be incorporated to reduce the vulnerability when exposed to a threat. Semi-active measures are response mechanisms that would be activated on identification of specific threats. These may involve shutting down or turning away of receivers when the incident signal strength crosses set limits, or manoeuvring the satellite away from danger in its orbital path. Active measures are offensive actions to deter any attack or as a response to an attack. Basic space protection measures should mandatorily include hardening and shielding against radiation and the use of basic electronic counter-measures like data encryption. Hardening and other on-board protection methods offer interim protection against potential threats. However, these measures are uneconomical and can be countered by a determined attacker. The possible options for space protection are listed below:[8]

- Hardening.
- Shielding.
- Electronic counter-measures like encryption and frequency hopping.
- Manoeuvrability for collision avoidance.
- Deception through stealth features and decoys.
- On-board self-protection weapons.
- On-board threat warning sensors.
- Autonomous operation to bypass ground data-links if jamming is encountered.
- System redundancy.

Obviating attacks by installation of threat-warning sensors on upcoming satellites to detect, identify, and classify attacks of various kinds could prove to be a game changer. This will have to become a basic requirement for satellite security, and private satellite manufacturers will have to understand the requirement, despite the additional costs involved. In the existing scenario, a satellite malfunction could be the result of cosmic radiation, a technical failure, a collision with space debris, or a deliberate attack, whether physical or electronic. Threat-warning sensors would not only provide an advance warning and threat classification, but will also give an opportunity to take preventive action by manoeuvring the satellite to safety.[9]

Space Denial

Space denial is an active space control option and is achieved by denying use of space to the adversary. Space denial can be achieved through hard kill as well as soft kill measures. Hard kill measures are kinetic ASAT weapons which have been in development and testing since the Cold War years. Use of space denial measures would be dictated by geostrategic imperatives; particularly, the use of hard kill techniques may result in escalation of a conflict. Space denial using soft kill techniques would play an important role in lowering the risk in the escalation matrix. A combination of cyber attacks, electronic interference and DEWs like lasers may go unnoticed and should be the preferred mode of space denial as compared to a hit-to-kill ASAT weapons in which escalation is imminent. The aim of space denial should be to achieve a graded effect towards space defence in the following sequence:[10]

- Disruption.
- Degradation.
- Denial.
- Destruction.

Space Situational Awareness

Space Situational Awareness (SSA) is a vital measure which is a pre-requisite for the other two components of space control, viz. space protection and space denial. A network of ground and space-based systems to monitor orbital objects is a precondition for any significant space defence or control capability. Coupled with this is the installation of threat warning sensors on satellites for enabling basic space protection.

Developments in Military Space Technologies

Space technologies of the 21st century, aided by miniaturisation and enabled by a software revolution have facilitated the accessibility to space, thus, fuelling the rapid growth of space objects in the Earth's orbit. These technological developments being dual use, will also have military utility and, thus, the fears of vitiating the space environment would always remain. Despite the deep military underpinnings of many of these space technologies, the reduction in costs for space companies has meant more commercialisation of space and a potentially booming space economy. Some major game changer technologies are given in the subsequent paragraphs.

Rendezvous and Proximity Operations: Rendezvous and Proximity Operations (RPOs) were being tested since 2005 by the US under the Demonstration of Automated Rendezvous Technologies (DART) project.[11] This is a primary capability required for automated docking of capsules to a spaceship. Besides docking with spaceships, the RPO has multiple utility. This one single game changer capability has enabled multiple options for civil and military satellite operators. RPO has been used for satellite-on-satellite approaches by Russia and China for unknown reasons. The US too has exercised this activity with its own satellites. The known purposes are for repair and servicing, refuelling of satellites and a satellite inspection. RPO, being a dual use phenomenon, the unknown activity could be for military purposes which vary from a flyby inspection to electronic jamming, lasing or even causing physical damage. This capability is also being planned for experiments to attach with dead satellites and bring them closer to the Earth's atmosphere for a burn up.

Satellite Servicing: RPO is also the primary capability required for satellite repair and servicing. This will include robotic repairs, replacement of solar panels and even refuelling of the target satellite. These activities—especially refuelling—give a fresh lease of life to satellite and can increase the satellite's life much beyond the design life of 7-8 years in Low Earth Orbit (LEO). Satellite servicing is set to change the economics of the space industry, the mantra being to '*Reduce, Reuse, Recycle, Repair, Refuel in space!*'.

Reusability: Reuse of space rockets has been the major factor in bringing down launch costs. From being able to reuse the first stage rocket engine, successfully being done by SpaceX for the Falcon 9 boosters, we are now on the verge of fully reusable rockets under trial. SpaceX's Big Falcon rocket and Blue Origin's 'New Shephard' rocket are set to be the first fully reusable rockets. The small rocket manufacturer 'Rocket Labs' is promising a game changer rocket called the 'Neutron' which will have full reusability and is expected to have a first launch in 2024.[12]

Spacelift: Space transportation is being envisioned in a novel concept which would entail passengers and logistics being spacelifted—not only to planetary destinations like the Moon and Mars, but from one place to another on the Earth. This will be made possible with fully reusable rockets like the Neutron becoming a reality. Spacelift is akin to airlift, the difference being in the mode of transport. A rocket with load and passenger carrying capacity could be launched, orbited, and made to land at a destination across the globe in a matter of a few minutes. Spacelift could be particularly useful for strategic transportation of military equipment and personnel.

Responsive Launch Options: Launching satellites on demand or responsive launch is a critical capability for enhanced national security requirements. This capability basically involves the ability to launch satellites at short notice or within a quick turnaround time. Such quick launches are used for tactical military reconnaissance, replacing lost satellites or even restoration of services caused by unserviceable satellite payloads. The responsive launch can happen from conventional land-based launch facilities, ship-based launch facilities or air-launched from a mother aircraft releasing a rocket at high altitude. 'Virgin Orbit' of the USA has demonstrated this capability with its 'Launcher One' rocket released from a modified Boeing-747 at 35,000-40,000 ft altitude and the facility has been operational since January 2021.[13] A more recent development in responsive launch capability is the concept of rockets orbiting in space for a payload release on requirement. The trend, therefore, is moving towards reduction in timeframes between launch preparations to 'on-orbit'. While this is a positive development for the space industry and military space strategists, it is a nightmare for the ever-increasing burden on airspace and orbital space, as the current air and space traffic regulating environment, and surveillance technologies are not conducive to such short notice space launches. Unless there is coordination at a global level for managing space bound traffic with corresponding tracking sensors, responsive launch will be a safety hazard with the present rate of growth in the satellite population.

Cost Reduction: A major driver for the growth of commercial space exploration is the cost factor. Innovative technologies have assisted in bringing down launch costs to affordable levels. Additive manufacturing is one such practice which has converted large multi-piece assemblies into a single part, leading to a reduction in volume, weight, cost, and lead time. Similarly, use of simulation systems has reduced the development time by several months. Software has been used to study the 3D flow of the rocket engine exhaust plume which has enabled reduction of exhaust temperatures by an order of magnitude.

Nuclear Powered Satellites: A major consideration for the life of a satellite, besides other factors, is the availability of on-board fuel to manoeuvre the satellite to keep it in the designated orbital slot. Nuclear power is an option, which has the advantage of providing unlimited life for generating power for propulsion as well as powering on-board systems, thereby replacing on-board batteries and solar panels. Though this is not a new phenomenon, there is a renewed effort in this direction. The US and the erstwhile Soviet Union had made use of nuclear power at the dawn of the space age to power their lunar missions using radio isotope power sources. These countries had also tested nuclear thermal propulsion systems and space reactors, but abandoned space nuclear research at the end of the Cold War.[14]

Today, nuclear propulsion provides an exciting opportunity to overcome the limitations to satellite propulsion and electric power, which could result in an era of satellites with unrestricted lives and manoeuvrability. There is a strategic mandate too for this. It gives the satellites and other spacecraft the ability to manoeuvre quickly to avoid emerging threats from adversaries, be it a kinetic ASAT weapon or a co-orbital satellite in proximity. Russia is pursuing several concepts, including a fission reactor to power an electronic warfare satellite and a reactor to power an ion engine to create a space tug. The US tested a small reactor in 2018—*tiny kilopower*–which is the first domestic reactor designed, built, and operated in decades by the National Aeronautics and Space Administration (NASA). China too is investing aggressively in nuclear powered spacecraft.[15]

Quantum Communication: Satellite communication and data-links are a critical vulnerability and will be an easy target for jamming and interference measures by an adversary during a conflict. Loss of communication with a satellite may render it useless, or much worse, may result in loss of control of the satellite. Hence, securing these data-links will be an essential measure to safeguard satellites from unlawful interference. Quantum communication techniques have enabled a different means of encryption which is secure. Quantum communication, or quantum key distribution, allows sharing of encrypted data that is transferred through particles known as qubits. These particles are also called photons—a unit of light—which can be bunched up in phases or entangled to give a coding effect. China has taken the lead on experimenting with the quantum communication techniques on satellites. In 2016, the Micius satellite in LEO communicated with two ground observatories in Delingha and Nanshan in China, which are separated by 1,200 km as proof of the concept. This satellite was used for an encrypted video call between Beijing and Vienna in 2017. In the same year, China also established the first long-distance quantum communication landline in the world, connecting Beijing with Shanghai.[16]

Artificial Intelligence: Artificial Intelligence (AI) has become a game changer by exponentially increasing the depth of possibilities for space exploitation and exploration. Although the list would be endless, some applications of AI in space are: processing of satellite images, system monitoring of satellites, development of satellites and spacecraft, autonomous spacecraft navigation, docking and proximity operations, supporting the large satellite constellations for relative positioning, communication and end-of-life management, etc. The military utility of AI is immense and could include shortening of the decision matrix, wherein a satellite could collect data and possibly evaluate the data and simultaneously assign the optimal weapon solution to eliminate a target. This will invariably enhance the capability in time sensitive targeting while shortening the sensor-to-shooter loop.

Robotics and AI are inherently linked. Robotics is already being used in space for some activities like spacecraft repair, satellite servicing and debris capture.

Another area for employment of AI which is fast developing is for an enhanced Space Situational Awareness (SSA) architecture. This would involve autonomous tracking and cataloguing of space objects and debris as well as an autonomous alerting service. It is also possible to see future satellites—especially large constellations—receive autonomous collision avoidance alerts and the satellites could perform autonomous avoidance manoeuvres.

Present Military Developments in Space Technologies

The Revolution in Military Affairs (RMA) in space has been made possible by the evolution in technology which has made space applications the backbone of the modern military strategy. The use of the space domain for the military has expanded into multiple disciplines like space surveillance, signal intelligence, strategic communications and data-links, tracking and data relay, navigation and precision strike, weather prediction, missile launch warning, etc., each of which has developed into a specialised military activity, with the availability of precise spaceborne sensors. Technology has also extended the war-fighting options into the space domain with the development of various counter-space weapons options. Space weapons and space-based Ballistic Missile Defence (BMD) are set to alter the space scape altogether, necessitating a much higher degree of the space surveillance regime.

Space Weapons

Space weapons would comprise not only weapons launched from the Earth but also weapons hosted in space and weapons that transit through space. The former variety of weapons launched from the Earth are a reality and are called the kinetic ASAT weapons. Now, we are increasingly seeing a shift towards hosting weapons in space under the garb of the dual use conundrum. These are in the form of lasers and electronic jamming equipment that could be hosted on satellites. These soft kill counter-space technologies may not destroy a satellite by fragmentation, but can make it dysfunctional, causing it to become unresponsive and move out of its orbital slot. Directed energy weapons which are soft kill weapons—like lasers, high power microwaves and electronic interference—have also been deployed on the Earth to target satellites in space. Weapons transiting through space are presently of the ballistic missile variety or even the hypersonic missiles and anti-ballistic missile. The possibility of intercepting ballistic missiles in the mid-course phase means an engagement in space, which qualifies these missiles as space weapons. As for the testing of kinetic ASAT weapons, there was an initial boom in the Cold War era, followed by a period of lull between 1995 and 2005. China's arrival as an ASAT weapon state in 2005 changed the scenario and there seems to be a resurgence in kinetic ASAT tests. These weapons are known to be deployed for operational use by China and Russia. The pointers are towards a renewed space race for gaining an edge in the quest to dominate the space domain.

Space-Based BMD

A space layer for missile defence and space-based weapons was first envisioned in the Star Wars Project of 1983 of former US President Ronald Reagan. Extensive research in this direction is said to have been done, but these weapons remained far from reality. However, the research done in the Star Wars project doesn't seem to have been futile. Ballistic missile defence as it exists today has many deficiencies. The missile technologies being developed by Russia and China are designed to circumvent the missile defences and, thus, are becoming more unpredictable. China reportedly tested a nuclear-capable hypersonic missile in October 2021 that circled the globe before heading towards its target, demonstrating an advanced strike capability through space that caught the world by surprise. Though not much evidence is available, a Chinese Foreign Ministry press briefing on October 18, 2021, clarified that it was a test of a reusable space vehicle. This gave rise to speculations of China possessing the capability to release a Hypersonic Glide Vehicle (HGV) from a missile that could travel around the globe, much like the Fractional Orbital Bombardment System (FOBS) of the erstwhile USSR in the 1960s. Russia too has developed a hypersonic weapon called the 'Kinzhal' that can reach a speed of Mach 10, and 'Avangard' that can supposedly touch a speed of Mach 27 using rocket boosters. In December 2019, Russia's Defence Ministry announced that a nuclear-armed HGV had been made operational, making Russia the first country armed with hypersonic weapons.[17]

The US has recognised the vulnerabilities of its existing missile defences like the Aegis Ballistic Missile Defence, Terminal High Altitude Area Defence (THAAD) and Patriot Advanced Capability (PAC-3). It has a system for missile launch detection on space-based sensors, called the Space-Based Infra-Red System (SBIRS), which has been operational since 2001[18]. However, there are gaps in detection, which can be exploited. The development of HGVs and warheads with Multiple Independently Targeted Re-entry Vehicles (MIRVs) and Manoeuvrable Reentry Vehicles (MARVs) necessitates a space layer for detection in missile defence. Over the past few years, the US has focussed its Research and Development (R&D) on space-based missile defences. The effort may see a new generation of missile detection satellites in space being called the Overhead Persistent Infra-Red (OPIR) which could be launched in 2025[19] as a replacement for the SBIRS.

Missile defence technologies are now moving towards an intercept layer in space. Space-based missile defences involving interceptors or non-kinetic technologies, like DEWs are capable of addressing some of the deficiencies of terrestrial missile defence systems, particularly the HGVs. Space-based defences are capable of engaging a missile in its boost phase, while its engines are still running. They could also be used to intercept ballistic missiles during their mid-course phase when they are unpowered and before decoys or reentry warheads can be deployed. In particular, directed energy weapons offer the potential to engage large numbers of warheads (and decoys).

Space-based missile defence will see a renewed thrust towards ASAT weapons to counter these systems. These missile defences could be the pre-emptive strike targets in any future war; the aim being to get the missiles through to their terrestrial targets.

The larger fear is the increase in the orbital population hosting missile defence payloads in LEO. To engage ballistic missiles during their boost phase, a missile defence system in space would need to be designed such that interceptors are always located relatively close to all potential missile launch sites. Satellites being in constant motion relative to the Earth's surface, hundreds of satellite platforms would be needed to cover potential launch sites.

Conclusion

The accessibility to space technologies has seen a shift due to various new concepts in manufacturing, miniaturisation and the digital revolution. There are already more than 82 countries which own satellites or have access to space services. The handful of nations having launch capability will also increase with the availability of commercial launch facilities and the demand for small satellite launch vehicles. Commercialisation of space is on the rise, making the possibilities for utilisation of space infinite. These developments have a profound effect in creating a positive impact for humankind.

Despite efforts to preserve space for peaceful utilisation, the space domain has transitioned from being an enabler for military operations to being an operational domain in itself. Emerging technologies in space have been instrumental in this transition, which is a disruptive phenomenon. The dual use possibilities of satellites and the proliferation of weapons into the space domain has necessitated possession of counter-space technologies by space-faring nations for ensuring freedom of operations in space. The emergence of 'space control' as a military strategy in space consisting of space protection and space denial measures ensures security of space assets while providing deterrence against attacks. The space domain has, thus, reached a tipping point and has disrupted conventional deterrence strategies. It is now possible that the first move in any future war would be in the space and cyber domains.

Ensuring safety of space operations is perhaps as important as the progress in space exploitation and exploration. While space control and counter-space measures can provide security against intentional attacks, there is also a need for securing space assets against unintentional mishaps. These may occur due to an unintentional collision with other satellites and space debris. Space situational awareness, therefore, is the foundational requirement for space operations. Technologies for space tracking sensors and satellite technologies for performing autonomous avoidance manoeuvres need to mature alongside other space technologies.

Notes

1. Hasan Suzen, "How Disruptive Technologies Affect Deterrence, Defence and Security", September 29, 2020. https://behorizon.org/how-disruptive-technologies-affect-deterrence-defence-and-security/. Accessed on January 22, 2022.
2. A K Cebrowski, *The Implementation of Network Centric Warfare* (Washington DC: Office of Force Transformation, US DoD, January 5, 2005), pp. 15-21. https://apps.dtic.mil/dtic/tr/fulltext/u2/a446831.pdf. Accessed on January 31, 2022
3. Andrew Jones, "China's Shijian-21 Towed Dead Satellite to a High Graveyard Orbit", January 27, 2022. https://spacenews.com/chinas-shijian-21-spacecraft-docked-with-and-towed-a-dead-satellite/. Accessed on January 28, 2022.
4. Brett Tingley, "Space Force Just Launched Satellites Capable Of 'Inspecting' Enemy Satellites", January 21, 2022. https://www.thedrive.com/the-war-zone/43980/space-force-just-launched-satellites-capable-of-inspecting-adversarys-satellites. Accessed on January 26, 2022.
5. Hitoshi Nasu, "NATO Recognizes Space as an 'Operational Domain': One Small Step Toward a Rules-Based International Order in Outer Space", March 4, 2020, https://www.justsecurity.org. Accessed on January 9, 2022.
6. Edward Hudgins and Charles Pena, "Should the United States 'Weaponise' Space? Military and Commercial Implications", *Policy Analysis*, No. 427, March 18, 2002.
7. TH Anand Rao, *India's Space Security Dilemma* (New Delhi: KW Publishers 2021), pp. 50-52.
8. Puneet Bhalla, "Weaponisation of Space", *Maneckshaw Paper*, No. 45/2014. http://www.claws.in/images/publication_pdf/1533354089_MP45Inside07-05-14.pdf. Accessed on February 5, 2018.
9. TH Anand Rao, "Space Control: The Next Step In India's Space Journey", *Expert View*, December 1, 2017. http://capsindia.org/expertview. Accessed on April 22, 2019.
10. Bhalla, n. 8.
11. DART, Gunters Space Page. https://space.skyrocket.de/doc_sdat/dart.htm. Accessed on December 25, 2021.
12. Loren Grush, "Rocket Lab Unveils Details of New Reusable Neutron Launcher", December 2, 2021. https://www.theverge.com/2021/12/2/22813819/rocket-lab-neutron-launch-satellite-reusable-mega-constellations. Accessed on December 24, 2021.
13. Robert Cardillo, "A Responsive Launch Capability will Deter Enemies, Boost National Security", September 3, 2021. https://www.defensenews.com/opinion/commentary/2021/09/03/a-responsive-launch-capability-will-deter-enemies-boost-national-security/. Accessed on January 4, 2022.
14. Alex Gilbert, "Nuclear Thermal Propulsion is Key to Keeping Peace in Space", February 14, 2022. https://www.thespacereview.com/article/4331/1. Accessed on February 15, 2022.
15. Ibid.

16. Passant Rabie, "Quantum Communication Takes a Major Leap with Satellite-Based Experiment", August 13, 2020. https://www.space.com/quantum-communication-major-leap-satellite-experiment.html. Accessed on February 15, 2022.
17. Sujay Bhattacharya, "Hypersonic Hyperdrive: China and Russia Ahead of US in Next-Generation Weapons Race". Indiatoday.in, October 21, 2021, at https://www.indiatoday.in/world/story/rocket-boosted-hypersonic-glide-vehicle-uk-russia-china-1867271-2021-10-21. Accessed on December 18, 2021.
18. Web article on '*SBIRS*', https://www.airforce-technology.com/projects/space-based-infrared-system-sbirs/. Accessed on December 18, 2021.
19. Theresa Hitchens, "Next-Gen OPIR Missile Warning On Schedule For 2025 Launch". Web article on August 25, 2021. https://breakingdefense.com/2021/08/next-gen-opir-missile-warning-on-schedule-for-2025-launch/. Accessed on December 18, 2021.

4. Impact of Electronic Warfare

Daljit Singh

Introduction

Armed forces fight wars in multiple domains of land, sea, air, space, and cyber space. One common domain, which pervades all other war-fighting domains is the Electro-Magnetic Spectrum Domain (EMSD), which ensures synergy in planning and conduct of operations through effective and integrated command, control, communication, and situational awareness. As the EMSD is a common and inseparable glue that bonds all other domains of operations, it is imperative that Electro-Magnetic Spectrum (EMS) superiority is achieved to ensure superiority in other operational domains. With massive technological developments in the last two decades, employment of EMS has expanded to the extremes of the spectrum, going beyond 100 Gigahertz, and significant employment of laser and Electro-Optical/Infrared (EO/IR) regimes. Despite such expansion of the EM spectrum bands, EMS employment has become increasingly congested, contested, and constrained. It is congested as the EM spectrum is copiously employed by both military and commercial and civilian organisations for communication, data storage, sensing, navigation, and urban planning. Introduction of 5G technology would further take away a significant segment of EMS for civilian use. The EMS domain is contested by hostile forces to extract intelligence, disrupt, destroy or deceive friendly EM capabilities while ensuring their own freedom of EMS operations. Freedom of action in the electro-magnetic spectrum, at the time, place, and in parameters of own choosing, is a required precursor to the successful conduct of operations in all domains.[1]

Electro-magnetic spectrum superiority is, therefore, considered essential to ensure the successful conduct of operations in all other domains.

Electronic Warfare (EW), which ensures friendly use of the electromagnetic spectrum and denies the same to the adversary, has gained crucial importance, as the armed forces depend increasingly on its employment. As the EMS is increasingly employed for commercial and civilian usage for national development, it requires attention and management at the national level to conform to international EMS regulations and ensure its smooth employment, without mutual interference, at the national level.

China has progressed significantly in all aspects of electronic warfare, with development of advanced Signal Intelligence (SIGINT) elements, both airborne and ground-based, fully integrated with operational formations, and multi-spectral and diverse air defence sensors. Pakistan has acquired EW systems from the USA, China and Turkey, and they are fully embedded in all operational elements. Their communication networks are jam resistant and encrypted. The Indian Air Force (IAF) and the other Services in India have lagged behind in secure communication networks, even though advanced communication systems acquisitions are likely to fructify soon. The Indian defence industry has yet to mature into providing modern EW systems to the armed forces for future operations, as Research and Development (R&D) in this field has not kept pace with the operational requirements of the armed forces. The Light Combat Aircraft (LCA) MkI is the fourth generation fighter aircraft inducted into the IAF for operations, without any comprehensive EW protection suite.

The Indian armed forces must prepare themselves for future wars with modern operational concepts of EMS dominance, which is a prerequisite for conducting effective operations in all other domains. It is, therefore, important to understand the historical technological development of EW, review the present status, analyse the future operational environment and strategy to dominate in EMS operations, in the years ahead.

Chronology of Electronic Warfare Technology

The EM spectrum was first operationally employed as a means of radio communication by navies of many countries at the dawn of the 20th century. As the transmissions were on single fixed frequency and without encryption, it was easy to monitor the transmissions and interfere with the communication by jamming.[2] This application of signal intelligence and communication jamming continues even today and will continue to occur in the future with more sophistication and complexities as the technology advances further. During World War I, the principle of goniometry for direction finding was employed to triangulate the location of communication transmitters. Now the principles of direction finding have improved to provide real-time geolocation capability, and the concept would continue to be employed in the future though the principles of geolocation have changed. World War II saw the development of radars and Integrated Air Defence Systems (IADS). The Germans and the British developed active counter-measures to jam the radars, and this led to expansion of the EM spectrum as the jammers could only jam single fixed frequency. This fight to gain freedom of operations in the EM spectrum led to the development of multi-frequency radars with doppler processing and employment of passive detection systems like searchlights. Integration of early warning and target tracking radars with anti-aircraft guns and airborne interceptors with communication networks, paved the way for multi-layered, multi-spectral integrated Air Defence (AD) systems. With the development of airborne navigational, airborne intercept and tail warning radars, Radar Warning Receivers (RWRs) were developed for aircraft and submarines, which improved the mission success and survival rates. SIGINT operations gained importance to map the electronic Order of Battle (ORBAT) and cryptography was developed to secure ground communications, passive counter-measures against radars were developed in total secrecy and deployed as 'chaff', as there was no antidote to counter them. However, in a short time, doppler processing radars and Very High Frequency (VHF) band radars were inducted and the operators learnt to differentiate real targets from chaff.

It is axiomatic that the EW technology and concepts progress fast during conflicts and then take a backseat during the intervening peace time. The Americans learnt this lesson the hard way during the Vietnam War, when the US F-4 Phantom fighter was shot down by the Soviet- built SA 2 Surface-to-Air Missile (SAM) on July 24, 1965. The US Air Force (USAF) lost 160 aircraft in the same year, most of them shot down by SAM-2 missiles.[3] The US defence industry got into the act to cover the lost ground and develop EW systems. SIGINT missions collated the relevant data to develop effective RWRs, jammers and evasive manœuvres. This prolonged war saw development of Remotely Piloted Vehicles (RPVs) for SIGINT, Anti-Radiation Missiles (ARMs), programmable self-protection jammers and communication jamming systems. Dedicated EW aircraft like the EA6B and EF 111 provided 'package EW' protection to the attacking aircraft formations. EW planning got integrated and enmeshed for operational mission planning. The Vietnam War saw operational concepts of 'hunter killer' missions to hunt for SAM sites and destroy them with the 'killer force' of ARMs. These were also known as 'wild weasel' missions. Suppression/Destruction of Enemy Air Defences (SEAD/DEAD) missions were operationlised to deny the enemy the freedom to employ the EM spectrum for operations. Another lesson learnt was that EW had emerged as one of the means amongst others to achieve success in the end game. Precision Guided Munitions (PGMs) were developed to mitigate the threat of anti-aircraft guns, by employing standoff PGMs. To counter the effectiveness of the Electronic Counter-Measures (ECMs) of the US forces, the Soviets supplied modified SA 2 SAM radars operating at much higher frequency bands as Electronic Counter-Counter-Measures (ECCMs) that were beyond the capability of the deployed jammers. Against the ARMs, the North Vietnamese deployed dummy SA 2 radar transmitters along the known route of the strike force, which resulted in the US forces exhausting the ARMs before they reached the real threat area. Due to EW effectiveness, the attrition rate of the US Air Force (USAF) dropped from 14 per cent at the beginning of the war to 1.4 per cent during the closing stages of the war.[4] EW played a key role in improving the mission effectiveness of the US forces. The 10-year Vietnam War ushered in many new technologies; the jammers became smarter by resorting to 'deception' jamming; programmable digital RWRs improved situational awareness; dedicated escort jammers protected bigger bombers; PGMs were inducted to improve survivability and weapon accuracy; and ARMs got inducted as DEAD weapons.[5]

While Israel achieved total surprise and decimated the opposing Egyptian forces during the Six-Day War of June 1967, the Israeli Air Force suffered heavy casualties during the opening day of the 1973 Yom Kippur War, as the Israeli intelligence failed to assess the deployment of newly inducted SA-6 SAMs operating with the Continuous Wave (CW) radar and the ZSU-23-4 Shilka Anti-Aircraft Artillery (AAA) equipped with the Ku band radars, that were beyond the capability of the US supplied jamming pods and RWRs. Updating of the hostile electronic ORBAT is crucial to conduct EW operations effectively. The Israelis learned their lessons well and during the Bekaa Valley operations in June 1982, they demonstrated the overwhelming impact of EMS dominance, when they jammed the Syrian communication network, blinded all radars, and stimulated a hostile AD network with decoys and decimated SAM sites through DEAD missions. The Syrian defence forces were left deaf, dumb, and blind, with their command set-up in total disarray. During this conflict, the Israelis created a template for future operations in which the control of the EMS dominated the entire concept of multi-domain operations, with overwhelming success. This template was replicated and enhanced during the first Gulf War, with the addition of space-based assets and more capable airborne EW, Intelligence, Surveillance, Reconnaissance (ISR) and communication jammers, better situational awareness, and stealth technology.

Recent conflicts in Syria once again highlight the importance of continuous R&D in the EW field to keep the EW tools sharp and adaptable to rapid changes in operational environments. Capability to detect and counter low Radar Cross-Section (RCS), low speed, armed drones in swarms could not have been produced in a short time. The physics and limitations of various frequency bands influence the selection of appropriate sensors, and deployment of multi-spectral sensors is the norm to cover the limitations of one frequency band of sensor over the other. Tension on the India-China border has once again highlighted the importance of monitoring the signature communication networks, associated with troop formations and the need to map them continuously and avoid surprises. The recent movement of the Russian troops with integrated and dedicated EW companies and brigades, close to the Ukrainian border, reaffirms the requirement to ensure EM spectrum dominance for ensuring superiority over the adversary[6]. The Russian concept is to monitor and map the hostile communication network continuously and jam it thoroughly in multiple frequency bands, which would result in disruption of the command and control elements. All the forces in future wars must be prepared to operate effectively in a Global Positioning System (GPS) denied environment.

Present EM Operational Environment

The EW operational environment for armed forces all over the world has changed dramatically with the induction of technologically advanced systems, sensors, and emphasis on net-centric operations. Most of the armed forces have inducted integrated air defence systems and networked other systems for better situational awareness, resilience, and redundancy against electronic counter-measures. Multi-spectral sensors and employment of the much diverse EM spectrum ranges require more agile, responsive, and adaptable EW systems for detection, identification, and effective counter-measures.

Net-centric Operations: All the armed forces are shifting from platform-centric to network-centric operations. Net-centric operations involve employment of a common data-link through which the sensors, shooters and decision-makers are networked. Networking of sensors, especially in multiple spectra of radio frequency, electro-optical and infra-red regimes improves target detection and location accuracy under all kinds of atmospheric environments. In the air, networking of platforms ensures improved situational awareness, faster decision loop and silent attack profile, as targets are designated from other sensors. Redundancy, resilience, and spectrum diversity are the hallmarks of net-centric operations that require more powerful, programmable, networked and agile communication jammers to counter such systems effectively. However, redundancy and multi-channel networking would ensure continuation of operations albeit in a degraded mode. On the other hand, mapping of the communication networks would reveal the deployment and disposition of the connected formations. Space-based Radio Frequency (RF) sensors on board Low Earth Orbit (LEO) satellites have the capability to map such networks and formation movements through artificial intelligence algorithms. Even though frequency hopping and spread spectrum techniques make it difficult to get intelligence from the networks, inputs on locational information and movement would be of immense importance.

Integrated Air Defence Operations: Conceptualised during World War II, the major air forces including the Chinese People's Liberation Army Air Force (PLAAF) and Pakistan Air Force (PAF) have well established, networked multi-layered and multi-spectral air defence systems that would be difficult to counter by just the self-protection suites on board attacking platforms. The attacking forces can resort to many types of attack profiles, varying from supersonic high level standoff attacks to low level last moment pop-up attacks. Various types of attack platforms like cruise missiles, ballistic missiles, fighter aircraft, helicopters, stealth platforms, standoff precision guided munition, Unmanned Aerial Vehicles (UAVs) and decoys necessitate multi-layered SAMs to cover the entire envelop of attack force. The Active Electronically Scanned Array (AESA) radars and software defined radios are much more resilient to active ECM action and EM interference. Passive electro-optical surveillance systems like the Sky spotter of the Rafael advance defence system and VERA passive surveillance system of ERA Inc, Czech Republic, would continue to provide detection capabilities as they remain unaffected by active ECM action or ARM attacks.

Standoff Attack Weapons: Improvement in sensor technology, propulsion systems and precision navigational systems has ushered in a variety of weapons that can be fired from standoff ranges of hundreds of kilometres. These weapons are capable of autonomous target engagement, and they could be data-linked to the mother aircraft for target updates and real-time bomb damage assessment. The IAF has acquired the SCALP air launched cruise missile which has stealthy features and an effective range of more than 250 km. The Rafael advanced defence system displayed the SPICE 250 ER Precision Guided Munition (PGM), during the last Aero India Show 2021, with an effective range of more than 150 km and capable of attacking moving targets. With such standoff ranges, the mother aircraft stays outside the lethal AD envelop and, therefore, does not require active ECM to degrade the hostile sensors, notwithstanding the requirement to protect itself from air threat. However, such standoff weapons employ some segment of EMS during the terminal phase of guidance, which could be vulnerable to interference.

UAVs: Unmanned Aerial Vehicles (UAVs) have been employed in most of the wars post World War II. The Israelis pioneered the employment of UAVs as decoys, SIGINT and Intelligence, Surveillance, Reconnaissance (ISR) platforms during the First Lebanon War, and the world took note of the UAV's potential as integral to all types of operations. Recent conflicts in Syria, Libya and Azerbaijan are testimony of the UAV's destructive power at the lowest cost. UAVs are being copiously employed as loitering munition for DEAD missions, airborne 'sniper' and persistent ISR, and SIGINT platforms. UAVs will have increased employment in EW operations either as autonomous platforms or as networked and 'teamed' platforms to enhance mission capabilities.

Space Applications: Space-based assets are being employed for communication, navigation, persistent Communications Intelligence (COMINT) and Electronic Intelligence (ELINT) applications. With advances in sensor technology, antennae designs and advances in cluster satellite applications, space is the expanding domain for EW applications.

Dense and Congested EM Spectrum: With allocation of frequencies for cell phone operations and other commercial use, the frequencies for military operations are getting restricted, and future implementation of the 5G network would further restrict frequency ranges. At the same time, net-centric operations demand a massive EM spectrum use within restricted frequency ranges. Due to the limitations of atmospheric attenuation, and data flow rate requirements, the frequency bands for military operators are getting increasingly congested in restricted frequency ranges. For example, many Airborne Interception (AI) radars on board fighters operate in the X band. The present IAF fighters and future inductions like the Light Combat Aircraft (LCA) variants and Advanced Medium Combat Aircraft (AMCA) would require frequency segregation at the design stage itself to avoid mutual electro-magnetic interference. Most of the data-links and voice communication for line of sight ranges are restricted to the Very/Ultra High Frequency (V/UHF) bands and frequency allocation to various military users would be essential. EM spectrum management for interference-free military operations amongst the three Services requires urgent and serious attention.

EW Suites

SIGINT: For effective conduct of EW, and for that matter, conduct of all domains of operations, intelligence on hostile sensors, weapon systems and disposition of formations, Air Defence Centres are a prerequisite. Signals intelligence provides information on hostile emitters in terms of their technical parameters, performance, location, and limitations. The electronic

ORBAT is required to be updated continuously during peace-time. Persistence and processing capabilities are key factors in employment of the SIGINT assets. The major forces have deployed space-based SIGINT systems which provide regular updates without fear of interference. The US has been deploying the 'Orion' series of SIGINT satellites, along with the 'Grab' series of ELINT satellites. The French have been deploying the 'Cerese' and 'Elisa' series of ELINT satellites. France has recently launched three satellite constellations in Low Earth Orbit (LEO) with a revisit time of 90 minutes. Russia and China have also deployed a sizeable number of such satellites. India launched its first ELINT satellite 'EMISAT' (Electro-Magnetic Intelligence Satellite) on April 31, 2019, and continues to plan the launch of more such satellites.[7] Private companies like Hawkeye 360 operate a first of its kind commercial satellite constellation. The low earth orbit and wide field of view of the satellites support frequent revisits anywhere each day[8]. Space-based SIGINT systems require a large antenna array and sensitive receivers to detect emitters. The location accuracy also suffers if the angle of arrival technique is employed. However, they are important assets for monitoring sea ships, submarines, and air defence mobile systems. Airborne SIGINT assets are more flexible for deployment and cover a wide swath of area. Large aeroplanes can carry many types of sensors including SIGINT, Electro-Optical (EO) and Infrared (IR) sensors which generate a more comprehensive data base, due to correlation of multi-spectral sensors. The Bombardier Global, Gulfstream and Falcon series of business jets are some of the platforms considered ideal due to their superior performance in range, cruise speed, altitude, and space for operators, internal fit, and accommodation of antennae. Other specialist aircraft like the Airborne Warning and Control System (AWACS), and for ISR and maritime reconnaissance also carry SIGINT sensors to improve situational awareness. Satellite communication ensures data downloads to ground stations even when the ground stations are beyond the line of sight of airborne assets. Most of the countries are in the process of upgrading the SIGINT airborne platforms with better performance platforms and modern SIGINT receivers. The IAF had issued a Request for Information (RFI) for seven SIGINT aircraft in the year 2017, however, it has not been progressed so far. Most of the UAVs have SIGINT sensors which are effectively deployed to cover the gaps in SIGINT operations, from other assets. Ground-based SIGINT systems have better processing capabilities, however, they suffer from line-of-sight limitations. Most of the Electric Support Measures (ESM) systems on board fifth generation fighters have ESM receivers with accurate geolocation capabilities for targeting, and they can supplement SIGINT data during peace-time as well as during hostilities. Analysis of the vast collated data is an enormous task which may take days to collate and disseminate. SIGINT data analysis requires modern tools and some level of automation to manage it within a reasonable period.

ESM Suites: Most of the airborne assets have radar warning receivers that are programmable and provide a display of Radio Frequency (RF) threats and associated weapons to the pilot or operator. Their geolocation accuracy has improved so much over the years that their inputs can be used to target hostile emitters with on-board munition or share the data on networks. Some of the fifth-generation fighters like the F-35 have ESM capability embedded in the AN/APG-81 radar.[9] The radar warning receivers have embedded digital technology with parallel wideband receivers. With extensive employment of lasers as ground-to-air weapons or guidance cues, modern airborne assets have started including Laser Warning Receivers (LWRs) as essential protection suites. To detect passive missiles (IR guided), the Missile Approach Warning Systems (MAWS) are now a standard fit for all modern fighters, military transport aircraft and helicopters. For aircraft operating at different altitudes, Ultra Violet (UV) based and Infrared (IR) based MAWS have been produced for operations. A few active radar-based MAWS are also operational on board some platforms. MAWS provide timely warning of the direction of approach of the missile and the 'time to impact.' For High Value Airborne Assets (HVAA) like AWACS and Very, Very Important Person (VVIP) carriage aircraft, MAWS are coupled with the Directed IR Counter-Measures (DIRCM) system which degrades the IR seeker by targeting it with laser rays. Northrop Grumman, Leonardo and Elbit are the leading companies that have such systems operational. In some configurations, MAWS activate IR flares to defeat IR guided missiles along with an appropriate manoeuvre.

ECM: Today, Self-Protection Suites (SPS) are essential integrated assets of all fighters. The SPS comprise the Self-Protection Active Jammer (SPJs),

Low Band Jammers (LBJs), RF towed decoys or expendable decoys, and passive counter-measure suites of chaff/flares The SPJs are programmable, auto-operated to counter multiple EM threats from many directions simultaneously. They are meant to counter tracking and weapon associated ground-based and airborne threats. Different deception techniques are generated to induce tracking errors in the weapon tracking systems and terminal guidance seekers, which should result in 'break lock', and keep the mother aircraft safe. The SPJs are fitted internal to the platform to leave the external stations for carriage of weapons. Podded Airborne Self-Protection Jammers (ASPJs) are inducted as add-ons to the earlier generation fighters. The SPJs cover the frequency band of 5.0 Ghz to 18.0 GHz, extendable to 40 Ghz to cover modern threats. SPJs are employed in conjunction with aircraft manoeuvre and chaff/flare deployment. Comprehensive simulation and exercises in a realistic threat environment are essential to ensure system effectiveness. AESA technology has brought in multi-functional radars which can be employed for surveillance, target designation and tracking. Low Band Jammers (LBJs) are, therefore, deployed against multi-functional low band radars for self-protection as well as for providing support jamming to the accompanying formation members. A configuration of low band jammers requires much larger antennae and high radiated power, which cannot be installed internally. LBJs are, therefore, in podded configuration. RF towed decoys are employed to create sufficient safe distance from the mother platform while 'luring' the missiles onto themselves, by generating a more powerful return. They are known to be effective against mono-pulse tracking seekers, against which normal embedded jammers may not be as effective. They are programmable and reel out quite fast to generate distinct targets for the hostile seeker. The RF decoys should not restrict the manoeuvring of the mother platform and should be retractable or dispensable. Passive counter-measure dispensing systems are employed as last-ditch measures against active RF seekers with chaff, and IR flares against IR guided weapons. It is important that chaff effectively cover the weapon seeker frequency band effectively and the flares must have a smart burn rate to avoid getting rejected by the IR tracking filters of the IR seekers.

Electronic Attack Systems: During the Vietnam War, the US Navy had deployed the dedicated EW aircraft, the EA 6B Prowler, twin-engine four-crew aircraft for providing effective jamming against hostile radars and communication networks. A total of 124 Prowlers were manufactured and they were employed during Operation Desert Storm, in Bosnia-Herzegovina, and in Kosovo, for enforcing the northern no-fly zone over Iraq and in Operation Iraqi Freedom. The Prowlers were armed with the High speed Anti-Radiation Missiles (HARM) the AGM 88, and carried up to five powerful ECM pods-ANALQ-99, covering frequency ranges from the VHF to the Ku bands.[10] The aircraft were retired in 2019, when the US Navy inducted the EA-18G Growler, the dedicated ECM aircraft. Presently the US Navy and Royal Australian Air Force have inducted Growlers as dedicated ECM aircraft, and Germany too has shown interest in them. They are used to counter powerful radars and communication networks as well as undertake DEAD missions with Anti-Radiation Missiles (ARMs). Other European countries like Germany and the UK have also considered the requirement of dedicated EW fighters to meet their own operational ECM requirements. The USAF inducted the EF-111 Raven dedicated ECM aircraft in 1981 as an EW aircraft. However, it could not undertake Suppression of Enemy Air Defence (SEAD) missions due to the lack of ARM carriage capability. The Ravens were retired in 1998 and the US Air Force (USAF) did not consider any replacement aircraft, as it has started development on stealth technology and did not feel the requirement of EW support to the stealth platforms. However, the USAF continued to share the EA-6B Prowlers as dedicated EW support aircraft with the US Navy. It is now evident that even stealth fighters like the F-35 require the EW suite to ensure their protection in the current EM environment. The USAF is once again considering induction of dedicated SEAD/DEAD aircraft. In Europe, there are plans to develop the Electronic Combat Reconnaissance (ECR) Typhoon fighter capable of SEAD and ECM operations. The EW configuration would be with two escort jammer pods, three 1,000-litre fuel tanks and six MBDA SPEAR-EW air-to-ground missiles (currently being developed for the Royal Air Force), in addition to the standard air-to-air compliment of four Meteor and two IRIS-T missiles. The escort jammer pods will be complemented by two emitter locator systems installed into the Typhoon's wingtips. Saab Industry has also test flown the Electronic Attack Jammer Pod (EAJP) on board the Gripen fighter, and the Swedish

Air Force has plans to acquire ECM escort jammers. The EAJP is from the family of Arexis ECM pods manufactured by Saab. China has developed the J-16D as the dedicated ECM aircraft against radars and communication nodes. Many other air forces have started focussing on acquiring dedicated ECM/SEAD platforms to address the rising demands of electronic attack capabilities. The Indian Air Force (IAF) has not yet considered induction of such platforms. With China deploying the S-400 class of AD systems, there may be a requirement of dedicated EW aircraft in the IAF for both communication and non-communication EW attacks.

Communication Jamming: Communication Jammers (COMJAMs) were resorted to as soon as the communication systems started operating for military operations at the dawn of the 20th century. COMJAM aircraft were employed effectively during the Vietnam War, Arab-Israeli conflicts, and during the Gulf Wars. Russia and China have elaborate COMJAM units integrated with army formations as well as airborne communication jammers. With proliferation of communication networks, COMJAM has gained a lot of importance in disrupting the command and control chains of the enemy. The USAF has recently deployed the Counter Communication System Block 10.2 to jam hostile satellite communications, which are crucial for beyond line-of-sight communications.[11] Twenty-five such systems are planned to be deployed by 2025. India has lagged in this field of communication jamming. The Indian Army is known to have an outdated communication jamming system. The IAF had clubbed the requirement of airborne COMJAM capability along with the SIGINT aircraft as part of the Request for Information (RFI) issued in July 2017. As the communication networks employ more advanced communication waveforms that have frequency hopping features, spread spectrum techniques and embedded encryption, it is important that the Indian armed forces and the defence industry invest in R&D and production of these systems. The IAF would need to consider this option on priority to counter the hostile net-centric advantage

GNSS Jammers: The Global Navigation Satellite System (GNSS) receivers are embedded in all military systems for navigation, tracking, time stamping and mapping purposes. As details of their operating frequencies and other technical parameters are officially known, and as the receivers are designed to be sensitive enough to receive low signal strength from satellites, the GNSS receivers are easily jammable. However, the Indian defence industry has taken a long time to manufacture such simple jammers and the Indian armed forces have not fully exploited these systems even to counter UAVs. Legal aspects of GPS jamming could be one of the reasons. Iraq had extensively employed GPS jammers during the first Gulf War and the Russians are known to have used powerful GPS jammers around Syria to counter suicide drones, however, the collateral impact has been felt in the Israeli airspace, by civil airliners. Finally, some progress in indigenous manufacture of such jammers systems seems to have been made in India.

Electronic Protection: Electronic Protection (EP) is one of the least addressed elements of EW, where this capability comes in 'by default' along with the system being procured, especially the radars and communication systems. Many modern radars employ the AESA technology which generates electronically steering beams that have better antenna gains and low sidelobes. Configuration of Transmit/Receive (T/R) modules makes it possible for the radars to transmit on multiple frequencies. Frequency agile radar transmitters force the jammer to dilute the jamming power as it is required to spread the jamming over the entire frequency range. The sector for radar transmissions can be selected by the operator, who can blank off the sector being jammed. Integrated and networked air defence sensors ensure a wide spread of frequencies, overlap of surveillance areas and integration of passive surveillance systems. All these measures provide good electronic protection capability against electronic jamming. However, some level of degradation does set into the system when tackling active jamming. Chaffs have been losing effectiveness against ground-based surveillance radars due to the incorporation of doppler processing, which filters out chaff returns. However, chaff against missile seekers could still be effective if deployed judiciously along with an appropriate manoeuvre. As passive sensors cannot be directly attacked with ARMs or active ECM, they provide an additional EW protected layer. Therefore, the Integrated Air Defence System (IADS) has inherent electronic protection against hostile EW action. Some of the surface-to-air missiles like David's Sling of Rafael have incorporated two terminal guidance seekers in the missile, which operate in the RF and EO regimes, and provides effective redundancy and resilience against offensive EW action. The DIRCM systems, equipped with lasers, provide effective electronic protection against incoming missiles and they are considered essential protection systems for high value airborne assets. Communication systems employing wide band frequency hopping transmissions with advanced modulations make them hard to detect and difficult to jam. The Indian armed forces are still in the process of acquiring such systems. As the employment of satellite-based communication has increased with greater dependency, it is important to ensure the resilience of Satellite Communication (SATCOM) against jamming. The US Space and Missile Command Centre has tested SATCOM anti-jamming capability and the system is planned to be deployed during 2022.[12] GNSS receivers are being hardened against GPS jamming and spoofing by altering the GPS receiver antenna pattern. In the future, more robust and jam resistant GNSS receivers would be an essential criterion for equipment induction.

Emerging Technology

AESA Technology: The AESA technology has matured sufficiently for radar applications. The same is being employed in manufacturing smart jammers. This will ensure much faster, agile, and simultaneous jamming of multiple threats emanating from different directions and RF frequency regimes.

Artificial Intelligence and Machine Learning: Typically, the first steps in EW operations are, gathering, sifting, and analysing SIGINT data, based on which identification and jamming libraries are created for the programmable systems to identify and jam as per the programmed techniques. The current EW systems can counter the presently deployed assets with known electronic characteristics that could be modified to a limited extent. However, with induction of software defined modern radars and radios, which can instantly change the transmission characteristics through software programmes, it would no longer be possible to analyse the huge heap of data in a brief time to update the identification and jamming 'libraries.' Due to technological advances in Artificial Intelligence (AI) and Machine Learning (ML), this labourious task would need to be performed by cognitive EW techniques that would employ EW algorithms to sift out known, unknown, new, or unusual signatures in a matter of minutes and generate appropriate jamming programmes for new and unknown threats. These 'libraries' would need to be transmitted and uploaded in the EW systems in a brief time for the forces to remain EW effective in a rapidly changing Electro-Magnetic Spectrum (EMS) environment. The future EW equipment itself would need to be upgradable and adaptable in a brief time and on site, to remain effective. The EW systems would have embedded AI and ML to tackle the rapidly changing EM environment during operations and generate an appropriate response to unknown or new target systems. The USAF has recently conducted a successful trial of uploading the EW data files from hundreds of miles away, to update the F-16 ALQ_213 counter-measure signal processor, in the air. This type of capability will ensure the shortest time for the EW systems to be updated during operations. An important aspect in the cognitive EW domain and AI/ML employment is the quality of the training data and improvement in action algorithms, as a continuous process. Expert EW operators would continue to be important and oversee the AI-based process.

Computer Technology: As the EW systems upgrade from reactive to adaptive and further to cognitive capable systems, computers with much higher processing powers and low latency would be needed to match the processing capabilities required. The enabling technologies would involve smart Field Programmable Gate Array (FPGA) with embedded processors to provide flexibility and reconfigurability. High performance embedded computing power would be an essential ingredient to run AI algorithms. Much faster Analogue to Digital (A/D) and Digital to Analogue (D/A) would be required for high performance high bandwidth applications of EW.

Directed Energy Weapons: There has been considerable progress towards fielding laser and high-power microwave Directed Energy Weapons (DEWs). The AN/SQ-3 laser weapon developed for the US Navy has been operationally deployed on board the US naval ship USS *Ponce* since September 2014. The weapon can destroy small UAVs effectively. The Self-protect High Energy Laser Demonstrator (SHiELD) is scheduled to be demonstrated in the USA, in 2024. Laser weapons require high power generation and creation of a narrow beam which should stay focussed sharply at a point on the manoeuvring target. The Israeli industry has successfully conducted a series of interceptions to shoot down drones with a powerful airborne laser system, installed on a civilian light aircraft. During the trials that were conducted over the sea, the high-powered laser fired from a civilian Cessna plane, and destroyed the unmanned targets at differing ranges and altitudes. The main consideration is to manage the size, weight, and power requirements of the airborne systems, to operationalise the airborne laser weapon. Israel plans to develop a ground-based laser weapon system which will be integrated with the Iron Dome system against rocket attacks, by 2024. The demand for laser weapons is increasing globally as they have low cost per shot, and are easy on logistical support and maintenance. The Leonardo Company is considering the option to install the laser weapons onboard the 'Tempest,' the UK led sixth generation fighter. There has been considerable development in high-power microwave energy weapons which would be effective against drone swarms. The US Army has funded one such project for future deployment against hypersonic targets. The directed energy weapons will complement the EW systems in the physical destruction or degradation of the electronic systems.

Other Technological Aspects

Modular and Open Architecture: It takes a long time to develop effective EW systems against a new threat as the operational systems cannot be upgraded fast due to propriety issues. Future EW systems would have to be modular in concept and upgradable to remain effective. Open architecture systems with common software standards would ensure faster upgrades during operations.

Interoperability. At present, the Indian armed forces are unable to access SIGINT or other intelligence data from the UAVs of the other Services, as the data-links are not common or interoperable. The armed forces must ensure interoperability of EW systems by incorporating common net-centric standards and SIGINT formats. This would ensure that all data will be shared through networks and made available for SIGINT analysis.

Networking of EW Assets: Individual ELINT assets would provide one level of geolocation accuracy and set of parameters, whereas networked ELINT assets would provide better geolocation accuracy and data parameters, just like the fused air situation picture obtained from networked AD sensors provides better results. Networking of airborne Electronic Support Measure (ESM) bearing aircraft would also result in improved situational awareness. Similarly, networked Electronic Counter-Measure (ECM) assets would be able to counter target sensors in a coordinated and synergetic manner. To achieve this, the EW systems need to have common ICDs and protocols for integration. This must be ensured during the procurement process of the systems.

EMS Management: The EMS environment would continue to grow more dense in the future as the armed forces would share it for commercial activities. EMS use and allocation of this limited resource would require strategic and dynamic management. The armed forces would require such a management organisation at the tri-Service level to manage this aspect right from the equipment induction phase.

Conclusion

Modern military operations are heavily dependent on the employment of the EM spectrum in all regimes of intelligence, command, control, communication, surveillance, targeting, defensive and offensive operations. The EM spectrum itself is the fundamental domain that enables conduct of operations in all other domains. Freedom of action in the EM spectrum, at the time and place of own consideration and EM segment, is a prerequisite for dominating operations in all other domains. Electronic warfare is a tool through which this freedom of action is achieved. Despite the spread of EMS employment, the regime is more congested, contested, and complex, as we share the spectrum for commercial and civilian use and contest for its freedom of operation, with hostile forces. The EW operational environment has changed dramatically with massive technological developments in the fields of communication, computer technology, electronics, sensors, and propulsion systems. Net-centric operations and IADS, with multi-spectral sensors and multi-layered weapons, require advanced, agile, and adaptive EW systems to ensure mission success. Software defined radars and radios can change their operating signatures and modes very rapidly. Under this environment, the SIGINT data so generated would require artificial intelligence tools to analyse and sift the known, unknown, unusual, and new EM signatures and generate appropriate jamming techniques. EW specialists would play a crucial role in overseeing effective AI functioning. Modern EW systems would need to be agile, adaptive, and upgradable to remain relevant in the rapidly changing operational environment.

While the Indian armed forces have laid more emphasis on non-communication EW capabilities, the capability to map the multi-spectral and secure networked communication systems and capability to degrade or destroy these networks through soft kill or hard kill, requires urgent consideration. Technological development of EW systems started at the same time that the EM spectrum was employed for military operations. Advanced technology has now been effectively adapted for employing many different types of ECM systems. EM spectrum management within the armed forces requires sincere consideration at the apex level to exploit its restricted useful range gainfully. Interoperability of systems should be achieved through standardised protocols, modular and open architecture systems. The history shows that EW is seen to have developed well during hostilities and its development takes a back seat during peace-time. This trend must change, as the outcome of any operation in any operational domain would significantly depend on the degree of dominance in the EM spectrum.

Notes

1. Department of Defence "Electromagnetic Spectrum Superiority Strategy," 2020, p. i.
2. Daljit Singh, *AIR POWER Journal*, Vol. 16, No. 2, Summer 2021 (April-June) p. 44.
3. Alfred Price, *The History of U.S. Electronic Warfare*, vol. III (Association of Old Crows, 1989), p. 36.
4. Abdul Karim Baram, *Technology in Warfare* (The Emirates Centre for Strategic Studies and Research), p. 224.
5. Singh, n. 2, p. 50.
6. Dr Thomas Withington, "Russian Radiation," *Armada International*, January 6, 2022.
7. STS http://stsfor.org/content/significance-elint-satellites-national-security-imperatives-india. Accessed on January 9, 2022.
8. https://www.he360.com/technology/. Accessed on January 8, 2022.
9. https://www.northropgrumman.com/what-we-do/an-apg-81-active-electronically-scanned-array-aesa-fire-control-radar/
10. https://www.airforce-technology.com/projects/prowler/. Accessed on January 7, 2022.
11. https://spacenews.com/l3-harris-wins-120-million-contract-to-upgrade-space-force-electronic-jammers/. Accessed on January 10, 2022.
12. https://www.c4isrnet.com/battlefield-tech/c2-comms/2020/08/26/space-force-tests-new-anti-jamming-capability/

5. Future of Aerial Warfare: Some Key Aspects

RK Sharma and VS Rana

Introduction

In the entire history of mankind, no two wars have ever been the same, even when taking place at the same time. This is primarily due to the differences in the geopolitical theatres, the cause of the wars, and the disparities in the military and technological capabilities of the adversaries. Therefore, it is always difficult to predict about future wars. Aerial warfare is dynamic in nature, and primarily due to the technological changes that continually take place and find their exploitation in aerial weapon systems, it becomes even more difficult to predict outcomes in future aerial wars. Indeed, all aerial warfare is a competition between offensive and defensive weapon systems; and along with a host of other factors, employment of technologically advanced platforms and weapon systems, can tilt the balance in favour of success or defeat. Since technology and aerial weapon systems continually evolve, it is for such reasons that predictions of future warfare can often be erroneous. It is also true that nobody has a crystal ball to predict the future of warfare, let alone an aerial war. However, a generally accurate assessment can be made through a process of net-assessments, appreciations and a logical review of capabilities that a potential adversary possesses. Nevertheless, militaries do need some sense of the future operational environment to be able to suitably prepare themselves for the imminent threats. This chapter will discuss the future of aerial warfare in general and develop a sense as to how the Indian Air Force (IAF) should be looking at certain key aspects of air power that are relevant for us in the future.

The rapidly changing technologies in the field of weapon systems and platforms will have a significant impact on the war-waging capability in the future. Manned and unmanned aircraft technologies have seen technological development in the past two decades that has never been seen before. Artificial Intelligence (AI) and the growth of compatible hardware have made aerial systems more accurate and lethal. The maturing of AI research will allow the employment of concepts that have always been desired but not been actionable due technological restrictions. The autonomous operations that AI technology affords will allow interesting concepts like drone mother ship, intelligent unmanned vehicles for reconnaissance, human-machine teaming, drone swarming, and so forth. This has been discussed in detail in subsequent chapters of this book. Since many such technologies have been absorbed into aerial systems, it has made air power that much more potent in nature. Due to the inherent characteristics of lethality, accuracy, range and response, air power is likely to spearhead the future wars, and the use of air power has been accepted as a first responder choice of force application by nations. Globally, the advanced nations continue to expand and exploit the technological gap between themselves and other nations that do not have advanced Research and Development (R&D) and a complementary manufacturing industry. Dominant aspects that are intrinsic to aerial warfare like Intelligence, Surveillance, Reconnaissance (ISR), robotics, AI, airframe and engine technologies, space and cyber warfare; and their roles in limited, hybrid and conventional wars have been discussed in the earlier chapters. This chapter will specifically deal with four aspects of aerial warfare, their inter-linkages and relevance in the foreseeable future in our context. These are: Tactical Operations, Effects-Based Operations (EBOs), Network-Centric Operations (NCOs) and the relevance of Centres of Gravity (CsOG).

Centralised Command and Decentralised Execution

To start with, it is important to recollect that the effectiveness of the employment of air power is contingent on the tenet of centralised control and decentralised execution. Joint plans and targeting objectives are laid out at the directional level. Dissemination of operational orders is made to the operational commanders. Depending on the force availability for target neutralisation, the responsibility for execution is at the tactical level. Complete tactical flexibility for execution of the mission is given to the operators. This structure contrasts with the concepts that land forces employ, wherein close command and control continue to be exercised, in one form/ way or another, right down to the tactical level, except, of course, in the case of special forces and special missions. Naval forces also provide flexibility towards the concept of decentralised execution with freedom to command and control provided to the "flag" at sea. The other distinguishing factor between land and air operations is that land forces work sequentially from objective to objective. The nature of the terrain, environmental conditions, speed of advance due to friction on the ground, logistical considerations and other such criteria, all play their part in the sequential ways the land forces operate.

Parallel and Dynamic Targeting

The ability to inflict damage on the enemy's identified multiple CsOG which are deep inside the enemy territory, bypassing fielded military forces, has seen an exponential rise ever since the aircraft's ability to carry the war into the enemy's heartland was first established. Over a period of time, various new concepts like parallel operations and dynamic targeting have emerged which have endorsed this versatile tenet of air power. In contrast to a sequential fight, air forces will usually employ the tactics of parallel and dynamic targeting. Parallel operations are aimed to neutralise a host of targets either simultaneously or in quick succession. These are best employed in offensive, counter-air as well as interdiction operations. These lend themselves to sustained pressure on the enemy through surprise, thereby enhancing room for manoeuvre by own land forces. Along with dynamic targeting and depending on the availability of offensive forces, parallel operations aid in creating several pressure points for the enemy and keeps his decision-making loops off-balance. However, such tactical operations succeed when they are part of a joint plan. The primacy of air power to create decisive advantages for the land forces through parallel operations has to be recognised and full flexibility provided to the mission executors. In effect, for such joint plans to succeed, they must be led by the air force. Similarly, dynamic targeting aims to wrest the offensive initiative and keep the enemy guessing.

Along with parallel operations, dynamic targeting is necessary to maintain a high battle tempo. However, these operations depend on the support of combat support elements like Airborne Warning and Control System (AWACS) and Intelligence, Surveillance, Target Acquisition and Reconnaissance (ISTAR) aircraft operating in an NCO environment. Smart aerial weapons with long range and high accuracy like air-to-surface precision weapons [employment of these weapons increased from 7 per cent overall in Desert Storm (1990), to 68 per cent in Iraqi Freedom (2003)] are also a prerequisite in such an aided environment to obviate attrition while causing destruction in very short timeframes. ISR builds the physical and electronic-Order of Battle (E-ORBAT) picture of the battlespace and with the support of AWACS and ISTAR, the initial missions will aim to destroy the enemy's command and control centres and neutralise surface-to-air threats using both passive and kinetic means. Short range Unmanned Aerial Vehicles (UAVs) and Loitering Munitions (LMs) will be part of the package to destroy sensors and create the necessary corridors for entering the enemy's airspace. Long range UAVs and LMs will attack other targets of the parallel targeting plan.

Net-Centric Operations

The future of aerial warfare will be contingent on working in an NCO environment. Net-centricity is essentially a communication environment which is cyber-secure, with redundancies and nodes, physically protected and robust in hardware, so as to provide information up and down the hierarchy as per shared protocols. Eventually, NCOs aim to aid decision-making for reducing the sensor-to-shooter time and enhancing time-sensitive targeting. In fact, NCOs will be the primary enabler in all future conflicts and an essential ingredient for employment of air power. Evolving a net-centric joint operational system with elements of each domain interwoven/linked at all levels to operate independently and/or in coordination with surface and maritime forces to achieve the desired effect emerges as an imperative capability for the future wars. The basis of an NCO is modularity. Sensors of all types, from satellites to Electronic Intelligence (ELINT), Signals Intelligence (SIGINT) aircraft, radars and UAVs provide real-time ISR to achieve Command and Control (C_2) interoperability. The net-centric architecture must have adequate bandwidth to handle the vast amount of data inflow and the complementary software for information fusion and providing the necessary situational awareness. An NCO environment must make the battlespace transparent to its own forces and through its own offensive action on the enemy's Command, Control and Communication (C_3) centres, make it opaque for the enemy. High and effective situational awareness that is essential in high-tempo operations is the eventual by-product of network-centric operations.

Let us now examine the linkage between the net-centric capabilities and the effects-based methodology. Net-centric capabilities are intrinsically linked to Effects-Based Operations (EBOs). The NCO is not a new concept; it has matured from hand signals to high Situational Awareness (SA), displays and secure communication systems through the years from World War I onwards. Air power doctrines evolved in the West from World War I onwards wherein air observation aircraft were essentially used to direct artillery fire and later for some nascent use of bombing from the air. World War II saw the use of air power as a much broader entity when aircraft had substantially developed as weapon systems. Aerial combat to create favourable air situations, interdiction, close-air support; and the use of bombers for industrial destruction, found articulation in the emerging doctrines. In the recent era, during the Falklands War, the Royal Air Force (RAF) came across issues of long distance command and control. While the success of air power during the Arab- Israeli Wars and later during Operations Desert Storm (1990), Kosovo, Allied Force (1999) and Enduring Freedom (2001) proved the primacy of air power, it is believed that Operation Iraqi Freedom (2003) was planned and fought using an emerging net-centric capability. NCO in its infancy can be described as the linkages among the sensor, decision-maker and shooter; the coalition forces in 2003 could bring together sensors of various forces, fuse the data on a common base, analyse and provide a common operational picture for the coalition air forces. Today, as well as in the future, the need for a robust NCO environment will be essential for effective conduct of all aerial warfare roles as per the air power doctrines, particularly when air forces have to operate in a multi-national and multi-domain environment. Multi-domain war-fighting entails knowledge of what is happening in the various domains that could affect the operational situation. Hence, a multi-domain connection through an encrypted data link architecture across each domain is necessary, if we are to integrate and exploit information from multiple sources, including intelligence, reconnaissance, surveillance, database, and sensor information to formulate an integrated response. The architecture should provide connectivity within the domain as well with other domains, and with a high degree of accuracy.

Effects-Based Operations (EBOs) and Net-Centricity

Historically, in conflicts post-World War II, one aspect that stands out is the evolution of an effects-based approach. What really is meant by the term "effects"? 'Effects' is basically the linkage between national security objectives and the application of military force. Basically, a national aim is connected from a strategic-level requirement, right through the operational and tactical objectives to achieve specific military tasks. It establishes the relevance of the objectives to be achieved at the strategic and operational levels, driven by a centralised and top-down targeting process. It also encompasses direct and indirect effects of diplomatic, psychological and economic instruments of a nation's net capability. An effects-based approach is, therefore, concerned with outcomes and is applicable at all levels of war (military, diplomatic and economic); and brings about a coherence towards a desired end state as per a nation's security policy.

For 'effects' to be effectively achieved at the planning and execution levels, the important prerequisites are a network-centric environment, precision weapons with combat-support elements in a top-down targeting process that is in consonance with operational objectives, with minimal attrition. It is also evident that to achieve the desired strategic, operational and tactical objectives; the tenet of centralised command and control and decentralised execution is the necessary and effective way of conducting all aerial warfare now and may be will be even more relevant in the future. As per RAF AP 3000 definition, centralised control will promote an integrated and joint multi-national effort. Since no single commander can personally direct all the actions of a large number of air force units, decentralised execution becomes necessary for mission success.

Centralised command in the application of air power, also prevents the frittering away of the air effort into smaller units and this sole reason exemplifies the way why air forces operate under this format. Finally, what comes out of the tenet is: if the objectives are clearly stated and controlled top-down, then mission execution will be effective. Objectives are then achieved with minimum control and maximum freedom to execute. Since there will always be constraints in execution of missions like availability of resources, environment, enemy opposition, etc., an enabled NCO environment, becomes necessary to address these constraints and provide quick decisions and responsive execution.

Working with the other Services in an NCO environment is a complex process that is largely driven by the physical environment. Maritime and land forces have low mobility and under conflict situations can be affected by logistical constraints, more so in the case of land forces. Land forces also have multi-layered command and control processes and spans of controls, which have become important. While network-centric operations enhance decision-making, mobility continues to be the big factor weighing on the speed of advance. For the air forces, speed and flexibility are positive characteristics. There are at most two or three levels of control feeding into well-defined execution plans. Command Headquarters issues the air-tasking orders based on targeting, enemy order of battle, threats and own resources. Execution is by package commanders and given an effective NCO environment, decision-making and speed of reaction are enhanced.

One critical issue in an NCO environment is air space management. The tasks performed at the Command Operations Centres and Air Defence Control Centres have to be seamlessly linked, so that there is no chance of fratricide. This issue becomes even more critical given that all future aerial warfare will have a very large number of UAVs operating in the Tactical Battle Area (TBA). This brings up the issue of employment of UAVs/Unmanned Combat Aerial Vehicle (UCAVs) of various sizes and specifications into the aerial warfare construct. In future, it is absolutely certain that UAVs/UCAVs and other robotic machines will play an enhanced role in battle. From hybrid to conventional warfare, UAVs and UCAVs will be utilised extensively in the ISR, targeting, communication relays and loitering munitions roles. Given the evolution of AI, they will be used in both standalone and consort modes. Rather, with the need to keep force attrition low, in some settings, UAVs will even play the leading offensive role. That said, the legal aspects of employing autonomous UAVs without the man-in-the-loop will continue to be debated.

Relevance of Centres of Gravity (CsOG)

The emergence of air power provided the most important and vital dimension of warfare, attacking the point of crucial vulnerability, directly circumventing obstacle and terrain imperatives. We now examine the aspect and relevance of selection of Centres of Gravity (CsOG) in an NCO environment and its lateral connection with EBOs. The COG is a concept that defines such target systems or points of crucial vulnerability of a critical capability against which, if a successful attack is carried out and it is destroyed, it will cause maximum effect in the defeat of the adversary. A COG can be at various levels i.e. strategic, operational, tactical and, may be, political also. At the start of a war, militaries will always expect to have unity of purpose, cohesion and clearly laid out objectives by the political authority. Fighting forces will always identify their CsOG, in their area of operations such that their destruction will cause a breakdown in the unity of the enemy forces. In a large theatre of air operations, centralisation of command enables unity of purpose for effective execution. However, if the air force units are dispersed, cohesion will become ineffective. This is one reason why air power is always centrally controlled so that effective concentration of force can be applied to destroy the adversary's CsOG and thereby his cohesion and unity. If one's own air power is deliberately divided into several smaller forces, it will not be possible to destroy the enemy's CsOG, especially those which require a large force offensive for their neutralisation.

The question is: will a COG always exist and will it always be identifiable? It is entirely possible that at the strategic level there may be none that can be identified that can cause the entire enemy armed forces to capitulate, particularly in limited wars of short duration. Nonetheless, there will always be identifiable CsOG at the operational and tactical levels that will still require application of air power, so as to disrupt the enemy's rhythm to progress the battle. Particularly in limited wars of short duration an NCO will always be essential to achieve rapid destruction of the CsOG.

The strategies followed during earlier wars were based on annihilation and attrition to render the enemy force ineffective. However, by employing an EBO approach, the same effect can be achieved with fewer casualties and in a cost-effective manner. The planning for on EBO would consider the effect desired at each level and identify the critical vulnerabilities, which, when neutralised, would cause the desired effect. The concept of CsOG too focusses on causing disproportionate effect by attacking crucial vulnerabilities where successful attacks are likely to be decisive. Hence, CsOG and EBOs are closely interlinked.

In joint operations, the fundamental difference in ascertaining the enemy's CsOG between the land and air forces is one of consequences. By their nature of being terrain-centric, land forces generally see the opposing concentration of force as a COG. Air forces, on the other hand, will identify several Cs OG in their geographical area of reach, such that their destruction will bring about the collapse of the adversary's entire system. Concentration of opposing enemy forces, if identified as a COG, will create a potential of getting into a war of attrition; which will be in contradiction to keeping the war swift, short and limited. On the other hand, application of air power has the larger objective of creating 'effects' through parallel targeting of CsOG in order to destroy a much larger system of the adversary. In the end, the complex part of identifying the enemy's CsOG lies in their relevance to the end-state that is desired in an acceptable timeframe.

Conclusion

It is difficult to predict the nature of future wars, but it is prudent to assume that they are likely to be uncertain, unknown, unexpected and unprecedented. There are no easy answers but it is more than likely that the type of war imposed on us would not be forethought. It is an accepted fact that aerospace power will continue to play a decisive and dominant role in future wars and it is also certain that the initial response will have to be provided by air power. The speed of action and reaction, the strategic agility of air power, the reach, the inherent capability of precision attacks where attendant damage is limited, the vast ambit of different roles and capabilities, and the wide variety of missions that are within the ambit of air power are attributes that are unmatched by land and naval power. We can now summarise the future of aerial warfare, particularly in the Indian subcontinental context wherein it is an acknowledged fact that the People's Liberation Army Air Force (PLAAF) will continue to have technological advantages and provide support of assets to the Pakistan Air Force (PAF). A two-front war is a distinct possibility. However, the initiative to control a dissuasive or a deterrent posture on any front is not a given. Neither are the geographical extent and timeframes of a conflict predictable. Preparedness to fight a long and vigorous conflict must be factored into the plans.

- Modernisation of air forces will continue in order to remain a primary deterrent, capable of swift punitive action. The focus will be on both, quantity and quality; and aerial warfare capabilities will encompass the entire spectrum from hybrid to conventional wars.
- The effectiveness of all air operations will be contingent on a robust and secure network-centric communications architecture. NCOs will enhance the effectiveness of centralised command and decentralised execution. Decision support systems, with ever increasing use of AI will be utilised to keep the decision cycle short.
- Air power will be employed to create many pressure points on the enemy's deployment of forces. Effective utilisation of offensive manned/ unmanned aerial assets will be the key to the success of manoeuvres by the land forces. Joint planning of such operations, with air power being central to the creation of the battlespace (along with accurate long-range surface weapons) will be necessary.
- Parallel and dynamic offensive operations will be planned in a high tempo scenario to disrupt the enemy's operational balance. For this, time-sensitive targeting with multi-purpose smart weapons and payload capability will be necessary.
- EBOs with centralised control will be necessary to cause effective destruction of the enemy's war-making capacity. Parallel and dynamic operations will be necessary for effective EBOs. Selection of targets at operational and tactical levels will be identified by the air force to facilitate rapid offensives by the land forces.
- CsOG targets will be identified to ensure that the air war proceeds in a manner to create severe pressure, leading to destruction of the enemy's operational capabilities. Selection of CsOG must be made by

air warriors of high operational calibre. Once identified, persistence and determination must continue through parallel EBOs.

- Highly accurate and lethal smart munitions will be needed in large quantities for the destruction of enemy targets and reduction of collateral damage.
- UAVs/UCAVs/drones will play an essential role in any future war. Air power will exploit the unmanned capabilities for ISR and offensive operations, in both consort with manned aircraft and in standalone roles. Unmanned systems will continue to evolve in performance, stealth and as intelligent weapon systems.
- The necessity for combat support elements [AWACS, ISTAR, jammers, ELINT, Air-to-Air Refuelling (AAR), etc.] will be essential prerequisites for the success of most missions.
- Since surface-to-surface missiles will be a part of any future war, it will be necessary to ensure de-confliction while carrying out offensive support missions. Accurate short and medium-range artillery assets along with unmanned systems are now a part of land forces. Hence, the need for classical Close Air Support (CAS) will be less in quantum. Land forces will need to ensure such support with the field weapon systems that they possess and will acquire in the future. Air power will be extensively employed for manoeuvre forces and depth targets with a focus on identified CsOG and EBOs.

6. Emerging Armament Technologies

SC Mukul, Bhanoji Rao, Abhishek Saxena and VS Rana

Introduction

Irrespective of the emerging new dimensions of warfare, armament technologies will be the key variable while prosecuting future wars and winning them with the least amount of attrition to own side. The evolution of armament technology in pursuit of the ever-changing art of warfare makes an interesting study. The art of warfare is a constantly evolving phenomenon. As the old adage proclaims, "The best guides to the future are those who understand the past well": a review of the defining moments that changed the face of warfare due to armament asymmetry for two centuries reveals that although each situation was unique in its origin, trajectory, and content, all shared common features. In each case, new combat methods arose through innovative use of next-generation armament technology that displaced earlier forms of warfare by shifting the balance between offence and defence, space and time, and fire and manoeuvre.

The nation-states which developed and harnessed the new technologies gained a significant advantage, compelling adversaries to match or counter them to be able to prevail on the battlefield. Those who adopted the new technologies flourished, while those who did not, declined, often precipitously. Examples of this phenomenon can be seen in the analysis of historic battles, e.g. the innovative use of longbow technology in 1415 at the Battle of Agincourt exhibited by the British, using a high proportion of longbow archers to decimate a French Army five to ten times larger; the advent of the mass army during the Napoleonic era of the late 18th and early 19th centuries; the embracing of the railroad, rifle, and telegraph in the mid-19th century, which heralded the industrialisation of warfare; and the German *blitzkrieg*. These were made possible by advances in internal combustion engine technology, aircraft design, radar and radio and associated armament innovations following World War I; and the development of nuclear weapons in the 20th century. The Gulf War provided a glimpse of emerging armament technologies through the large-scale use of space, the effectiveness of Precision-Guided Munitions (PGM) and the use of the Global Positioning System (GPS) to coordinate operations. The current increasing use of PGMs, Unmanned Aerial Vehicles (UAVs), and Unmanned Combat Aerial Vehicles (UCAVs) further consolidates the influence of evolving armament technologies on the conduct of warfare. The use of hypersonic cruise missiles by Russia during the ongoing Russia-Ukraine conflict clearly indicates that emerging armament technologies will play a decisive role in future warfare.

Evolutionary Growth Pattern

As a rule, every armament technology follows an evolutionary growth pattern. UAVs are at the pinnacle of the technological pursuit that goes back to the invention of slings and arrows centuries ago. The process, which brought catapults and later artillery and Intercontinental Ballistic Missiles (ICBMs) into the picture, today has reached the current state allowing long-range UAV missions with much more flexibility and capacity for everyday use. The swarm UAV attacks in Syria and the use of drones during the Russia-Ukraine conflict illustrate the potential and direction of growth in this field.

The quest for accurate delivery of bombs and munitions gained added urgency in the Vietnam War and the Laser Guided Bomb (LGB) soon became the most sought after weapon. The LGB can, however, go awry due to smoke, clouds, and other atmospheric obscurities. The limitations of the LGB resulted in the development of Joint Direct Attack Munitions (JDAMs) and later the Joint Standoff Weapon (JSOW) family of weapons that relied on the Inertial Navigation System/Global Positioning System (INS/GPS) for guidance and made it possible to deliver these even in bad weather as long as the correct geographical position of the target was available.

The introduction of precision-guided munitions and the employment of unmanned aerial vehicles have separated the warriors mentally and physically from the act of killing in the real world. The skill level required to fire unguided bombs accurately to destroy targets was of a very high order. During the firing of LGBs, the operator was required to designate the target with a laser and keep it illuminated throughout the bomb's flight, a process that took seconds. Delivering a GPS-guided bomb simply requires feeding the coordinates of the target into a computer. Similarly, UAV operators are physically present at a distance from the combat zone.

Effectiveness/Breakthrough Cycle

The operational or strategic problems faced by the operators on the battlefield resulted in the emergence of armament innovations. The recent military-technological revolution shows that the advantage in warfare goes to those who can most effectively utilise/harness the emerging technologies. Armament innovations display a common structure: a cycle of innovation, diffusion, and refinement. As British Army officer and military historian J.F.C. Fuller put it, "Every improvement in armament is eventually met by the counter-improvement which gradually or rapidly whittles down its power. Although technical and operational counter-measures rarely succeed in nullifying the effectiveness of new military practices, they do, over time, erode it somewhat. The competition between measure and counter-measure becomes a defining feature of the ensuing military regime".[1]

The impact of emerging space technologies and military systems to make military operations more effective on a large scale was demonstrated for the first time during the Gulf War. In addition, the importance of GPS to coordinate military operations, the effectiveness of PGMs, the significance of stealth technology, and the potential value of theatre missile defence were demonstrated. The United States embraced precision weaponry in the decade that followed the Gulf War. The combination of precision-guided munitions and stealth provided the US Air Force (USAF) the ability to strike adversaries from the air with near impunity.

During the ongoing Russian-Ukrainian War[2], the strategic strikes against military targets using cruise missiles, and short range ballistic missiles like the Iskander-M and Kaliber, bombarding of the cities with rocket artillery and cluster munitions, use of the Bayraktar TB-2 drone, and multiple launch rocket system BM-21 all indicated that usage of state-of-the-art armament systems will be an important consideration in future wars. Russia used the 'Kinzhal' hypersonic missile successfully against Ukraine for the first time after its development. Its hypersonic missile, the 'Zircon', was also test-fired from the *Admiral Gorshkov* frigate stationed in the Barents Sea and hit the target located 1,000 km away in the White Sea successfully.[3] How the employment of hypersonic weapons will shape future wars, only time will tell.

Operational Environment and Impact of Emerging Armament Technologies

Predicting the future is always a difficult proposition. One can go drastically wrong. However, the future has to be anticipated. Based on future operating environments, the strategy, force structure, weapons and equipment, profile, doctrine, training, and human resources management are evolved. This is a dynamic process. Depending on changes in the security environment, mid-course corrections can always be made.

So what is going to be different in the use of armaments around 15 to 20 years hence? There are some important areas that we need to be particularly mindful of. First, is 'time', or the 'timeframe for action'. Through the medium of air, we can wield power in, let's say, minutes to hours, through space, in seconds to minutes, and through cyberspace, in milliseconds. Second, space and cyberspace do not respect geographical boundaries, and for that matter, distance becomes irrelevant in the cyber domain. Rapid advances in information and information-related technologies are enabling detection, identification, and tracking of a large number of targets over a wide area, for a longer time, with better accuracy and speed. Complementing these exponential increases in information warfare capabilities are major improvements in the range, accuracy, and lethality of conventional munitions which have resulted in building confidence to destroy or neutralise targets in a relatively short period. Innovative computer-simulation software and techniques are being developed to train and equip combatants far more effectively and efficiently. There will be active competition for creating or denying an information advantage. There will be high levels of integration in all the mediums of warfare: air, land, maritime, cyber, and space. Space will increase in importance as it will emerge as a major medium for conducting and supporting military operations. These factors are going to govern the growth and utilisation of future armament technologies.[4]

As a part of the ongoing transition, our dependence on wireless and wired mediums is converging. Computer and communication networks are becoming indistinguishable. The transmission of digitised packets on Internet Protocol (IP) and space-based networks is revolutionising information sharing and media broadcasting. It has led to the integration of overlapping areas of network operations, information operations, and the more focussed areas of electronic warfare, signals intelligence, electromagnetic spectrum operations, and military information support operations, changing the very face of emerging armament technologies and related platforms.[5]

Future trends in armament growth are characterised by a fusion of technologies relating to the physical, digital, and biological spheres—futuristic armaments are evolving in biotechnology, robotics and autonomous vehicles, additive manufacturing (such as 3-D printing), and nanotechnology. The energy that underpins everything is undergoing several different types of transformation. Directed Energy Weapons (DEWs) appear to be the most promising field. These systems inflict damage on a target by the emission of highly focussed energy—microwave, laser and acoustic, and electric propulsion. Potential applications of DEWs include anti-personnel weapon systems, surface-to-air weapons, airborne lasers, and anti-satellite weapons. Simultaneously, defensive systems, denying the effects of DEWs such as dazzlers and anti-radiation coating/paints are already in widespread use and many more are on the drawing boards.[6] Some of the other factors[7] influencing the growth drivers are:

- Evolution of a new generation of less-than-lethal/non-lethal weapons and disabling technologies to avoid collateral damage and reduction in civilian casualties.
- Information Warfare (IW) will emerge as a key technology that will greatly affect the future of conventional armaments.
- Advanced propulsion technologies involving the development of improved low vulnerability solid propellants and acquisition of technologies for Electro-Thermal-Chemical (ETC), Solid Fuel Ramjet (SFRJ) electromagnetic propulsion.

- Advanced armament electronics for sensors and fuze technologies for projectiles and warheads for next-generation smart munitions.
- Technologies for next-generation explosives, warheads, and munitions, like case bonded composite propellant technology, metal-based fuel-rich propellant, polymeric hydrocarbon-based fuel propellant, fuels for Fuel Air Explosive (FAE) bombs, etc.

The emerging field is vast and dynamic. The progress of newer armament technologies reaching the frontline will be dependent on the amount of research funding allocated and the push to field new weapon systems by the sides engaged in an ongoing war—as witnessed in Syria, Yemen and Ukraine. Research on DEWs hypersonic weapons and drones' utilisation has been progressing at a breakneck pace and we are likely to witness an array of these weapon systems being fielded shortly. Russia, the US, and China have been devoting large sums to defence Research and Development (R&D) and are the frontrunners in the race to field newer armament technology weaponry. In this chapter, we will dwell upon a few major armament technologies, including smart weapons and hypersonic weapons, and their likely employment in future wars.

Smart Weapons

With the increase in demand for long standoff ranges and higher accuracies with low collateral damage, the need for smart weapons has gained importance. The miniaturisation of electronics, new generation navigational and guidance systems, and fast computing techniques have paved the way for better and more accurate mid-course and terminal guidance. The 'Make in India' push has now led to an infusion of smart weapon technology from foreign firms. Indian R&D is also catching up with the technology thanks to rapid developments in the electronic industry over the last decade. Glide bombs and loitering munitions will rule the world. In the future, there will be more low-cost solutions for smart weapons compared to missiles and hypersonic weapons. The seeker technology has changed rapidly with new generation Electro-Optical (EO) and Infra-Red (IR) systems. Using these high-end sensors and fast computing possibilities, the technology is now available in most countries. There is a need to analyse the types of smart weapons available and their trends in the future.

Smart weapons provide guidance to ensure a higher stand-off range with enhanced accuracy. Smart weapons may be categorised into powered and unpowered ones. The powered smart weapons are provided with a propulsion system of either a propellant or a battery as the power source. However, a low-cost solution for smart weapons is the conversion of existing unguided bombs into guided bombs with smart technology. The laser-guided bombs have lost their relevance as the lasing of targets in enemy territory is becoming complicated and risky. Therefore, laser guidance for long-range weapon systems has lost its importance. However, for border conflicts, rockets and some of the short-range weapon systems are still being used with laser correction rounds.

Laser-Guided Weapons

The unguided bombs and rockets can be fitted with laser guidance for better accuracy with a marginal increase in range, especially for bombs. In the case of bombs, the tail could be an extendable fixed-wing or a smart tail, with the nose portion fitted with a laser guidance kit. The Pulse Repetition Frequency (PRF) codes of the guidance kit and the laser designation pod are to be matched prior to fitment. The canards of the laser kit will act as control surfaces. The extendable wing provides lift. Therefore, unlike the unguided bombs, the laser bombs give a marginal increase in range and better accuracy. The accuracy depends on the type of control. If the error signal is proportionally fed to the control system, then it is called proportional control and ensures better accuracy. However, the majority of the laser kits comprise bang-bang control wherein irrespective of the amplitude of the error signal, the control surfaces deflect to the maximum. With the development of glide bombs and loitering munitions with exceptional EO/IR seekers, laser guidance kits lost their relevance for bombing. However, the short-range artillery rounds and unguided rockets could be retro-fitted with the laser guidance kit for better accuracy.

Glide Bombs

The majority of the glide bombs have a smart tail. For glide characteristics, the glide kits (foldable wings) are to be fitted to the warhead which will provide higher ranges. The smart tail will ensure higher accuracy as per the Inertial Measurement Unit/Global Positioning System (IMU/GPS) inputs. The GPS/IMU-aided weapon will provide accuracies of 5 to 10 m. To achieve higher accuracies, terminal guidance kits may be fitted. However, terminal guidance will greatly increase the cost of the bomb. If the warhead is of 250 kg and above, the IMU/GPS will be adequate as the lethality of a 250 kg warhead will offset the accuracy issues. In case the user wants to have a man-in-loop control over the terminal guidance weapon, then there is a need to incorporate a data-link system which will confirm the target destruction. The data-link will have its own negative aspects as maintenance of data-links will be difficult for longer ranges.

The unguided bombs could be fitted with a smart tail which will have either GPS (immune to jamming) alone or GPS coupled with IMU. The smart tails will have servo-actuators that will get the input from the GPS/IMU signals through a flight control unit. The target coordinates are to be fed to the IMU/GPS. Based on the aircraft inputs, the smart tail will communicate with the aircraft systems and provide continuously computed impact point/release point. The bombs with a smart tail will provide a maximum range of 50 km with trajectory shaping when released at high altitudes and maximum speeds for sea level targets. At times, bombs with a smart tail will also be installed with the terminal guidance of EO/IR or laser seeker for better accuracy. The smart tail with a terminal seeker will have better trajectory management for higher impact angles. For enhancement of range beyond 100 km, there is a need to install foldable wings on the bomb body along with the smart tail. The folding position of the wings can be programmed to suit the control laws for the impact angle and impact speed management. The glide kit, along with the smart tail, will maintain the glide characteristics as per the target coordinates. To enhance the accuracy of the bombs, the glide bombs can be fitted with terminal seekers like EO/Imaging Infra-Red (IIR).

The maximum range of the glide bombs is generally around 100 km. However, if the range is to be enhanced, increasing the wingspan to enhance the glide characteristics is not an option. But, there is a possibility to install a rocket booster at the tail which will enhance the initial velocity after release. The rocket-boosted glide bombs generally have sleek warheads for better range enhancement up to 150 km. Since the payload for this kind of bomb is very high (up to 1,000 kg), these variants of smart bombs are the best option instead of missiles where the payload of 1,000 kg requires a very big missile with a heavy rocket motor for ranges of 150 km. In the future these would be widely used by most armed forces.

Loitering Weapons

The advent of unmanned aerial vehicles paved the way for loitering munitions. Most of the UAV manufacturers offer a very primitive solution of carrying a warhead by a quadracopter or fixed wing UAV. However, portability and the ability to carry it on a backpack or multiple tube launcher by ground/air/sea is the main requirement. It means that the munition should have foldable wings and tail and a simple release/launch mechanism. The loitering munitions are controlled through data-links as per the target location and impact angle/direction management. This means that the munitions will loiter, identify the target (by the person controlling the munitions), and control the direction and angle of impact on to the target. This would be ideal for a top attack or for attacking moving targets. The weight category could be from 5 kg to 1,000 kg, depending on the type of the munition and, the size of the warhead. The range could be from 20 km to 1,200 km.

The loitering weapons are powered either by a battery or by small Integrated Circuit (IC)/turbine engines. The most important aspects of loitering munitions are the data-link and terminal seeker. Depending on the data-link capability, and the power source of the munition, the range would be determined. The airborne data-link pod or data-link with a third party control (the aircraft launching the munition and the aircraft which controls the weapon with the data-link pod being different) like the Airborne Warning and Control System (AWACS) is the new norm. The munition, once launched, could also be controlled through ground control data-link systems located in a forward area near the target. The range depends on the antenna size.

The launch speeds of the loitering munitions depend on the type of launch mechanism from the tubes. With compressed air launched from the tube, the speeds would be much lower than those of helicopters or fighter aircraft. However, with rocket-boosted launch, the launch speeds of loitering munitions could match those of helicopters/fighter aircraft. Since the munitions could be launched through tubes, the unguided rocket pods would be replaced with loitering munitions of various sizes in the future. Depending on the size of the munitions, the launcher pods could be reconfigured on UAV/helicopter/fighter aircraft. This will become a game-changer. While the launch vehicle launches the weapons, the ground station or airborne station will control and ensure target destruction. Multiple loitering munition launches on the same target will not only ensure redundancy, but also provide the battle damage images to the ground control station. With miniaturisation of EO/IR seekers and improvements in resolution, the terminal guidance of loitering munitions has improved. Some of the seekers will also carry laser range finders and be integrated with EO/IR seekers for better terminal guidance. With high precision gimballed angles and response rates, target tracking and guidance will show improved results.

Low-Cost Missiles

Generally, when we refer to air-to-ground missiles, we consider them as an expensive proposition as they need good seekers and complication on-board navigational systems and reliable propulsion systems. With the development of low-cost IMU and immune GPS systems and the wide range of servo actuators, the high-end missile systems are no longer an option for the majority of ground targets. The low-cost option does not need high-end seekers. A missile with IMU/GPS guidance ensures an accuracy of 5m. If need be, low-cost uncooled IR and EO seekers can be installed for better accuracies in the terminal guidance phase. The Indian Regional Navigation Satellite System (IRNSS) programme is ensuring consistency in GPS guidance accuracy. Therefore, the new generation missile systems are provided with good rocket motors and IMU/GPS guidance. For extended ranges, and good manoeuvrability in the terminal phases, two pulse and three pulse rocket motors are being used. With accurate GPS inputs of the target, the low-cost missiles would be very effective. Since the propulsion systems have a limited life, the glide bombs will score over the missiles in terms of life cycle cost and payload delivery capability.

Directed Energy Weapons

Though directed energy weapons like lasers or electromagnetic pulse are being talked about and countries like the US and Israel have been working on the weaponisation of this class, these weapons are not in combat use even in the ongoing Russia-Ukraine conflict. After spending billions of dollars, the US government dropped a joint programme with Israel. Theoretically, ground-based laser weapons can address air targets—the power requirement for the laser and cooling system used for generating the laser are the limiting factors for their large-scale use. For laser ranges up to 5 km, the cooling system is as big as a 6.5 ton truck. Installing the laser equipment along with the cooling system on an aircraft will be a challenge. Moreover, the directed energy laser weapon can engage only one target at a time. For additional targets, once the laser pulse is fired on the target, a minimum time gap is needed for engaging the second target. In the future, the technology may mature for better laser power management and cooling systems so that DEWs may become cost-effective.

Hypersonic Weapons

Hypersonic weapons are generally defined as objects flying at speeds surpassing 5 Mach or five times the speed of sound.[8] The speed-based definition of hypersonic systems is very broad and incomplete. If we go by the standard of speed, most ballistic missiles travelling at hypersonic speed in their mid-course and terminal phases would fit into the classification of hypersonic weapons. Also, emphasising the kinetic aspects of hypersonic systems overshadows their fundamental attributes, such as manoeuvrability and low-altitude flying.

The three key attributes distinguishing hypersonic weapons from ballistic and cruise missiles are speed, manoeuvrability, and low-altitude flying.[9] Hypersonic weapons fly at an altitude of around 20 km to 60 km within the earth's atmosphere. Hypersonic flight, by definition, is an atmospheric flight.[10] Atmospheric flight exposes hypersonic vehicles to thermal, aerodynamic, and material challenges such as overheating, laminar flow disruption, ionization of surrounding gases, and plasma formation which are unencountered by ballistic objects travelling faster than most hypersonic weapons in a low-density near-space environment.[11] Objects undergoing hypersonic flight experience a tremendous amount of flow friction and viscous dissipation, which can lead to extreme temperatures (more than 2,000 degrees Celsius). Extreme surface temperatures of aerodynamic vehicles can ionize and disassociate the surrounding gases, leading to the formation of a plasma state. The plasma reacts vigorously with the airframe's surface, disrupting the laminar flow and destabilising the hypersonic flight. Due to the cruise missiles' relatively lower—subsonic and supersonic—speed, they do not encounter hypersonic flight conditions despite flying in atmospheric conditions at a much lower altitude than hypersonic weapons.

Categories of Hypersonic Weapons

There are primarily two types of hypersonic weapons: rocket-boosted Hypersonic Glide Vehicles (HGVs) and scramjet propelled Hypersonic Cruise Missiles (HCMs).[12]

Hypersonic Glide Vehicle

Hypersonic Glide Vehicles (HGVs) are rocket-launched aerodynamic vehicles that go across space. Gliders perform a pull-up shortly after launch to reenter the atmosphere and achieve equilibrium gliding.[13] Gliders rely on aerodynamic lift to sail unpowered over large distances within the earth's atmosphere during their mid-course. When the weapon is close to its target, it uses internal boosters to exit the gliding trajectory, performs evasive terminal manoeuvres, and hits the target. In some sense, hypersonic flight combines the best attributes of ballistic and cruise missiles: the speed of ballistic missiles and the low altitude flying and manoeuvrability of cruise missiles.

Hypersonic Cruise Missile

Hypersonic Cruise Missiles (HCMs) are nothing but faster versions of conventional cruise missiles. While the key difference between ballistic missiles and HGVs is the latter's ability to carry out extreme manoeuvres, not speed, what differentiates cruise missiles from air-breathing hypersonic cruise missiles is speed, not manoeuvrability. Like their subsonic and supersonic cousins, HCMs are powered throughout their trajectory and, thus, are capable of executing manoeuvres throughout their flight.

The key distinction lies in the disparate propulsion modes. Hypersonic cruise missiles are propelled by supersonic combustion ramjet or scramjet engines, whereas cruise missiles are propelled by turbofan or ramjet engines. Scramjets are ramjet engines that have superior technology. A scramjet engine's airflow is supersonic, whereas a ramjet engine's airflow is subsonic. As a result, scramjet-powered cruise missiles (HCMs) outrun traditional cruise missiles.

Limitations of HGV/HCM Dichotomy

While the HGV/HCM bifurcation may help understand hypersonic weapons, it oversimplifies hypersonic missile design possibilities.[14] The characteristics of glide vehicles and cruise missiles may be combined in future hypersonic weapons. Scramjet engines, for example, may be incorporated with glide vehicles to improve range, manoeuvrability, and speed. The HGV/HCM divide does not capture many of these possibilities.

Strategic and Tactical Uses of Hypersonic Missiles

The most prominent military application of hypersonic weapons, driving the world powers towards a hypersonic arms race, is their ability to counter and evade Ballistic Missile Defences (BMDs).[15] The combination of speed, low-altitude flight, and manoeuvrability poses a unique challenge to the missile defence regime, designed to engage predictable parabolic missile threats. While the defensive or retaliatory role is the well-recognised use of hypersonic weapons, there is nothing implicit about the technology that limits its deployment only for defensive purposes. The ability of hypersonic weapons to get through missile defences can be employed with added utility in an offensive role to gain a first-strike advantage. In the early stages of the war, before the adversary's missile defences are neutralised, hypersonic weapons may be used to strike strategic targets such as command-and-control nodes or the missile defences themselves. Notably, since the United States does not face any serious missile defence threat from Russia and China, the US Conventional Prompt Strike (CPS) programme might be intended to wage preemptive strikes on the adversary's strategic assets and command-and-control systems.

In addition to strategic offensive and defensive operations, hypersonic cruise missiles can be effectively employed to gain tactical advantage during a conflict. For example, a swarm of hypersonic tactical systems can sink an aircraft carrier or a surface ship in a crisis situation. John Venable, a senior Defence Fellow at the Heritage Foundation, noted that China might employ hypersonic weapons to "sink the flattops while they're in the harbor in Norfolk, (Virginia), or off the coast of California (as a surprise attack)."[16]

Strategic Implications

Hypersonic weapons would impact future warfare and strategic stability in various ways. The attributes of hypersonic weapons such as speed and manoeuvrability make them the preferred choice of weapons as compared to existing cruise and ballistic missiles. Their low altitude flight, coupled with speed and manoeuvrability, poses a formidable challenge to existing air and ballistic missile defence. Even if the ground and space-based radars can detect the hypersonic missile launch, tracking, engaging, and intercepting it is extremely challenging. The inability of the existing missile defence regime to counter hypersonic vehicles makes them highly survivable strike weapons. Their ability to evade missile defence also increases their ability to successfully destroy targets, bestowing them with a high success rate.

The high kinetic energy of hypersonic weapons—directly proportional to the square of their velocity—makes them potent munitions against long-range hardened, underground, or stationary targets. The ability of hypersonic precision strike weapons to penetrate protected targets was demonstrated by Russia in the 'special military operation' in Ukraine. The Russian military used its newest Kinzhal hypersonic missiles for the first time in Ukraine to destroy an underground hangar with weapons and ammunition.[17] The ability of hypersonic weapons to execute extreme manoeuvres during the terminal phase also allows them to be used against time-sensitive and mobile targets.

The ability of hypersonic weapons to target long-range strategic assets amounts to their significant deterrent value. A prominent Indian military expert argues, "Indian HCMs should act as a deterrent against high-value targets such as Chinese aircraft carriers which are set to foray into the Indian Ocean."[18] The deterrent value of hypersonic weapons has also been compared with nuclear deterrence, in that "hypersonic deterrence could be the new equivalent of nuclear deterrence."[19] While conventionally-armed hypersonic weapons would not replace nuclear weapons, they could be used in combination with their nuclear cousins to deter conventional and nuclear threats effectively. In the near future, hypersonic weapons could also carry out missions delegated to nuclear weapons, such as demonstration and de-escalation strikes.

Hypersonic Arms Race

Although hypersonic missile technology is based on the potential of aerodynamic concepts, the idea of using a booster to launch a reentry vehicle was foreseen way back in the 1940s, and military installations worldwide have been working on it for decades now, but it was only in the last few years that countries prioritised its development and started deploying these weapons. All the world's major powers are developing hypersonic weapons and are in various stages of research and development. Among them, the United States, China and Russia are the standouts.

In December 2017, Russia deployed the MiG-31K fighter jets armed with the Kinzhal hypersonic missiles on preliminary combat duty.[20] At the 70th National Day parade in October 2019, China showcased the dual-capable DF-17 medium-range ballistic missile carrying the DF-ZF HGVs.[21] Aside from the DF-ZF HGV, China is working on the 'Starry Sky 2' hypersonic cruise missile.[22] Multiple programmes sponsored by the US Navy, Army, Air Force, and Defence Advanced Research Projects Agency (DARPA) are pursuing hypersonic weapons.[23] DARPA is working on a wedge-shaped ground-launched Tactical Boost-Glide (TBG) system. The US Air Force (USAF) is developing the AGM-183 Air-Launched Rapid Response Weapon (ARRW), an air-launched hypersonic glide vehicle based on DARPA's TBG technology.[24]

Hypersonic weapons will become a reality in India sooner rather than later.[25] The Defence Research and Development Organisation (DRDO) successfully flight-tested the Hypersonic Technology Demonstration

Vehicle (HSTDV) on September 7, 2020, demonstrating hypersonic air-breathing scramjet technology.[26] In addition to the HSTDV, India is developing the BrahMos-II, a Mach 7 HCM based on the Russian Tsirkon missile, in partnership with Russia.[27]

Countering the Hypersonic Missile Threat

In addition to developing hypersonic missiles, countries are looking for counter-measures to address emerging hypersonic threats.[28] In a recent report published by the Centre for Strategic and International Studies (CSIS), Tom Karako and Masao Dahlgren argue, "Defending against hypersonic missiles is strategically necessary, technologically possible, and fiscally affordable, but it will not be easy."[29] In other words, defence against hypersonic missiles is tough but tractable.

While Russia and China are leading the race in hypersonic missile development, the United States is far ahead of both its adversaries in the development of hypersonic missile defences. In the 2017 National Defence Authorisation Act (NDAA), Congress designated the Missile Defence Agency (MDA) as the executive agent for missile defence. The MDA is working closely with the Space Development Agency (SDA) to develop defences against hypersonic threats.[30] Russia has claimed that its most advanced missile defence system, the S-500, deployed around Moscow, can defend against hypersonic threats. Also, the S-550, the lighter version of the S-500, expected to enter service in 2025, would field a mobile launcher deployed with a hypersonic interceptor missile to defend against hypersonic threats.[31] China has made remarkable progress in developing an infra-red heat-seeking hypersonic missile that could target objects such as stealth aircraft, aircraft carriers, and hypersonic missiles.[32]

Conclusion

Rapid growth in the field of armament technologies has made it even more difficult to ascertain the type of war we are going fight in the future. The wars fought in the last two decades have indicated that technologies are going to play an important and decisive role in the future battlefields. From dumb bombs to smart weapons, from A4Ms to Beyond Visual Ranges (BVRs), loitering munitions, directed energy weapons, Multiple

Independently-targetable Reentry Vehicles (MIRVs), hypersonic missiles, the list is endless. From the 'man behind the machine' to Artificial Intelligence (AI) enabled autonomous aerial platforms, armament technologies are growing by leaps and bounds. It is difficult to keep pace with technological advancements by most of the nation states barring the great powers like the United States, Russia and China, that can afford to invest heavily in Research and Development (R&D) and harness these technologies.

India is working towards absorbing the armament technologies in the field of hypersonic missiles, air-to-ground smart weapons and other significant weapon systems. Many significant projects, including the 'Akash' surface-to-air missile system, 500 kg prefragmented bomb, 120 mm Penetration-Cum-Blast (PCB) and Thermobaric (TB) ammunition for the Main Battle Tank (MBT) Arjun, Cannon Launched Missile Development Programme (CLMDP), GPS/INS guidance and control kit for the 450 kg High Speed Low Drag (HSLD) bomb, guided Pinaka rocket system, Prithvi missile warheads[33], Bi-Modular Charge System (BMCS) for 155mm ammunition, thermal imaging sight Mark-II for the T-72 tank, Light Combat Aircraft (LCA) 'Tejas', Lakshya parachute for the pilotless target aircraft, etc. have been manufactured in the country under the 'Make in India' initiative of the government in the recent past. The government has introduced several policy measures under the 'Make in India' initiative and brought reforms to encourage indigenous design, development and manufacture of defence equipment and weapons, thereby reducing dependence on imports.[34] India has collaborated with Russia to develop the BrahMos-II hypersonic cruise missile and also an indigenous hypersonic cruise missile as part of the HSTDV programme.

Technology has transformed the traditional employment philosophy of militaries to hi-tech modern armed forces which are endeavouring to gain dominance over the enemy through qualitative means of harnessing advanced technologies. The relative combat effectiveness is being enhanced by integrating evolving technologies. Future trends in armament growth will be characterised by a fusion of technologies relating to the physical, digital, cyber and space spheres—futuristic armaments are evolving in robotics and autonomous vehicles, and nanotechnology. Armament technologies will be the key variable while prosecuting future wars and winning them with the least amount of attrition.

Notes

1. Thomas G. Mahnken, "Weapons: The Growth and Spread of the Precision-Strike Regime", *Dœdalus, The Journal of the American Academy of Arts & Science*, 140(3) Summer 2011, pp. 45-57. https://www.mitpressjournals.org/doi/pdf/10.1162/DAED_a_00097
2. https://graphics.reuters.com/UKRAINE-CRISIS/WEAPONS/lbvgnzdnlpq/. Accessed on May 30, 2022.
3. https://www.thehindu.com/news/international/russia-tests-hypersonic-missile-zircon-amid-ukraine-war/article65470023.ece. Accessed on May 30, 2022.
4. Gen. C. Robert Kehler, Commander, Air Force Space Command, Air Force Association, Orlando, Fla., "2009 AFA Air Warfare Symposium (Cross Domain Integration)", February 27, 2009. Accessed on May 30, 2022.
5. "Redefining Information Warfare Boundaries for an Army in a Wireless World". https://www.rand.org/pubs/monographs/MG1113.html
6. Ralph Tillinghast, Andrei Cernasov, James Zinuno and Capt Thomas Murphy, US Army ARDEC, RDAR-WSF-M, "Future Technologies and Concepts: Robotics, Artificial Intelligence, Exoskeletons, and Sensors", US Army RDECOM. https://ndiastorage.blob.core.usgovcloudapi.net/ndia/2016/armament/18399_Tillinghast.pdf
7. "Future Trends in Armament Technology". drdo.gov.in/drdo/pub/techfocus/oct2001/trends.htm
8. Dinakar Peri, "Understanding Hypersonic Weapons", *The Hindu*, March 23, 2022. https://www.thehindu.com/news/national/understanding-hypersonic-weapons/article65249442.ece. Accessed on March 24, 2022.
9. Abhishek Saxena, "Russia Launching Hypersonic Missiles Heralds a New Era of Warfare—High Speed, More Lethal", *The Print*, April 3, 2022. https://theprint.in/opinion/russia-launching-hypersonic-missiles-heralds-a-new-era-of-warfare-high-speed-more-lethal/898194/. Accessed on April 3, 2022.
10. Tom Karako and Masao Dahlgren, "Complex Air Defense: Countering the Hypersonic Missile Threat", Centre for Strategic and International Studies, February 2022, p. 3. https://www.csis.org/analysis/complex-air-defense-countering-hypersonic-missile-threat?msclkid=d9f1c1c5cf4f11ecb525200a64d52720. Accessed on February 10, 2022.
11. James M. Acton, "Hypersonic Boost-Glide Weapons", *Science and Global Security*, Vol. 23, Issue 3, 2015. https://www.tandfonline.com/doi/abs/10.1080/08929882.2015.1087242. Accessed on July 24, 2021.
12. Kelley M. Sayler, R45811, "Hypersonic Weapons: Background and Issues for Congress", Congressional Research Service (Washington, DC: Congressional Research Service, 2022), p. 2.

13. The alignment of local horizontal and velocity vectors in the same direction is called equilibrium gliding.
14. Karako and Dahlgren, n. 10, p. 9.
15. Steven Simon, "Hypersonic Missiles Are a Game Changer", *The New York Times*, January 2, 2020. https://www.nytimes.com/2020/01/02/opinion/hypersonic-missiles.html. Accessed on July 27, 2021.
16. Stephen Losey, "What Should be the United States' Next Move on Hypersonic Tech?", *DefenseNews*, March 14, 2022. https://www.defensenews.com/air/2022/03/14/what-should-be-the-united-states-next-move-on-hypersonic-tech/. Accessed on March 18, 2022.
17. "Russia Says it Used Hypersonic Missiles in Ukraine for First Time", Al Jazeera, March 19, 2022. https://www.aljazeera.com/news/2022/3/19/russia-uses-advanced-hypersonic-missiles-in-ukraine-for-first-tim. Accessed on March 21, 2022.
18. Anil Chopra, "Hypersonic Weapons: Realities and Challenges", Centre for Air Power Studies, July 23, 2021. https://capsindia.org/hypersonic-weapons-realities-and-challenges/. Accessed on May 11, 2022.
19. Ibid.
20. "Russia Picks MiG-31 Fighter as a Carrier for Cutting-Edge Hypersonic Weapon", TASS, April 6, 2018. https://tass.com/defense/998221. Accessed on November 8, 2021.
21. "China Displays New Hypersonic Nuclear Missile on 70th Anniversary", Al Jazeera, October 1, 2019. https://www.aljazeera.com/news/2019/10/1/china-displays-new-hypersonic-nuclear-missile-on-70th-anniversary#. Accessed on October 4, 2021.
22. Holmes Liao, "China's Development of Hypersonic Missiles and Thought on Hypersonic Defense", *The Jamestown Foundation*, Vol. 21, Issue 19, 2021. https://jamestown.org/program/chinas-development-of-hypersonic-missiles-and-thought-on-hypersonic-defense/. Accessed on October 11, 2021; Liu Zhen, "China's Hypersonic Aircraft, Starry Sky-2, Could be Used to Carry Nuclear Missiles at Six Times the Speed of Sound", *South China Morning Post*, August 6, 2018. https://www.scmp.com/news/china/diplomacy-defence/article/2158524/chinas-hypersonic-aircraft-starry-sky-2-could-be-used. Accessed on October 9, 2021.
23. Amy F. Woolf, R41464, "Conventional Prompt Global Strike and Long-Range Ballistic Missiles: Background and Issues", Congressional Research Service (Washington, DC: Congressional Research Service, 2021), pp. 1-55. https://crsreports.congress.gov/product/pdf/R/R45811. Accessed on October 25, 2021.
24. "AGM-183A Air-launched Rapid Response Weapon", *Airforce Technology*, September 2, 2020. https://www.airforce-technology.com/projects/agm-183a/. Accessed on October 12, 2021.
25. Lalit K Jha, "India Among Few Countries Developing Hypersonic Missiles, US Congressional Report Says", *The Print*, October 22, 2021. https://theprint.in/defence/india-among-few-countries-developing-hypersonic-missiles-us-congressional-report-says/754703/. Accessed on October 25, 2021.

26. "DRDO Successfully Flight Tests Hypersonic Technology Demonstrator Vehicle", Press Information Bureau, September 7, 2020. https://www.pib.gov.in/PressReleasePage.aspx?PRID=1651956. Accessed on October 25, 2021.
27. Prakash Manda, "BrahMos-II Missile Program To Greatly Benefit From The Successful Test Of Russian Zircon Hypersonic Missile", *The Eurasian Times*, July 22, 2021. https://eurasiantimes.com/brahmos-ii-missile-program-to-greatly-benefit-from-the-successful-test-of-russian-zircon-hypersonic-missile/. Accessed on September 11, 2021.
28. Abhishek Saxena, "Hypersonic Missile Defence System: A Perspective", Centre for Air Power Studies, *Issue Brief* 159/22, March 7, 2022. https://capsindia.org/hypersonic-missile-defence-system-a-perspective/. Accessed on March 7, 2022.
29. Karako and Dahlgren, n. 10, p. 1.
30. "Missile Defense Agency Pivots Focus to Hypersonic Systems", *Government Matters*, February 20, 2022. https://govmatters.tv/missile-defense-agency-hypersonic-systems. Accessed on February 21, 2022.
31. "Russia Tests S-550 System Capable of Hitting Spacecraft, Hypersonic Targets", *TRT WORLD*, December 29, 2021. https://www.trtworld.com/europe/russia-tests-s-550-system-capable-of-hitting-spacecraft-hypersonic-targets-53127. Accessed on December 30, 2021.
32. Stephen Chen, "China Says it has Hypersonic Missiles with Heat-Seeking Tech – Years Before US", *South China Morning Post*, December 31 2021. https://www.scmp.com/news/china/military/article/3161762/china-says-ithas-hypersonic-missiles-heat-seeking-tech-years. Accessed on January 2, 2022.
33. https://www.drdo.gov.in/technology-cluster-links/labs-products/174?title=&sort_by=title&page=2. Accessed on June 2, 2022.
34. https://pib.gov.in/PressReleasePage.aspx?PRID=1796164. Accessed on June 2, 2022.

7. Future of Uninhabited Aerial Systems and India's Challenges

RK Narang

Introduction

This paper deliberates on the future of Uninhabited or Uncrewed or Unmanned Aerial Systems (UAS). The rise of air power in the last century can be attributed to manned aircraft, which ruled the civil-military aviation landscape since the first manned flight by the Wright brothers in 1903. The entry of air power, with enhanced reach and firepower, changed the dynamics of warfare. The US bombers' dropping of atom bombs on the cities of Hiroshima and Nagasaki in Japan in August 1945 indicated the revolutionary and devastating impact of air power in warfare. However, the same manned aircraft had made a transformational impact in civil aviation by connecting different continents and transforming the world into a global village. On the other hand, unmanned aircraft could not keep pace with manned aircraft despite their early start with the conversion of the Curtiss N-9 trainer aircraft into an unmanned aircraft in 1917. The UAS remained in the periphery of civil-military aviation applications for the last century despite coming into play 14 years after the first flight of manned aircraft. However, recent developments in unmanned technologies are challenging the preeminent position of manned aircraft.

A few of the significant developments in the military UAS that could impact the trajectory of air power in the near future include Intelligence Surveillance and Reconnaissance (ISR) and armed strike UAS; Unmanned Combat Aerial Vehicles (UCAVs), autonomous UAS; and Manned and Unmanned Teaming (MUMT). In addition, small intelligent UAS operating individually, collaboratively or in swarms are increasingly being adopted for a number of commercial and military applications that are also likely to have a significant impact on air power. The small UAS also pose a new challenge for Air Defence (AD) forces that were found ill-equipped and unprepared to counter this new threat. The limitations of AD elements in preventing and providing protection against small armed UAS were visible in the small UAS attacks that took place around the world in the last few years. The ineffectiveness of the Armenian AD systems against Azerbaijan's armed UAS led to the defeat of Armenia in the Azerbaijan-Armenia War of 2020. The unsuitability of existing AD systems for detecting, identifying and neutralising small, slow and low flying UAS necessitated the development of new technologies to counter the small UAS threat. This paper, therefore, deliberates on the following issues:

(i) What has been the trajectory of UAS?
(ii) Examining the emerging UAS technologies such as ISR and armed UAS, High Altitude Long Endurance (HALE), UCAVs, Hypersonic Uncrewed Aerial Vehicles (HUV) and MUMT.
(iii) Why are small UAS, operating individually, collaboratively or in swarms, becoming an AD challenge?

Background

The unmanned aircraft, after following a slow and incremental development trajectory in the last century, have seen a significant upswing in the recent past. Despite the first flight of the UAS having taken place in 1917, it took 44 years to fly the first unmanned flight of the fighter aircraft with limited automation (by the US) in 1961. The stimulus for UAS development came from the shooting down of the U-2 spy plane of the USA over Russia in 1960 and over Cuba in 1962. Thereafter, the UAS were predominantly employed for the ISR role by a few countries, led by the US. They came into the limelight globally with the innovative employment of low cost UAS as decoys by Israel during the Bekka Valley operations in 1982. As a result, many defence forces started employing UAS for the ISR role as well as for tracking insurgents and terrorists. However, it was realised that after the detection of targets by the UAS, the strike aircraft took a long time to reach them, and this time loss often allowed critical high value targets to escape. The firing of the Hellfire missile from the turboprop engine Predator UAS in

February 2001[1] provided the UAS the much needed firepower to reduce the reaction time between sensing and shooting, which was effectively used by the US in anti-terror operations undertaken in an environment of complete air superiority. However, these turboprop UAS had limitations in combat as they could be easily detected and shot down in contested airspace.

Emerging UAS Technologies

The recent transformation in UAS has been stimulated by the rapid expansion of their commercial applications in the last few years. The associated technological advancements in Artificial Intelligence (AI) and Machine Learning (ML), miniaturisation and automation are also contributing to the development of new capabilities and military applications of UAS. These developments substantially increased the capability of UAS and initiated a chain reaction that is contributing to increased focus on the development of new capabilities such as armed UAS, UCAVs, rapid adoption of UAS in aerial combat, air logistics, aerial surveillance and other applications by the military.

UAS and UCAVs

The UAS and UCAVs differ in terms of their ability to be operated by a pilot and in the degree of their autonomy. The UAS have limited autonomy and are operated by remote pilots while the UCAVs have a high level of autonomy and can take a significant number of critical operational actions and manœuvres without needing inputs from remote pilots.

UAS

The UAS can be divided into two broad categories: propeller-driven UAS and jet engine UAS. Both categories of UAS are used for ISR and armed strike roles for the military.

Propeller-UAS

The necessity for the development of armed UAS was first felt by the US during its war on terror when it converted its propeller driven Predator ISR Medium Altitude Long Endurance (MALE) UAS into an armed UAS and carried out the first armed strike in October 2001.[2] The Predator

UAS (MQ-9A) and its advanced version, the MQ-9B (Reaper)[3] UAS were employed against Al-Qaeda in Afghanistan for the counter-terrorism role. China, with the active involvement of its defence forces, Research and Development (R&D) organisations and academic institutions [like Beijing University of Aeronautics and Astronautics (BUAA) and Harbin Aviation Group (HAIG)] developed the BZK-005 turbo-prop ISR UAS.[4] It also developed the CH-3 tactical propeller-driven armed UAS and soon exported it. Thereafter, China developed the larger CH-4 and CH-5 MALE armed UAS with an aim to match their performance with the US Predator and Reaper class of UAS. Turkey also developed the Anka turboprop MALE UAS that carries payloads of up to 200 kg.[5]

The US employed the turboprop Predator MALE UAS in its war on terror in complete air superiority, which created a false sense of their invincibility. However, it was difficult for the slow moving MALE and High Attitude Long Endurance (HALE) propeller UAS to survive in a contested environment. Therefore, a need was felt for developing a high performance jet UAS.

Jet UAS

China developed a number of jet UAS for the ISR and armed strike roles such as the WZ-2000[6] and WJ-600 UAS, while the US developed the MQ-9C (Avenger (Predator-C)[7] jet engine UAS. These jet engine UAS, having high speed and higher survivability could not be called UCAVs as they did not have the desired level of autonomy, AI and other capabilities to undertake combat operations.

Wing Shadow or Cloud Shadow UAS: China's Chengdu Institute of Aviation Industry (Chengei) developed the Pterosaur series of ISR and armed UAS. Its Feng Ying (Wind Shadow) or Pterossaur-10 (or Wing Loong-10) twin WS-500 turbojet engine (with 500 kg thrust) armed UAS was developed for domestic use and equipped with the binary jet pipe for reducing the infrared signature. However, its export variant named the Yunying (Cloud Shadow) UAS, is equipped with a single jet engine WP-11 C turbojet engine (with 1,000 kg thrust)[8] with round engine exhaust.[9] Weighing more than 3,000 kg, it can carry a 400 kg weapon payload, operate up to an altitude of 14 km and fly at a speed of 630 kmph. It can carry the

BA-7 air-to-ground missile, YZ-212 laser guided bomb, YZ-102 A anti-personnel bomb and L-6 50 kg miniature guided bomb.[10] This UAS was employed for meteorological experiments involving estimation of the centre of Typhoon 'Senrak' under the Haiyan Project.[11] Its earlier version, the Sky Wing-III (Tian-Yi-3) was displayed during the Paris air show in 2007.[12]

Heron UAS: The experience of developing and successfully employing ISR and decoy UAS in the Arab-Israel War of 1982 helped Israel in becoming the leading exporter of tactical, MALE, HALE and loitering UAS. Its Heron TP UAS, equipped with the Pratt Whitney PT-6A 1200 bhp engine with a maximum speed of 220 kts, endurance of 30 hours, maximum weight of 5,670 kg and payload of up to 2,700 kg is emerging as a capable ISR and armed HALE UAS.[13]

Global Hawk HALE UAS: The Global Hawk HALE UAS developed by Northrop Grumman in 2001, with gross weight of 1,136 kg and payload of 863 kg, has been providing the US with day and night ISR capability. Its Rolls Royce (North America) Allison AE-3007 H turbofan engines rated at 3,410 kg of thrust at sea level, maximum speed of 335 kts, endurance of 31 hours and operating altitude of 65,000 ft with Imagery Intelligence (IMINT), Signal Intelligence (SIGINT) and Moving Target Indicator (MTI) provided global ISR coverage.[14] The Global Hawk, equipped with two Integrated Mission Management Computers (IMMCs) developed by Vista Controls Corporation, California, two KN-407 Inertial Navigation System/ Global Positioning System (INS/GPS) supplied by Kearfott Guidance & Navigation Corporation, New Jersey, and KN-4072 Monolithic Ring Laser Gyros (MRLG) in conjunction with an embedded differential ready Coarse Acquisition (C/A) code receiver remained an important unmanned platform in the US' global war on terror.[15] The Global Hawk, with the ability to fly safety well above the normal operating altitude of civil airliners, was accorded authorisation by the US Federal Aviation Administration (FAA) to operate in the US national airspace. Its mission planning system was developed by GDE Systems (now BAE Systems, Electronics & Integrated Solutions), and Raytheon Intelligence and Information Systems mission control ground systems provided secure uplink, downlink, launch and recovery capability. It became the key Command and Control (C_2) and ISR platform for the US ground forces deployed across the continents. However, its strength was in undertaking operations away from war zones and the adversary's AD networks. The vulnerability of the Global Hawk was exposed with its shooting down by the Surface-to-Air Missile (SAM) fired by Iran on June 20, 2019.[16] Also, the rising cost became a concern that led to reduction in the procurement of the Global Hawk UAS.

Avenger HALE UAS: The Avenger HALE UAS was developed by General Atomics of the USA and its first flight was conducted in April 2009. Its fuel-efficient Pratt & Whitney turbofan engine, having over 2,272 kg of thrust, reduces its take-off to below 5,000 ft and provides more than 20 hours of endurance. Its high speed of 400 kts and altitude of 50,000 ft and internal precision munitions of 1,363 kg make it a potent ISR and armed strike platform.[17]

Soaring Dragon HALE UAS (WZ-7): The Chinese Xianglong Soaring Dragon or Divine Eagle is a 10-12-ton class tandom joined wing design HALE UAS powered by a single WP-13 turbojet engine for the ISR roles. It project was unveiled at an air show in China in 2005 and its prototype was seen at an airport of the Aviation Industry Corporation (AVIC) of China in 2011.[18] It was initially designed with a single vertical tail, which was later modified into the V-tail configuration.[19] It has a maximum cruise speed of 750 kmph, flight range of 7,000 km and combat range of 2,000 km. It can operate up to 10 hours at an altitude of 18 km.[20] The WZ-7 is designed with stealth features such as ridgelines on the side of the fuselage, the backpack air intake and triangular tail nozzle. It has a satellite communication antenna, advanced battlefield communication equipment, side view phased array radar, electronics jamming equipment, and can provide target data for long-range missiles such as the DF-21.[21] These UAS have been in service with the People's Liberation Army Air Force (PLAAF) and started operating close to the Indian border since 2017—they could become unmanned airborne early warning systems in due course.[22]

Shan Diao or Divine Eagle HALE UAS: China's Shenyang Aircraft Corporation developed the Shan Diao or Divine Eagle twin fuselage twin vertical fin HALE UAS, which is the largest UAS built so far.[23] The Divine Eagle is influenced by the S-62 UAS design of the Sukhoi Bureau of Russia as China had collaborated with Sukhoi for the co-development of the S-62 UAS; however, the modus of acquisition of its design is not yet known.

China arm-twisting the cash strapped Sukhoi for acquisition of the design or abandoning the co-development project midway and building it after gaining knowledge during the co-development phase or obtaining design information through clandestine means cannot be ruled out.

Its unique design involves the twin boom attached to the front fuselage and inverted Pelican tail rear wing, which houses twin turbofan engines. The aircraft is expected to be in between the 15-20 ton weight category with an operating speed of 0.8 Mach and ceiling of 25 km. The twin fuselage provides an option for carrying more fuel, missiles for satellite launch, anti-satellite and anti-ship missiles; and a number of sensors.[24] According to popsci.com, it carries seven radars including the X/UHF Airborne Moving Target Indicator (AMTI) Active Electronically Scanned Array (AESA) radar on the front two X/UHF AMTI/ Synthetic Aperture Radar (SAR)/Ground Moving Target Indicator (GMTI) AESA radars on its twin boom; two X/UHF AMTI AESA radars on either side of the engine nozzles and two more radars on the boom. The AMTI and GMTI radars track air (fighter jets and missiles) and surface targets respectively and the SAR provides detailed ground installations images.

China has also developed the JY-26 long wave radars, which are expected to detect stealth fighters such as the F-22 as their stealth features are effective only against the current generation short wave radars. The Divine Eagle could be equipped with a smaller airborne version of the JY-26 radar.[25] It is difficult to ascertain the actual capability of the Divine Eagle since most of the reports are based on assessments and a few assumptions made by Western authors; however, considering its large size and unique design, it has enormous potential for long range ISR and combat support applications.

Feilong-2 Unmanned Long Range Stealth Bomber UAV: The Zhong Tian Guide Control Technology Company (ZT Guide), a private company based in Xian Prefecture of China, claimed to have developed a prototype of a multi-role high subsonic long range flying wing stealth bomber UAS named Feilong-2 or Flying Dragon-2 in 2021. The Feilong-2 could be deployed for precision strikes on the adversary's airfields, Command and Control (C_2) centres and aircraft carriers. It would also be able to launch and employ on-board swarm of drones to carry out the ISR and strike missions. It is being designed to fly up to a speed of 780 kmph, carrying a 6,000 kg payload and is expected to have an operating range of 7,000 km. It will be equipped with optical and radar sensors for target detection and have special coating to reduce its radar signature.[26]

The Feilong-2's performance is estimated to be closer to that of the US B-21, which is a manned long-range manned stealth bomber under development by the US under its Long Range Strike Bomber (LRS-B) programme. During the 2019 China air show, the company made a special effort to market the Fellong-2 as a product with lower cost, high operational life and less maintenance as compared to the B-21. An endeavour was made to highlight that the proposed induction of the Feilong-2 was ahead of the induction of the B-21 by the US in 2026.[27] China compared the unmanned Feilong-2 with the US' B-21 manned stealth bomber instead of comparing it with the manned stealth Xian H-20 bomber. This could either be an attempt to deliberately attract the attention of the international media on this programme to gain publicity or take the limelight away from the H-20 project.[28]

UCAVs

The definition of UCAVs has differed from commentator to commentator as some have even described the armed turbo-prop UAS as a UCAV while others view the UCAV to be a replacement of fighter aircraft. However, the current class of UCAVs being developed lies between these two extremes, probably due to technological challenges. The UCAV can be described as a high performance stealthy UAS capable of flying at high speed, carrying weapons internally, with a high level of automation, and a desirable capability of air-to-air combat.[29] The development cycles indicate that the trajectory of UCAV development has been long and slow.

X-45 and X-47 UCAV: The US Navy initiated the X-47 programme in 1999 with the US Air Force (USAF) launching the X-45 UCAV programme in parallel. These UCAVs have been tested for release of precision weapons, air-to-air refuelling and operations from an aircraft carrier. Also, the operating environment for the UCAVs was revised several times from 'operations in protected air space' to 'operations in deep-denied enemy territory', 'high threat environment'; and 'highly contested and uncontested light strike permissive for low end contested environment'. The increasing cost, frequent changes in the operating environment and delays in operationalisation of the UCAVs indicate numerous challenges faced during the process of their design and development. Also, their qualitative requirements were modified several times on confronting technological challenges and gaining experience.[30] However, neither of the two UCAVs has been inducted into operational service despite changes in the operating environment.

nEUROn UCAV: The low observable nEUROn UCAV project, led by France and supported by six European Union (EU) countries was launched in 2003. The aim was to achieve very low radar and Infra-Red (IR) signature, autonomous flight consistent with airworthiness regulations, air-to-ground weapon delivery from the internal bay, and automatic detection and recognition of relocatable ground targets.[31] A total of 123 test flights were flown between 2012 and 2015. The nEUROn has successfully completed air-to-ground subsonic missions, autonomous undetected reconnaissance of ground targets, low Radar Cross-Section (RCS) and IR trials. The nEUROn was tested for collaborative operations with fighters and Airborne Warning and Control System (AWACS) in 2020; however it is yet to be inducted into operational service.[32]

Taranis UCAV: The UK formally unveiled the Taranis UCAV technology demonstrator in 2010 and its first flight took place in 2014. Taranis' development was aimed at assessing the employability of future UCAVs in ISR, AD, battlefield interdiction and battlefield strike missions in a hostile environment as well as understanding the complexities of manned and unmanned operations. It has not yet been inducted into operational service.

Future Combat Air System (FCAS): In 2014, France and the UK, leveraging their experiences in the development of the nEUROn and Taranis, decided to work together on the two-year feasibility study on the FCAS, which was aimed at replacing the Dassault Rafale and Eurofighter Typhoon fighter aircraft by 2040. In 2016, they signed an agreement to develop the FCAS with 50 per cent cost sharing.[33] However, their collaboration did not move forward towards the design and development phase. France, Germany and Spain jointly launched the FCAS project in 2017 and concept studies were completed in 2020. The FCAS is being developed as a 'system of systems' having a fighter, UAS, sensors and a remote carrier.[34]

S-70 (Okhotnik) UCAV: Russia was late to start the development of the UCAV when Sukhoi began work on the flying wing shaped S-70 in 2009. The contract was signed in 2012 and S-70 Hunter UCAV made its first flight on November 23, 2018. It flew in a joint exercise under the control of the fifth generation Su-57 fighter on September 27, 2019. The Hunter, smaller than the Su-57 fighter, equipped with Electro-Optical (EO) and other reconnaissance systems and RCS reduction measures such as special materials and coatings, is likely to enter service in 2024. Russia had earlier tested the Hunter communication, avionics and other systems on the Su-57 fighter aircraft.[35] The Hunter is equipped with the AL-31 F turbofan engine or AL-41F jet engine, afterburner and flat engine exhaust jet nozzle to reduce its heat signature. Each Su-27 would be able to control four Hunter UCAVS. The Hunter weighs 20 tons, carries a payload of about 5.5 tons including air-to-air and air-to-ground missiles, has a range of 6,000 km and a maximum speed of 1,000 km an hour.[36]

Lijian or Sharp Sword (GJ-11) UCAV[37]: The Lijian, a stealthy flying wing shaped jet engine powered UCAV technology demonstrator project was launched in 2009. According to Global Security, the PLAAF provided funding for the Sharp Sword UAS in its Twelfth Five-Year Plan (2011-15). A total of seven different models were developed, with design variations on a basic model, which was named the AVIC 601-S. The Lijian was designed by the Shenyang Aircraft Design Institute (SYADI) of the Aviation Industry Corporation (AVIC), also known as the 601st Institute of the Aviation Industry, Shenyang Aerospace University (SAU) and manufactured by Hongdu Aviation Industry Group (HAIG).[38] The Lijjian has two weapon bays located between the landing gears, which can carry four small diameter satellite guided bombs in each internal weapons bay, with the potential to carry different types of weapons and missiles.[39] Its first flight took place in 2013, and the GJ-11 is the ground attack version of the Lijjian. It was initially equipped with the WP-7 aero-engine which was replaced by the WP-13 turbofan engine having 5.4 ton thrust. It has a Blended Wing Body (BWB).[40] It has a serpentine intake or S-duct with triangular entrance, and its engine was moved inwards into the fuselage, and the exposed area of the nozzle was rearranged into the fuselage to shield its exhaust to reduce radar signature. There are unconfirmed reports about China using tungsten, having a high melting point, in its shrouded jet nozzle to withstand high temperatures arising due to its design. It is likely to be employed as the uninhabited wingman of the future H-20 stealth bomber.[41] In addition, there is a possibility of the GJ-11 joining as the "loyal wingman" to Chinese fifth generation fighters such as the J-20 and FC-31. The GJ-11, equipped with precision air-to-surface missiles and glide bombs could be employed for the reconnaissance, aerial refuelling and armed strike roles against heavily defended high-value targets.[42] The GJ-11, in its, present configuration, is not suitable for naval carrierborne operations as it lacks folding wings, tail hook and reinforced undercarriages.[43]

Tian Ying UCAV: The China Aerospace Science and Industry Corporation (CASIC), a leading manufacturer of missile systems unveiled the fully autonomous 3-ton class Tian Ying (Sky Hawk) flying wing shaped UCAV technology demonstrator prototype in late 2018. The Tian Ying, with a relatively small wingspan of 11 m, robust undercarriage, long endurance and automatic take-off and landing capability, has the potential to be developed for undertaking carrier-based reconnaissance and armed strike missions.[44]

Anjian or Dark Sword Supersonic UCAV: China's Shenyang Aircraft Corporation developed the low observable Anjian/Dark Sword supersonic UCAV, with high swept back wing and two vertical fins, which was first displayed in 2006 and is believed to have been test flown in 2012.[45] The Dark Sword is expected to operate at up to 740 miles per hour (1,190 kmph). It is the only UCAV of its kind and differs significantly from the current generation flying wing configuration high subsonic stealth aircraft being developed globally.[46] It has a slender delta wing with wide splayed tail section, twin slanted vertical stabilisers, swept forward chin mounted intake and is powered by a single jet engine. Its design incorporates stealth features including Diverterless Supersonic Inlet (DSI) technology, which allows supersonic flight without using the manœuvring ramps that slow the air to subsonic speeds before entering the engine and provides stable and consistent airflow without needing non-stealthy splitter plates and other structures. The Dark Sword, with characteristics of a fighter, is likely to be used in combat and could act as a loyal wingman to manned aircraft.[47] It is estimated to weigh around 15-tons, perform 9g rate turn and operate up to a radius of action of 1,000 km. In Dark Sword, China demonstrated a UCAV that does not exist in the inventories or development programmes of the Western countries and, thus, cannot be termed as a reverse engineered UCAV.[48]

Hypersonic Uninhabited Aerial Vehicle

The Hypersonic Uninhabited Aerial Vehicle (HUV), an emerging technology with potential applications in conventional and nuclear weapons, can provide significant advantage to AD and strike forces. The term hypersonic represents the speed of an object beyond Mach 5, i.e. five times the speed of sound at which the physical speed of the object roughly varies between 5,000-6,000 km, depending upon its altitude.[49] The Hypersonic Glide Vehicles (HGVs) or hypersonic unmanned glide vehicles like hypersonic missiles are taken to the upper atmosphere by high velocity booster rockets and then one or more hypersonic glide vehicles are deployed. These HGVs rely on momentum and control surfaces to manœuvre towards their targets.[50] In order to land an HGV, its engine would need to be shut down around 125 miles short of the intended place of landing. Its current generation of engines, designed for hypersonic flights, cannot be used for subsonic flight, which adds to the complexities. Also, slowing down of the hypersonic vehicle prior to landing is challenging, and the controller may resort to S-turns while keeping stress levels on its structure within limits. The hypersonic glide vehicle moves so fast that air pressure in front of it forms a plasma cloud as it moves, absorbs radio waves and becomes invisible to radars. Also, these weapons, with more than five times the speed of sound, have much higher speeds than current generation AD missiles. Their ability to fly at low level and manœuvre makes them an extremely difficult target for AD systems to neutralise.[51]

The development of emerging hypersonic unmanned vehicles is steered by the defence forces, i.e. the USAF and PLAAF personnel, in collaboration with their academic institutions. The PLAAF and Beihang University in Beijing, College of Automation Engineering at Nanjing University of Aeronautics and Astronautics (NUAA) are conducting research on hypersonic technology and contributing to China's hypersonic programme.[52]

Avangard Hypersonic Missile and Glide Vehicle

Russia has led the development of HUVs and inducted the Avangard missile equipped with the Hypersonic Boost Glide Vehicle (HGV) in its missile regiment in December 2019. The Avangard, first tested in 2004, can manœuvre to avoid the adversary's AD systems.[53]

Wu Zhen-8 (WZ-8) Supersonic-Hypersonic UCAV[54]

China unveiled the WZ-8 tri-cycle undercarriage reusable UCAV air launched from the H-6N bomber during a military parade in 2019. It lacks air intake and air breathing engine and is instead equipped with two rocket boosters units positioned on both sides of the fuselage with about 200 seconds of operation. It has an arrow shaped design, with the wing body blending, pointed nose, tri-cycle undercarriage, vertical outward canted fins and internal weapon bay. It is estimated to travel at speeds between supersonic to hypersonic[55], out-running SAMs, and covers a distance up to 5,000 km.[56] It can operate at near space altitudes, undertake reconnaissance, carry out post strike damage assessment and provide details of strategic high value targets to long range missiles. It can be launched from the H-6N bomber and was reported to be part of the PLAAF's 10th Bomber Division at Anquing in Anhui province, located west of Shanghai.[57] China had earlier tested the DF-ZF hypersonic glide vehicle to validate the hypersonic flight operations capability.[58]

The PLAAF team of personnel led by Dai Fei reportedly contributed in the development of the Chinese HUV. Researchers of another PLAAF unit working with the Nanjing University of Aeronautics and Astronautics (NUAA) claimed to have improved software to predict landing scenarios. The development of the flight control mechanism for hypersonic vehicles is an extremely complex process, and China is actively pursuing development of landing technology for HUVs, which is essential to make them reusable and economical. The induction of HUVs would change air combat and armed strike capabilities. Chinese University Professor Wang Xing, in an academic conference, observed that the F-22 and F-35 classes of stealth fighters would become visible on releasing a missile or bomb and, thus, can be chased by hypersonic drones and neutralise retreating fighter aircraft.[59]

USAF HGV

The USAF Air Launched Rapid Response Weapon (ARRW) hypersonic boost glide vehicle launched from a B-52 bomber failed the tests that were conducted in April 2021 and July 2021 as the hypersonic missile failed to light up. The failure is a setback for the USAF as well as for its manufacturer, Lockheed Martin.[60] The USAF announced in August 2021 that it would test the hypersonic drone in partnership with the start-up Hermeus Corporation (based in Atlanta, USA). The test would be conducted on the Quarterhorse hypersonic plane powered by the Turbine Based Combined Cycle (TBCC) engine modelled on the GE J85 turbojet engine. The project is steered by the Air Force Innovation Hub (AFWRX) of the USAF and is funded by the Air Force Life Cycle Management Centre of the Air Force Research Laboratory (AFRL).[61]

HTDV: India successfully tested the Hypersonic Technology Demonstration Vehicle (HTDV) in 2020. It used an indigenously developed cryogenic engine and demonstrated air breathing scramjet technology, which is being developed in collaboration with Russia. It is launched by a solid fuel ballistic missile rocket launcher; and after separation from the launcher, it gets its propulsion from a supersonic combustion ramjet or scramjet engine. It flew at six times the speed of sound (Mach-6) at 30 km altitude for 20 seconds.[62] Indian hypersonic technology is expected to mature in the next four to five years. The missile test places India along with Russia, China and the US, which are developing hypersonic systems. India's first missile test failed in 2019. China's increasing assertiveness on the border; inducting hypersonic missile and testing hypersonic glide vehicles, make the HTDV test crucial for India to deter its adversaries.[63]

Hypersonic Cargo Plane

The Russian company Destinus headed by Mikhail Korkorich is building a hydrogen-powered, zero-emission transcontinental cargo drone that would be able to fly up to a speed of Mach 15. This hypersonic cargo drone would take off from a regular airport runway using a turbojet engine in the first stage; and thereafter its rocket engine would lightup and accelerate to Mach 13 to Mach 15 in the mesosphere at an altitude of over 50 km. The aim is to fly the hypersonic cargo plane through the atmosphere of least resistance to reduce aerodynamic losses. The challenge would lie in developing reusable rocket engines, and a hydrogen cooling system to protect aircraft structures from melting while operating at very high temperatures. The company made the Jungfrau prototype; however, obtaining funding for this project and untested technologies are the key challenges. The development of hypersonic vehicle landing technology, super-computing autonomous complex command and control system, improvement in safety, reliability, and overcoming limitations of unavailability of the engine in the landing phase are challenges which could take some time to overcome before it is operationalised.[64]

MUMT

The advancements in AI and ML have significantly enhanced the capability of UAS and UCAVs, and designers are working towards collaborative operation of Unmanned Aircraft (UA) with manned aircraft, also known as MUMT. The MUMT concept involves manned aircraft staying behind, and acting as the mother ship; and controlling multiple air and ground launched UCAVs, missiles and small UAS swarms. A typical MUMT for ground forces would comprise soldiers, manned aircraft, armoured vehicles, UAS and Unmanned Ground Vehicles (UGVs).

The US Navy and US Marine forces demonstrated a MUMT comprising the UH-1Y Venum and AH-1Z Viper attack helicopters for manœuvre and attack and the MQ-8C Fire Scout Unmanned helicopter for support.[65] The German Air Force and Airbus carried out a MUMT experiment with the Airbus A-400 transport aircraft launching a Do-DT25 drone from its cargo door in the air in February 2022, and the drone transmitting data back to the mother aircraft through the Modular Airborne Cloud Services (MACCS). The Airbus A 400 will carry up to 40 drones in the future. In an earlier experiment, the Eurofighter had tested networking and tasking of two Do-DT25 drones.[66] The US is planning to develop two classified UCAVs that would be controlled from the F-22 and F-35 manned fighter aircraft or B-21 bombers.[67] US companies are developing a number of UCAVs, including Boeing's MQ-25, Krato's Valkyrie-58 and Unmanned Tactical Aerial Platform (UTAP)-22, General Atomics' MQ-20 Avenger; and development of two more new UCAVs was announced recently. The designers are exploring the feasibility of developing a cost-effective manned aircraft for controlling networked UCAVs and UAS. Some experts have advocated the development of new light fighter aircraft that are designed to control UAS and UCAVs. It was observed that existing light fighter aircraft such as the Light Combat Aircraft (LCA) or Tejas of India, and the Korean F-50 and L-159 are not designed for controlling UCAVs.[68] However, the Indian company Hindustan Aeronautics Limited (HAL) that is developing the LCA, launched the Combat Air Teaming System (CATS) project the during the 2020 Bangalore air show, and declared that it would be exploring the feasibility of developing the LCA as a mother ship.

Combat Air Teaming System (CATS)

Hindustan Aeronautics Limited (HAL), with the tacit approval of the Indian Air Force, initiated development of MUMT under the CATS project and its full scale model was displayed during the Aero-India project 2021 at Bangalore in February 2021. The CATS comprises four elements:

(i) CATS-MAX, a two-seat fighter aircraft such as the LCA trainer, Su-30, etc.

(ii) Warrior UCAV with 300 km radius of action.

(iii) Hunter missile with approximately 200 km range.

(iv) Air Launched Flexible Assets (ALFAs).

CATS-MAX operates at a altitude of up to 50,000 ft within Indian territory and controls four 1.6 ton smart stealthy armed UCAVs named CATS-Warrior. The CATS-Warrior is proposed to be equipped with two PTAE-W engines. Presently[69], HAL is collaborating with Bharat Electrical Limited (BEL), another public sector company and a private sector company to integrate the Hunter missile and ALFA swarms. The project is in the developmental stage. This programme is in line with most MUMT programmes in which fifth generation fighters are being developed as mother ships, i.e. the US'F-35, Russian Su-57, and Chinese FC-31 and F-20 fighter aircraft. Subsequently, India's Advanced Medium Combat Aircraft (AMCA) is also expected to be teaming up with unmanned combat aircraft to undertake dangerous and dirty combat missions. The CATS project would obviate the need for sending a pilot over enemy territory and deny opportunity to the adversary for adverse media coverage.

Long Shot Air Launched Unmanned Porter Programme

The Defence Advanced Research Programme Agency (DARPA) of the USA launched a programme in 2021 to develop an air launched "Unmanned Porter" capable of carrying multiple air-to-air weapon systems to extend engagement ranges, increase AD mission effectiveness and reduce risk to manned aircraft. It allocated $22 million funding for the first year to Lockheed Martin, General Atomics and Northrop Grumman to commence the design.[70]

Manned-Unmanned Teaming

Collaborative Operations in Denied Environment (CODE)

DARPA's CODE programme launched in 2014 is aimed at enhancing the capability of existing UAS, increasing their automation, survivability and enabling multiple UAS to engage highly mobile ground and maritime targets in a denied environment at low cost. The propeller driven RQ-23 Tigershark UAS, similar to the Rustom-I of India, was used for the trials. Phase-III of the project commenced in 2019 and the trials are focussed on validation and strengthening the network and their ability to operate collaboratively. These capabilities will improve the ability of the UAS to undertake offensive and defensive operations.[71]

Unmanned Air Mobility and Air Logistics

Future unmanned aircraft are going to transform air mobility with a number of emerging civil-military applications. In the commercial sector, Unmanned Aerial Mobility (UAM) and Advanced Aerial Mobility (AAM) are emerging capabilities that would provide transportation within and between cities. India, with its large population, high vehicular traffic congestion, increasing need for faster intra-city and inter-city transportation services, and favourable civil drone policies, could become a potential designation for the development and adoption of UAM and AAM. Indian start-up companies Vinata Aeromobility[72] and the Indian Institute of Technology (IIT), Madras-incubated start-up ePlane[73], both based in the South Indian state of Tamil Nadu, are developing manned flying air taxis for transportation of passengers and cargo. The cost of travel is expected to be 1.5 to 2X times that of a normal taxi initially; however ,it would reduce travel time significantly.[74] The Vinata Aeromobility's air taxi is powered by an electric engine while ePlane is building a propulsion system having a combination of electric and combustion engines.[75] However, technological solutions for air space integration, reliability of the platforms, safety, social acceptance, security of command and control systems, cyber-security concerns, market potential and value addition would be decisive factors in their adoption for civil-military applications.

The UAS, with increasing capability, are likely to be employed in logistics supply, Combat Search and Rescue (CSAR), medical evacuation, insertion/ extraction and other operations in conflict zones. Unmanned vehicles could overcome several limitations of manned platforms such as the risk of the pilot being captured, physical and bio-medical limitations of the pilot, weather, etc. The ability to operate in poor visibility and overcome other human limitations would make UAS key enablers in future wars.

Feilong-1 (FL-1) MALE UAS: ZT Guide unveiled the large payload long endurance, universal unmanned transportation platform in the air show in China in 2018, and reportedly conducted the first test flight of the FL-1 UAS in January 2019. The FL-1, with an All Up Weight (AUW) of 3,200 kg and payload of 1,400 kg (including fuel) resembles the CH-5 MALE UAS. It carries Electro-Optic (EO)/Infra-Red (IR) sensors and has two hard points under each wing, with each hard point having the capability to carry a 250 kg payload.[76]

Fei Long-71 (FL-71) Supersonic Unmanned Transport UAV: ZT Guide also unveiled its plans to develop a 3,000 kg supersonic unmanned transport platform, with maximum speed of 2,200 kmph and a range of 900 kms. This is at an early stage of development.[77]

High Altitude Pseudo Satellites (HAPS)

HAPS are predominantly UAS, airships or balloons that are placed at an altitude of 20 km in the stratosphere for surveillance and providing communication links to unmanned and manned aircraft at a lower altitude. HAPS are cost effective, easier to launch UAS that overcome the performance and capability limitations of satellites. HAPS can remain on station for two to three months and are useful in providing communication in remote areas and over seas. Hindustan Aeronautics Limited (HAL) is developing HAPS in collaboration with a private sector start-up company, and they are expected to become operational by 2024-25.[78]

Small, Autonomous and Swarm UAS

The small intelligent UAS operating individually, collaboratively or as swarms are having a significant impact on air power dynamics. Their easy availability in the commercial market, the low cost, ease of operation and the ability to be launched from a restricted space has made it easier for terrorists, insurgents and criminals to use these for smuggling of arms, drugs, counterfeit currency and armed strike missions with insignificant or negligible warning to the military and internal security agencies. The use of AI, ML, increasing accuracy of sensors and navigation equipment, lethality of weapons, small size and unsuitability of existing AD systems have made small UAS a serious military and internal security threat.

Counter UAS (CUAS) Systems

The employment of small, slow and low flying UAS for armed attacks in many countries in the last few years has highlighted the gaps in the existing AD networks to counter this threat. The existing AD systems, designed to detect large and fast aircraft, were unsuitable to detect small, slow and low UAS, which were manufactured by using composites and plastics, had a low radar signature and insignificant noise levels. The employment of multiple small UAS collaboratively during some of the attacks highlighted the enormity of the threat and challenges for AD planners. This stimulated intensive Research and Development (R&D) activity directed towards the development of new CUAS systems. A number of detection, identification and neutralisation systems were developed, including the short distance, doppler Active Electronically Scanned Array (AESA), Passive Electronically Scanned Array (PESA), Multiple Input Multiple Output (MIMO) radars, Electro-Optic (EO), Infra-Red (IR), Radio Frequency (RF), acoustic detection and identification systems. Also, soft kill systems such as RF and Global Navigation Satellite Systems (GNSS) jamming and GNSS spoofing were found useful in neutralising commercial drones operating on known

C_2 and GNSS frequencies; however, these soft kill systems may not be able to neutralise military UAS with encrypted C_2 and GNSS systems.

The hard kill or kinetic neutralisation systems such laser, High Power Microwave (HPM), defender UAS, defender UAS swarms, modified shot guns, AD guns with upgraded ammunition, drone nets and other innovative solutions are being developed to counter this threat. Most CUAS systems being developed are hybrid systems since no single UAS neutralisation system was found to provide assured neutralisation. Future aviation combat platforms may need to be equipped with suitable CUAS to protect themselves as well as to protect Vital Access (VAs) and Vital Points (VPs). There is increasing emphasis on achieving safe automation, with human oversight, to reduce the reaction time to counter rogue small UAS launched from nearby locations.

UAS Integration in National Airspace

The increasing employability of UAS in civil-military applications, and the high traffic density of UAS traffic is making the airspace congested. The current practice of operating UAS in segregated airspace is adding to the complexities of air operations and there is a need to integrate them in the civil airspace as well as in the battlespace with technological and procedural measures. Countries around the world are pursuing extensive R&D programmes to develop low-level Unmanned Aircraft Systems Traffic Management Systems (UTM), automatic collision avoidance, uncooperative detection and other technologies to facilitate seamless operation of small UAS in non-segregated airspace.

The Indian Drone Rules-2021 and UTM policy have identified collaborative identification systems such as Real Time Remote Identification and Tracking (RIT), No Permission No Take-Off (NPNT) and other systems, however, corresponding R&D programmes to develop these systems and test their suitability for the integration of drones in the Indian airspace are yet to be launched. These systems would need to be integrated into the digital sky system of the Directorate General of Civil Aviation (DGCA), civil-military Air Traffic Services (ATS) and the AD networks of the defence forces. Accordingly, protocols, standards and symbols for data exchange between UTM and other systems would need to be created to facilitate seamless integration of UAS in the Indian airspace.

The Ministry of Civil Aviation (MoCA) in collaboration with the Indian Air Force (IAF), Department of Science and Technology (DST), Ministry of Electronics and Information Technology (MeitY) and industry could explore launching suitable programmes for the development of UTM, collision avoidance and other technologies to facilitate integration of UAS in the Indian airspace.

India's Unmanned Challenges

The increasing capability of India's neighbours, China and Pakistan, to develop and deploy unmanned systems in combat and clandestine operations, is posing new challenges for India. The US, Russia and Europe had led the aviation manufacturing industry in the seven decades after World War II. However, recent developments in UAS technology provided an opportunity to new players like Israel, China and Turkey to establish a foothold in the UAS industry. Israel was one of the first countries to take the lead in the development and manufacture of tactical MALE and loitering UAS. Israel supplied advanced military UAS to India; however, it had also supplied combat and loitering UAS to China in the past. The supply of loitering UAS to China was discontinued under pressure from the US; however, technological gains in the unmanned domain from such deals added to the Chinese domestic manufacturing capability, which would need to be factored in by India.

India has been facing rogue small UAS being used for cross-border surveillance, trafficking of arms, ammunition, drugs and contraband items along its western border with Pakistan. The clandestine activities reached a new high with the armed UAS attack on India's Jammu airbase located barely 15 km from its western border with Pakistan on June 27, 2021

China: China took UAS manufacturing to a different level and scale by developing a number of new military UAS with diverse capabilities. Its ongoing development of a number of ISR, armed, logistics supply and other UAS indicates its emphasis on optimising these designs before their induction and export. Also, development of unmanned stealth high-subsonic bombers and supersonic stealth unmanned fighter-bombers and marketing these as new technologies ahead of other global players indicate its deep desire to establish itself as leading exporter of niche unmanned aircraft technologies. China manufactured a number of small civil UAS and their components in large quantities at low cost in the last decade, to become the leading exporter of civil UAS in the world. It achieved this by creating an enabling aviation and UAS research, design, development, testing, manufacturing and export eco-system and associated policy framework. Several Chinese civil military academic and research institutions undertake focussed academic research that contributes to the research database, such as the China Aerodynamics Research and Development Centre under the aegis of the China Aerodynamics Association, and Department of Journal of Aerodynamics that contribute to aeronautics and UA development programmes.

Emboldened by the advancements in its UAS industry, China unsuccessfully attempted to gain a psychological edge over India by demonstrating UAS swarms delivering food to its soldiers during the Galwan conflict along the Ladakh region of India in 2020. China deployed small, MALE/HALE UAS in the Himalayan region against India for the first time in 2021.

An Indian UAS of Israeli origin, flying a surveillance mission along the border, crashed in the adjoining Chinese territory.[79] This crash could have been stimulated by a cyber attack from the Chinese side. The Chinese are known to have been involved in hacking and clandestine acquisition of technology as well as in leveraging knowledge gained from the analysis of crashed Russian and American UAS to replicate and develop such capabilities and technologies in its homegrown military UAS since 1960s.

Turkey: Turkey has developed armed UAS and supplied TB-2 tactical UAS systems to few countries including Azerbaijan and Ukraine. Turkish UAS played a significant role in Azerbaijan's win over Armenia in the Armenia-Azerbaijan war of 2020. The war exposed lack of preparedness of Armenian military for drone warfare. Non-availability of counter-drone technologies with Armenian forces gave freedom to Azerbaijani drones to strike at will. The role of Turkish UAS was highlighted during the Russia-Ukraine conflict of 2022, as they were employed to neutralise Russian armour and military targets. However, there is a need to exercise caution in drawing lessons as role played by Turkish armed drones was exaggerated in propaganda videos. These wars established Turkey as a serious player in global UAS market.[81]

China-Turkey-Pakistan: The increasing capability of China and Turkey in the unmanned domain and their close defence relations with Pakistan is a factor that has implications for India. The Pakistani armed forces possess modest UAS capability, with the acquisition of the Burraq UA (CH-3) and CH-4 from China,[82] the Falco from Selex, Italy, and the Luna X-2000 UA from Germany. Its public and private sector companies have been manufacturing tactical and small UAS for more than a decade and have also exported small UAS. The indigenous UAS industry provides additional capability to the Pakistani armed forces and intelligence agencies that have been covertly employing them for clandestine operations against India.[83]

China proactively arming Pakistan as part of its strategy to keep India engaged has added to the complexities for India. Turkey has provided diplomatic and political support to Pakistan on the Kashmir issue against India in international forums in the recent past.[84] Turkey's relations with Pakistan in the unmanned aircraft domain are expanding: the Pakistan Aeronautics Complex (PAC), Kamra, manufactured components of the Turkish Anka MALE UAS for the first time in 2013, and Turkish Aerospace (TUSAS) and the National Engineering and Science Commission (NESCOM) of Pakistan signed a contract to manufacture the Anka UA in Pakistan in 2021.[85] The Pakistan Air Force reportedly also acquired an undisclosed number of the Turkish Bayraktar TB-2 tactical armed UA in this deal. The Bayraktar is powered by the Rotax-912 internal combustion engine, carrying Micro Smart Munitions (MAM), Micro Smart Munitions Lightweight (MAM-L) and UMTAS missiles. The increasing cooperation of China and Turkey with Pakistan in UAS would add to the challenges for the Indian defence forces.[86]

Conclusion

The emerging capabilities of UAS would have a transformative impact on air power in the future. The significance of UAS was reinforced in the devastating UAS attacks on the Saudi Arabian oil facilities in 2019, the crushing defeat of Armenia in the Armenia-Azerbaijan War in 2020, and employment of UAS for surveillance, attack and propaganda operations in the Ukraine-Russia War in 2022. The UAS, with miniaturisation, advancements in AI and ML, are becoming potent platforms and are being increasingly employed for diverse civil-military applications. The development of UTM, collision avoidance and other technologies is essential to facilitate collaborative operation of manned-unmanned aircraft operations in the congested civil-military airspace.

The small UAS operating individually, collaboratively and as a swarm have raised a new threat as well as added a new dimension in AD dynamics, which necessitated development of new and innovative CUAS technologies. The soft kill systems have evolved in due course; however, hard kill CUAS systems to neutralise rogue UAS operating in autonomous mode are yet to reach the desired degree of maturity. Therefore, concerted efforts would be needed to develop CUAS systems to neutralise the emerging threats from multiple UAS operating in swarms with the reasonable degree of assurance. Also, these CUAS systems would need to be integrated in the AD networks to enhance their effectiveness and reduce attrition.

The employment of propeller driven UAS during recent conflicts demonstrated their potential in undertaking deception, psychological ISR and armed strike operations. They were employed in the uncontested and semi-contested airspace to cause physical damage as well as create a psychological impact on the morale of the enemy forces. However, their survivability in a contested airspace is suspect. Therefore, future combat UAS are expected to be jet engine powered, intelligent, and stealthy, and would operate in collaboration with manned, and other unmanned aircraft, swarms and missiles to undertake risky missions in the contested airspace. The new age UAS would operate in a networked environment using secure communication in dense manned-unmanned traffic.

Chinese hypersonic, swarm, armed, logistics supply and other innovative UAS, and MUMT are in the advanced stage of development and induction. Pakistan is indigenously developing small and tactical UAS as well as acquiring MALE, armed and other advanced UAS from China, Turkey and other countries. The use of commercial UAS for clandestine armed strikes, surveillance, identifying infiltration routes for terrorists, smuggling of drugs, and weapons, counterfeit currency and other operations by Pakistan is adding to the complexity of AD of India.

The Indian military UAS development programme appears promising with its public sector entities, i.e. DRDO and HAL pursing the development of the Rustom-I, Rustom-II, Ghatak UCAV, CATS and other UAS programmes. These programmes are under different stages of development and would need hand-holding and active involvement of stakeholders as partners to succeed. India's private sector companies are contributing to its military UAS capabilities by developing a variety of small UAS that include logistics supply, armed swarm and ISR UAS. In the civil UAS industry, India has taken several policy initiatives for civil UAS operations; however, it needs to launch associated technological initiatives to facilitate integration of UAS in the Indian airspace. Also, a focussed indigenous capability development programme is needed to reduce Indian industry's dependence on Foreign Original Equipment Manufacturers (FOEMs) for critical components. India would need to focus on building its civil-military manufacturing industry to optimally leverage commercial and military UAS capabilities for stimulating its economic growth and addressing its security challenges.

Notes

1. Chris Cole, "Rise of the Reapers: A Brief History of Drones", https://dronewars.net/2014/10/06/rise-of-the-reapers-a-brief-history-of-drones/. Accessed on December 27, 2017.
2. Chris Woods, "The Story of America's Very First Drone Strike", *The Atlantic,* May 30, 2015. https://www.theatlantic.com/international/archive/2015/05/america-first-drone-strike-afghanistan/394463/. Accessed on February 6, 2022.
3. "Top 5 Best Combat Drones (UAVs) in the World", BulgarianMilitary.com, August 3, 2020. https://bulgarianmilitary.com/2020/08/03/top-5-best-combat-drones-uavs-in-the-world/. Accessed on February 6, 2022.
4. "BZK-005 Harbin/ Sea Eagle" http://www.navaldrones.com/BZK-005.html. Accessed on February 24, 2016.
5. "The World's Top Combat Drones", *Army Technology,* June 27, 2019, https://www.army-technology.com/uncategorised/top-combat-drones/. Accessed on February 7, 2022.
6 BZK-009/WZ9/WZ-2000, https://www.globalsecurity.org/military/world/china/bzk-009.htm, Accessed on February 6, 2022.

7. "Top 5 Best Combat Drones (UAVs) in the World", BulgarianMilitary.com, August 3, 2020, https://bulgarianmilitary.com/2020/08/03/top-5-best-combat-drones-uavs-in-the-world/. Accessed on February 6, 2022.
8. WP-11 C is a derivative of the 1950s' French engine Fouga Magister.
9. https://www.globalsecurity.org/military/world/china/wing-loong-10.htm. Accessed on February 7, 2022.
10. "China's Cloud Shadow – Flexible but Short Endurance", *UAV VISION*, November 24, 2017. https://www.uasvision.com/2017/11/24/chinas-cloud-shadow-flexible-but-short-endurance/. Accessed on February 7, 2022.
11. "Pterosaur 10 was Successful! How did the Pterosaur Family Affect the Global Situation?", August 5, 2020. https://www.sohu.com/a/411606552_120266948. Accessed on February 7, 2022.
12. "CAIG Wing Loong-110 Explained", *Everything. Explained, Today*. https://everything.explained.today/CAIG_Wing_Loong-10/. Accessed on February 7, 2022.
13. "The World's Top Combat Drones", *Army Technology*, June 27, 2019, https://www.army-technology.com/uncategorised/top-combat-drones/. Accessed on February 7, 2022.
14. Yvonne Gibbs, "Global Hawk – Performance and Specifications", *NASA TV*, March 13, 2014. https://www.nasa.gov/centers/armstrong/aircraft/GlobalHawk/performance.html. Accessed on February 7, 2022.
15. "RQ-4 A/B Global Hawk HALE Reconnaisance UAV", *Airforce Technology*, July 13, 2020. https://www.airforce-technology.com/projects/rq4-global-hawk-uav/. Accessed on February 6, 2022.
16. Kyle Mizokant, "Iran is Rebuilding the US Drone It Shot Down Last Year", *PopularMechanics*, July 16, 2020. https://www.popularmechanics.com/military/weapons/a33338100/iran-drone-rq-4-global-hawk/#:~:text=The%20RQ%2D4%20Global%20Hawk%20drone%20was%20shot%20down%20on, costs%20approximately%20%24123%20million%20each. Accessed on February 7, 2022.
17. "Predator C Avenger", *General Atomics*. https://www.ga-asi.com/remotely-piloted-aircraft/predator-c-avenger. Accessed on February 6, 2022.
18. Zhao Lei, "Soar Dragon Drone to Strengthen PLA Aerial Capabilities", *China Daily*, December 5, 2016. https://www.chinadaily.com.cn/china/2016-12/06/content_27591837.htm. Accessed on March 20, 2022.
19. R. K. Narang, *India's Quest for UAVs and Challenges* (New Delhi: KW Publishers, 2020).
20. "Chinese Soar Dragon HALE UAV Unmanned Aerial Vehicle Used to Spy on US Navy USS *Antietam*", armyrecogniation.com, August 4, 2019. https://www.armyrecognition.com/august_2019_global_defense_security_army_news_industry/chinese_soar_dragon_hale_uav_unmanned_aerial_vehicle_used_to_spy_us_navy_uss_antietam.html. Accessed on March 20, 2022.
21. "Xianglong WZ-7 Drone Commissioned to Guide Carier-Killer Missiles", China-arms.com, December 18, 2020. https://www.china-arms.com/wz7-drone-help-carrier-killer/. Accessed on March 20, 2022.

22. Rick Joe, "China's Growing High End Military Drone Force", *The Diplomat,* November 27, 2019. https://thediplomat.com/2019/11/chinas-growing-high-end-military-drone-force/. Accessed on March 23, 2022.
23. Narang, n. 19, pp. 169-170.
24. Bill Gertz, "China Unveils New Long Range Drone", *The Washington Free Beacon*, May 29, 2015. https://freebeacon.com/national-security/china-unveils-new-long-range-drone/. Accessed on March 19, 2022.
25. Lin and Singer, "China Flies Its Largest Ever Drone: The Divine Eagle", *Popular Science,* February 6, 2015. https://www.popsci.com/china-flies-its-largest-ever-drone-divine-eagle/. Accessed on March 20, 2022.
26. Mark Episkopoa, "China's Feilong-2 Drone Is No Match for the B-21 Raider", *The National Interest*. https://nationalinterest.org/blog/reboot/china%E2%80%99s-feilong-2-drone-no-match-b-21-raider-194047. Accessed on April 16, 2022.
27. Kristin Huang, "Chinese Firms Claims New Stealth Drone May Rival US Air Force's B-21 Raider", *South China Morning Post*, April 21, 2021. https://sg.news.yahoo.com/chinese-firm-claims-stealth-drone-101822373.html. Accessed on March 23, 2022.
28. "Chankalyee 2, China's New Stealth Drone 'Feilong-2' Already Ahead of US' B-21 Stealth Bomber: Chinese Experts", May 6, 2021. https://tiananmenstremendousachievements.wordpress.com/2021/05/05/chinas-new-stealth-drone-feilong-2%E2%80%B2-already-ahead-of-us-b-21-stealth-bomber-chinese-experts/. Accessed on April 16, 2022.
29. Narang, n. 19, p. 38.
30. Ibid., pp. 51-58.
31. "nEUROn UCAV: Development and Operational Assessment Campaign", *NATO OTAN*. https://www.sto.nato.int/publications/STO%20Meeting%20Proceedings/STO-MP-SCI-269/MP-SCI-269-15.pdf. Accessed on February 11, 2022.
32. "France Tests, nEUROn Stealth Combat Drone With Rafale Jets, AWACS Aircraft", DefenceWorld.net, February 22, 2020, https://www.defenseworld.net/news/26394/France_tests_nEURON_stealth_combat_drone_with_Rafale_Jets__AWACS_Aircraft#.YgWEofVBz8M. Accessed on February 11, 2022.
33. Narang, n. 19, pp. 62-63.
34. "The Future Combat Air System (FCAS) Towards the Next Generation Fighter Aircraft", FINABEL, European Army Interoperability Centre, April 20, 2021. https://finabel.org/the-future-combat-air-system-fcas-towards-the-next-generation-fighter-aircraft/. Accessed on February 11, 2022.
35. "Top 5 Best Combat Drones (UAVs) in the World", bulgariamilitary.com, August 3, 2020. https://bulgarianmilitary.com/2020/08/03/top-5-best-combat-drones-uavs-in-the-world/. Accessed on February 26, 2022.
36. Alexander Bratersky, "Russia Unveils Upgraded S-70 Hunter Drone, with Plans for Fielding in 2024", December 17, 2021. https://www.defensenews.com/unmanned/2021/12/16/russia-unveils-upgraded-s-70-hunter-drone-with-plans-for-fielding-in-2024/. Accessed on February 26, 2022.
37. GJ or Gong Ji refers to the attack/strike UAV.

38. "Gongji-11 (GJ-11) Sharp Sword/Lijian". https://www.globalsecurity.org/military/world/china/lijian.htm. Accessed on March 23, 2022.
39. Mike Yeo, "Chinese Airshow Offers Glimpse at Military's New Drones", defensenews.com, September 30, 2021. https://www.defensenews.com/unmanned/2021/09/30/chinese-airshow-offers-glimpse-at-militarys-new-drones/. Accessed on March 23, 2022.
40. The Blended Wing Body (BWB) is a hybrid shape that resembles a flying wing, but also incorporates features from conventional transport aircraft. This combination offers several advantages over conventional tube-and wing airframes. The BWB airframe merges efficient high-lift wings with a wide airfoil-shaped body, allowing the entire aircraft to generate lift and minimise drag. This shape helps to increase fuel economy and creates larger payload (cargo or passenger) areas in the centre body portion of the aircraft. https://www.nasa.gov/centers/langley/news/factsheets/FS-2003-11-81-LaRC.html. Accessed on March 23, 2022.
41 "Gongji-11 (GJ-11) Sharp Sword/Lijian". *Global Security,* https://www.globalsecurity.org/military/world/china/lijian.htm. Accessed on February 26, 2022.
42 "Gongji-11 (GJ-11) Sharp Sword/Lijian", https://www.globalsecurity.org/military/world/china/lijian.htm. Accessed on March 23, 2022.
43. Joe, n. 22.
44. Jr Ng, "China's Next Generation Unmanned Assassins", *Asian Military Review*, June 5, 2019. https://www.asianmilitaryreview.com/2019/06/chinas-next-generation-unmanned-assassins/. Accessed on March 23, 2022.
45. Narang, n. 19, p. 62.
46. Harry Pettit, "China Unveils its Unmanned 'Dark Sword' Fighter Jet that Could Fly at Supersonic Speeds and Prove a Nightmare for US Defences", Mailonline, June 6, 2018. https://www.dailymail.co.uk/sciencetech/article-5811677/China-unveils-unmanned-Dark-Sword-stealth-combat-drone-prove-nightmare-US.html. Accessed on March 20, 2022.
47. Tyler Rogoway, "Image of China's Stealthy 'Dark Sword' Fighter-Like Dombat Drone Emerges", *The Warzone,* June 5, 2018. https://www.thedrive.com/the-war-zone/21324/image-of-chinas-stealthy-dark-sword-fighter-like-combat-drone-emerges. Accessed on March 20, 2022.
48. Chen Chuanren, "China Reveals a Supersonic UCAV", AINonline, June 12, 2018. https://www.ainonline.com/aviation-news/defense/2018-06-12/china-reveals-supersonic-ucav. Accessed on March 20, 2022.
49. Brockmann and Schiller, "A Matter of Speed? Understanding Hypersonic Missile System", SIPRI, February 4, 2022. https://www.sipri.org/commentary/topical-backgrounder/2022/matter-speed-understanding-hypersonic-missile-systems. Accessed on March 15, 2022.
50. Alex Hollings, "Here Are The Hypersonic Weapons Russia and China Have in Service", *Sandbox,* December 16, 2021. https://www.sandboxx.us/blog/here-are-all-hypersonic-weapons-russia-and-china-have-in-service/. Accessed on March 15, 2022.

51. Blake Stilwell, "Why Russia's Hypersonic Missiles Can't Be Seen on Radar", Military.Com, https://www.military.com/equipment/weapons/why-russias-hypersonic-missiles-cant-be-seen-radar.html. Accessed on March 16, 2022.
52. John Feng, "China Hypersonic Drone Program Confirmed by Military Researchers", *Newsweek,* July 9, 2021. https://www.newsweek.com/china-hypersonic-drone-program-confirmed-military-researchers-1626616. Accessed on March 15, 2022.
53. "First Regiment of Avangard Hypersonic Missile Systems Goes on Combat Duty in Russia", TASS, December 27, 2019. https://tass.com/defense/1104297?utm_source=google.com&utm_medium=organic&utm_campaign=google.com&utm_referrer=google.com. Accessed on March 15, 2022.
54. Wu Zhen (WZ) refers to "unmanned reconnaissance" UAV.
55. i.e. equal to five times the speed of sound.
56. Mike Yen, "Chinese Airshow Offers Glimpse at Military's New Drones", *DefenceNews.* https://www.defensenews.com/unmanned/2021/09/30/chinese-airshow-offers-glimpse-at-militarys-new-drones/. Accessed on February 24, 2022.
57. Ibid.
58. "AVIC WZ-8", military factory.com, November 22, 2021. https://www.militaryfactory.com/aircraft/detail.php?aircraft_id=2435. Accessed on February 27, 2022.
59. "China's Air Force Allegedly Had Way of Landing Hypersonic Drones", *VOI,* September 7, 2021. https://voi.id/en/technology/82663/chinas-air-force-allegedly-has-way-of-landing-hypersonic-drones. Accessed on March 15, 2022.
60. "U.S. Hypersonic Glide Vehicle Test Fails Again", Arms Control Association, September 2021. https://www.armscontrol.org/act/2021-09/news-briefs/us-hypersonic-glide-vehicle-test-fails-again. Accessed on March 15, 2022.
61. "Mother of All Drones: US Prepares to Test Hypersonic Drone That Can Fly 5 Times the Speed of Sound", *The Eurasian Times,* August 8, 2021. https://eurasiantimes.com/mother-of-all-drones-us-prepares-to-test-hypersonic-drone-that-can-fly-5-times-the-speed-of-sound/. Accessed on March 16, 2022.
62. "Does India Have Hypersonic Missile Technology? The Country Gets Ready to Strengthen its Capabilities: Know More", *Financial Express,* December 20, 2021. https://www.financialexpress.com/defence/does-india-have-hypersonic-missile-technology-the-country-gets-ready-to-strengthen-its-capabilities-know-more/2384494/. Accessed on March 18, 2022.
63. Kelsey Davenport, "India Tests Hypersonic Missile", Arms Control Association, October 2020. https://www.armscontrol.org/act/2020-10/news/india-tests-hypersonic-missile. Accessed on March 15, 2022.
64. Loz Blain, "Russia's Elon Musk is Developing Hypersonic Rocket Cargo Planes", *New Atlas,* February 9, 2022. https://newatlas.com/aircraft/destinus-hypersonic-aircraft/. Accessed on March 16, 2022.
65. Joe Saballa, "US Navy, Marines Demonstrate Manned-Unmanned Teaming", *The Defence Post,* March 16, 2022. https://www.thedefensepost.com/2022/03/16/us-manned-unmanned-teaming/. Accessed on March 18, 2022.

66. "Future Combat Air System: A400M Clears the First Hurdle as a Remote Carrier Launcher", *Airbus,* February 21, 2022. https://www.airbus.com/en/newsroom/news/2022-02-future-combat-air-system-a400m-clears-the-first-hurdle-as-a-remote-carrier. Accessed on March 17, 2022.
67. Kimberly Johnson, "FLYING", January 19, 2022. https://www.flyingmag.com/air-force-looking-to-manned-unmanned-aircraft-teaming/. Accessed on March 18, 2022.
68. Alex Biegalsky, "The Light Fighter is the Air Force's Manned-Unmanned Team Solution", *War on the Rocks*, February 8, 2022. https://warontherocks.com/2022/02/the-light-fighter-is-the-air-forces-manned-unmanned-team-solution/. Accessed on March 18, 2022.
69. Ajai Shukla, "HAL Looks to the Future with Lethal New Warfighting System", *Business Standard,* January 1, 2022. https://www.ajaishukla.com/2021/12/hal-looks-to-future-with-lethal-new.html. Accessed on March 15, 2022.
70. Rachel S Cohen, "Design Gets Underway on DARPA's 'LongShot' Drone", *AirForce Magazine,* February 8, 2021. https://www.airforcemag.com/design-gets-underway-on-darpas-longshot-drone/. Accessed on March 15, 2022.
71. "CODE Program Enters Phase-III", *ArmyTechnology,* January 11, 2018. https://www.army-technology.com/news/darpas-code-programme-enters-phase-iii/. Accessed on March 15, 2022.
72. "Vinata Aeromobility". https://vinataeromobility.com/. Accessed on November 22, 2021.
73. "ePlane". https://www.eplane.ai/. Accessed on November 22, 2021.
74. https://timesofindia.indiatimes.com/city/chennai/coming-soon-from-iit-madras-stable-flying-taxis/articleshow/82058951.cms?utm_source=twitter.com&utm_medium=social&utm_campaign=TOIDesktop
75. https://www.financialexpress.com/industry/technology/the-eplane-company-flying-taxis-for-a-roof-to-roof-commute/2207434/
76. Kelvin Wong, "China's FL-1 MALE UAV Performs Maiden Flight", *Janes,* January 22, 2019. https://www.janes.com/defence-news/news-detail/chinas-fl-1-male-uav-performs-maiden-flight. Accessed on March 23, 2022.
77. "China's Next Generation Unmanned Assassins", *Asian Military Review,* June 5, 2019. https://www.asianmilitaryreview.com/2019/06/chinas-next-generation-unmanned-assassins/. Accessed on March 23, 2022.
78. PNBS, "Meet Hindustan Aeronautics Limited's HAPS: India's Futuristic Defence Satellite", newsonair.com, July 14, 2021. https://newsonair.com/2021/07/14/meet-hindustan-aeronautics-limiteds-haps-indias-futuristic-defence-satellite/. Accessed on February 27, 2022.
79. AVM Manmohan Bahadur, "The Indian Drone that Crashed in China Could be Goldmine for Chinese Weapons Engineers", *The Print,* December 7, 2017. https://theprint.in/opinion/if-the-fallen-uav-fell-into-chinese-hands-they-would-strip-it-for-technology/20975/. Accessed on January 30, 2022.

80. "Turkey In Talks With 10 Nations Including Pakistan To Sell Its Most-Powerful Drone – Baraktar TB2 UCAV?", *The Eurasian Times,* August 7, 2021. https://www.pakdefense.com/blog/pakistan-air-force/pakistan-air-force-officially-deploys-turkish-bayraktar-tb2-medium-altitude-long-endurance-tactical-combat-drone-for-combat-missions/. Accessed on January 9, 2022.
81. Turkey In Talks With 10 Nations Including Pakistan To Sell Its Most-Powerful Drone—Baraktar TB2 UCAV?, *The Eurasian Times,* August 7, 2021, https://www.pakdefense.com/blog/pakistan-air-force/pakistan-air-force-officially-deploys-turkish-bayraktar-tb2-medium-altitude-long-endurance-tactical-combat-drone-for-combat-missions/. Accessed on January 9, 2022.
82. Lt Gen Prakash Katoch, "China-Turkey Arming Pakistan", *SP's Naval Forces,* November 2, 2021. https://www.spsnavalforces.com/experts-speak/?id=477&h=China-Turkey-Arming-Pakistan. Accessed on January 9, 2021.
83. Narang, n. 19, pp. 203-242.
84. Vinay Kaura, "The Erdogan Effect: Turkey's Relations with Pakistan and India", Institute of South Asian Studies, National University of Singapore, October 16, 2020. https://www.isas.nus.edu.sg/papers/the-erdogan-effect-turkeys-relations-with-pakistan-and-india/. Accessed on March 10, 2022.
85. "Turkey Expands Cooperation with Pakistan on Long-endurance Drone", *The Week,* August 22, 2021. https://www.theweek.in/news/world/2021/08/22/turkey-expands-cooperation-with-pakistan-on-long-endurance-drone.html. Accessed on March 10, 2022.
86. "Pakistan Air Force Officially Deploys Turkish Bayraktar TB2 Medium Altitute Long Endurance (MALE) Tactical Combat Drone for Combat Missions", *PAKDEFENCE,* January 8, 2021. https://www.pakdefense.com/blog/pakistan-air-force/pakistan-air-force-officially-deploys-turkish-bayraktar-tb2-medium-altitude-long-endurance-tactical-combat-drone-for-combat-missions/. Accessed on January 9, 2021.

8. Emerging Technologies and Air Defence

Anil Khosla

> It may be said that warfare has acquired a new phase—technological war. The kind and quality of systems that a nation develops can decide the battle in advance and make the final conflict a mere formality or can bypass conflict altogether.
>
> —General Bernard Schriever

Introduction

The origin of warfare is coincident with the origin of living beings. Human beings have made it into a specialised art by applying the knowledge of science to it. The nature of warfare is constantly changing with advancements in technology. Warfare essentially has two facets: offensive and defensive. Offensive action is aimed at causing damage to the enemy, and defensive action is to save oneself from the enemy's offensive action. In the olden days of fighting with hand-held weapons, swords were used as an offensive weapon and shields were used to protect oneself.

Air power appeared on the warfare scene quite recently as compared to other domains of warfare. Aviation itself started about 120 years ago, however, within a very short time, it made forays into warfare, giving birth to a new Service. Warfare, since then, has gone through a rapid change with the use of the third dimension of air and space. Air warfare also has two facets of offensive application of air power and defensive actions to mitigate the enemy's offensive air actions. In air warfare, the division between the offensive and defensive campaigns is not as simple as it seems. The two campaigns are intrinsically interconnected.

In the last decade, the Air Defence (AD) operations have undergone an extensive change with new technologies being employed. Research is already in progress on new technologies like quantum computing, Artificial Intelligence (AI), hypersonics, nanotechnologies, unmanned systems, etc. These new technologies will have a transformational impact on AD as well. It is worthwhile to trace the historical evolution of AD operations over the years, take stock of the present situation and crystal gaze into the future.

AD Perspective

Understanding AD

The term Air Defence (AD), simplistically means defence of a nation's assets from an enemy's air attacks. However, AD today means much more than that. It means ensuring the sovereignty of a country's airspace in peace and additionally, in war, ensuring freedom of all friendly air and surface operations. It involves a wider responsibility which includes networked and integrated surveillance, command, control and decision-making system and kinetic/non-kinetic, defensive and offensive protective measures. Various facets of AD operations are as follows:

- During both peace and war, the basic task of AD is to monitor round the clock, the entire airspace of interest. AD operations are no longer restricted in volume to own continental or maritime airspace. It covers the entire national airspace along the land borders, the Exclusive Economic Zone (EEZ) and beyond, both the seaboards, and looking deep even into the enemy territory is required. Further, with the use of space for warfare, the envelope has expanded and Air Defence is being renamed as Aerospace Defence.
- AD is the first line of defence and it is the first activity to be raised to a higher level of readiness and alertness during the heating up of a situation.
- Airspace management and control is one of the tasks of AD activities. The intensely busy and dense volume of airspace needs close monitoring and control, to ensure timely detection, identification and engagement of hostile air threats while permitting full freedom of operations to own

users. In peace-time, this no easy task is primarily to avoid accidents and fratricide. During hostilities, the aim is to maximise the effectiveness of combat operations without adding undue restrictions on the users. This role is generally misconstrued as an exclusive claim of use of airspace by the air force.

- AD protection is required not only to the Vital Areas and Vital Points (VAs/VPs) but also to own airborne platforms like the Airborne Warning And Control Systems (AWACS), Airborne Early Warning and Control (AEW&C), and Flight Refuelling Aircraft (FRA), combat support aircraft, helicopters, ground-attack aircraft and unmanned aerial platforms.
- Even offensive air missions are closely integrated with AD elements located on the ground as well as those airborne. AD forms a protective bubble around these offensive packages.
- Air defence is the *raison d'être* of the air force. AD activities are an integral and vital element of every air operation and cannot be executed as a separate campaign.

AD Activities

AD activity has four subsets: Detection, Identification, Interception and Destruction (DIID).

- Surveillance plays a key role in effective AD. A coordinated gap-free, multi-tiered and layered coverage of airspace is required for the detection of air threats as far away as possible. Detection of a likely threat is with the help of radars, electronic sensors and observers. The radars could be long or short-range, static or mobile on the ground or mounted on an airborne platform (aircraft, balloons or drones).
- Identification and classification of air tracks as hostile or friendly is carried out based on electronic means and systems (IFF- Identification Friend or Foe), track behaviour and correlation with known plans.
- Interception and destruction of the hostile track are carried out by interceptor aircraft, Surface-to-Air Missiles (SAMs) of various ranges and close-in weapon systems (AD guns).
- For the protection of ground VAs/VPs, a multi-tiered, layered defence concept is used. Various sensors and weapon systems of different

capabilities are employed to detect and destroy hostile tracks at different ranges, forming four to five protective layers in the 'AD kill chain'.

- With the advancement of technology, the entire gamut of AD operations and activities has got integrated into a network. All the AD elements are interconnected by high speed integrated and secure networks and fused with advanced command and control systems. The advantage is that the AD kill chain has become swift and efficient by reducing the sensor-to-shooter cycle.
- AD flying missions involve both defensive and offensive missions. Defensive Counter-Air (DCA) missions include Combat Air Patrol (CAP) missions over high-value assets on the ground. On the other hand, Offensive Counter-Air (OCA) missions include AD fighters tasked to go into hostile enemy airspace to draw out and shoot down enemy aircraft.
- Own attack packages going across into the enemy airspace are provided full AD cover. The package includes dedicated AD escorts and aircraft for suppression/destruction of enemy AD systems (using electronic warfare jammers and anti-radiation missiles). These missions are executed under the AD surveillance and control provided by the AWACS and AEW&C aircraft which provide AD cover deep inside enemy territory.
- Passive AD (PAD) measures are another facet of AD protection. These include measures to prevent detection by enemy sensors and protection from enemy attacks. Camouflage, concealment, decoying, dispersion, protective shelters and runway rehabilitation schemes, etc. would fall under this category of such activities.

AD Needs of the Army and Navy

Both the army and navy have sizeable AD assets for defending their combat assets against enemy aerial attacks.

- **Army:** Protection of friendly surface forces in the Tactical Battle Area (TBA) comes under the classification of defensive AD. The air force provides a big and wider AD umbrella over the entire area of interest. The army's defensive formations, automatically and adequately, get covered by the multi-tiered air force AD umbrella, and they only need terminal defences. The offensive formations need highly mobile, quick reaction systems for their terminal AD. The army needs radar systems and surface-to-air guided weapons that are mobile and quick to deploy for terminal defence. Even these need to be integrated into the network to avoid fratricide.

- **Navy:** The navy needs to protect its fleets and carrier battle groups. The naval ships are equipped with radars, surface-to-air missiles and close-in weapon systems. Carrierborne fighter aircraft provide an air AD umbrella. The flotilla AD gets augmented by the shore-based aircraft when within their reach. The naval AD weapons and systems work independently of the continental AD network when sailing on the high seas. However, they need to get integrated into the overall AD network when in harbour or close to the shore.

Cost-Benefit Debate

The cost-benefit debate takes place, wherein a simplistic comparison is made between the incoming cheaper hostile projectiles versus the costly AD systems and missiles used to counter them. The classic case is the recent rocket attack on Israel and the use of the Iron Dome system for protection. The cost of VAs/VPs and the extent of damage caused to them by hostile projectiles also needs to be considered, in this comparison. As far as the cost offset is concerned, other options of punitive actions and destruction of enemy launch sites and equipment need to be exercised. Even an increase in deterrence value and display of resolve to retaliate would dissuade enemy attacks.

Concept of AD Command

In the last four decades, AD capability has increased manifold. From point defence, it has become fully networked, covering the entire landmass (including island territories) following the strategy of active defence. For the active defence strategy to work, the AD operations have to be enmeshed with the overall air plans. AD as a separate function cannot be isolated from air warfare. The multi-role, swing-role and now omni-role platforms can achieve much more—even in the same mission. Separating them as role-wise platforms would be gross underutilisation of their capability. A limited number of strategic assets like AWACS and AEW&C are required for other tasks besides AD operations. None of the major powers has a separate AD Command, because it is unviable and the serious operational disadvantages far outweigh the limited gains.

Evolution of AD Concepts

The first use of aerial platforms in war was for aerial reconnaissance. Thereafter, aerial bombing originated with the throwing of hand-held grenades from aircraft. For these aerial threats, passive AD measures like camouflage and concealment were sufficient.

Air warfare and AD operations have come a long way since then and evolved into an intricate facet of warfare. The evolution of air defence and its concepts has been possible with the advancement of technology and improvement in capabilities of terminal weapons, surface-to-air missiles, ground-based and airborne radars, air-to-air missiles, fighter aircraft performance, combat support aircraft and networked command and control systems. AD concepts have evolved and expanded over the years.

- **Point Defence:** During the World Wars, the ground assets were protected by anti-aircraft guns. These provided a limited AD umbrella, with the biggest disadvantage being that they did not prevent the enemy from carrying out an attack. The AD umbrella got slightly bigger with limited range SAMs and fighter aircraft equipped with Airborne Interception (AI) radar and Air-to-Air Missiles (AAMs).
- **Limited Area Defence:** With improvement in the performance of ground-based radars, and fighter AD aircraft (AI radar and AAMs), the limited area defence concept came into being. The concept was to integrate some of the sensors and weapon systems to form bigger AD umbrellas. The biggest advantage of this concept was that an attempt was made to intercept the enemy attack package before it reached the target, reducing the weight of the attack. The attack aircraft were engaged by terminal weapons over the target area and once again, interception was attempted in the egress mode to cause maximum attrition. This concept had the limitation of the existence of large gaps, which could be exploited by the enemy by resorting to tactical routing to avoid the defences.

- **Area Defence:** The next step in the evolution of the AD concept was obviously to remove the gaps and expand the coverage to provide an even bigger AD umbrella covering the entire airspace. This was possible not only by increasing the number of AD assets but also due to further improvement in platforms, sensors and weapons. Long-range sensors mounted on AWACS and AEW&C aircraft, fighters with long-range AI radars armed with Beyond Visual Range (BVR) AAMs and increased range of SAMs enabled this concept. This concept allowed shooting down the enemy aircraft enroute before they could reach the target. Even the AD bubble being provided by fighter escorts to own attack packages got bigger.
- **Integrated Area Defence (Networked):** An Integrated Area Defence (IAD) system comprises a network of all the AD systems, including sensors, platforms, weapons and command and control centres. The Integrated Air Command and Control System (IACCS) of the Indian Air Force (IAF) is an ideal example of such a network. It enables the entire air and AD activity to be closely monitored and controlled. The network effectively links all sensors to provide an 'Integrated Air Situation Picture (IASP)'. Such an integrated system essentially has a three-tiered network i.e. a network of ground elements, a network of aerial platforms through Operational Data-Links (ODLs) and a network linking the ground and air elements. The networked concept provides lots of advantages like clarity, quick decision-making, flexibility of operations and reduction of the sensor-to-shooter cycle.
- **Offensive Defence:** The concept of AD is no longer defensive. It has become proactive and offensive. It is no longer limited to own friendly airspace but takes the fight into the enemy territory and airspace.

Effect of Technology

The air force is a technology-intensive Service. The air force in general and AD operations, in particular, have been influenced by advancements in technology. AD operations have changed over the years mainly due to advancements in terminal weapons, surface-to-air-missiles, ground-based and airborne radars, air-to-air missiles, fighter aircraft performance, combat support aircraft and networked command and control systems. The existing technology features in AD platforms and systems are as follows:

- **Fighter Aircraft:** The fighter aircraft remains the main instrument of prosecution of the air war and air defence. Advancements in fighters include agility, super cruise, stealth, multi-function Active Electronically Scanned Array (AESA) radars, network-centric systems, integrated glass cockpits, fibre-optics data-transmission, multi-spectral sensors, fused situational picture, helmet-mounted sights, and Precision Guided Munitions (PGMs).
- **Airborne AD Sensors:** Airborne radars enhance the look range much beyond the visual ranges. Most of the airborne platforms now have AESA radars. These radars allow simultaneous surveillance, tracking and attack on multiple targets. Ultra-long-range Unmanned Aerial Vehicle (UAV) radar systems are useful in early detection and weapon slewing and designation for the fighters. Passive Infra-Red Search and Tracking (IRST) sensors also form an important part of the of aircraft suite. These can provided good situational awareness.
- **AWACS and AEW&C Aircraft:** These aircraft can detect aircraft and even projectiles at long ranges. They can simultaneously perform command and control and battle management functions. These aircraft are packed with electronics and numerous active and passive systems.
- **Aerial AD Weapons:** Air-to-Air Missiles (AAMs) typically have kill ranges of as far as 200 km. Long-range anti-radiation missiles have been developed as AWACS killers. The range of these weapons goes up to about 400 km. Electro-optical sensor missiles are being used against low-heat targets such as UAVs and cruise missiles.
- **Ground-Based Radars:** High and medium powered surveillance radars, tethered aerostat radar balloons, missile acquisition and guidance radars and tactical battlefield mobile radars are part of the ground sensor network. The ground-based radars have features that could include detection capability of low, medium and high altitude threats, transportability, 3-dimensional air search, long-range surveillance and over-the-horizon look capability. Systems to beat stealth technology are also being developed.

- **Ground-Based AD Weapons:** For conventional threats, SAMs cover the middle AD layers with the inner ring being covered by Close-In Weapon Systems (CIWS) i.e. short-range quick-reaction SAMs and anti-aircraft guns. On the other hand, Ballistic Missile Defence (BMD) requires very long-range interceptor missiles. Now the trend is of integration of multiple missiles with ranges from 40 to 400 km into one system itself (e.g. the S-400).
- **CIWS:** The Anti-Aircraft (AA) guns have improved with features like ballistic and high explosive high-calibre shells, optical or radar control systems, and high rates of fire. However, Man-Portable Air Defence (MANPAD) missiles and Quick Reaction Short-Range Missiles (QRM) are being preferred over the AA guns. The trend is towards smaller and faster missiles with guidance for mid-flight course correction. Hybrid systems with guns and missiles have also been developed.

Future Technologies

New technologies are emerging at a fast pace. These technologies are impacting the nature of warfare (especially air warfare) like never before. Some of the important ones are:

- Quantum computing.
- Hypersonic weapon systems.
- Artificial intelligence.
- Robotics.
- Nanotechnology.
- Unmanned platforms, drones and swarm technology.
- Network-centric environment/internet of things/system of systems.
- Stealth.
- Sensors and seekers.

AD Specific Technology Advancement

Over the years, the number of threats from drones, other platforms and projectiles have resulted in the development of counter-AD systems that can either reduce the effectiveness of such attacks or completely nullify them. The trends include multiple-object kill vehicles, electro-magnetic rail guns, space-based sensors, space-based interceptors, and Hypersonic and Ballistic Tracking Space Sensors (HBTSS). Other AD specific technologies that are advancing are as follows.

- **4D Active Electronically Scanned Array Radar:** The 4D AESA radar is the latest innovation in radar technology. It is designed for close to long-range ground-to-air surveillance and identification.
- **Counter-Hypersonic Weapon System:** Rapid advancements in the field of hypersonic weapon technology and the resultant strategic threats have made the development of counter-hypersonic weapon systems a necessity.
- **Directed Energy Weapons (DEWs):** These systems are at various stages of testing and development. They will give a much higher magnitude of precision. Very narrow beams of lasers, microwave radiation and particle beams would destroy or damage guidance systems or trigger warheads of incoming projectiles.
- **Laser-Based Missile Interception System:** High energy laser weapons are being developed to intercept and destroy threats from missiles, mortars, unmanned aerial vehicles, and other aerial threats.
- **High Power Microwave Weapon:** A High Power Microwave (HPM) weapon signifies a class of non-lethal weapons designed to disable the electronic systems of enemy drones with jolts of powerful electrical energy.
- **Boost Phase Laser-Based Missile Defence System:** The boost phase missile defence system is involved in the obliteration of a hostile missile during the earliest stages of its flight while it remains within the Earth's atmosphere. Slower and easier tracking of missiles is possible during the mid-course or terminal stage, thus, making them vulnerable toward interception. Boost phase laser-based missile defence systems are designed in such a way that they can eliminate missiles during this phase.
- **Neutral Particle Beam Weapons:** Neutral particle beam weapons comprise technology based on the propagation of neutron particles without an electric charge at the speed of light, and directing them toward the target. Particle beams can be more effective than lasers because they can penetrate beyond the surface of the enemy's missile,

igniting its fuel supply, melting its mechanical components, and damaging its electronic system.

Harnessing Emergent Technologies

Technology superiority needs to be a cornerstone of the national military strategy. A comprehensive defence science and technology strategy needs to be defined. It should contain the plan to harness technology and convert it into decisive military capability. It would provide strategic focus by making long-term and medium-term technology plans for guidance, with a periodic review. A top-down approach, guided by a policy document and supported by adequate monetary allotment would ensure success. A suitable ecosystem needs to be developed to bring users (defence in this case), academia, Research and Development (R&D) [Defence Research and Development Organisation (DRDO)] and industry [Defence Public Sector Undertakings (DPSUs and private)] to work in unison. Some of the existing projects that need impetus are:

- Hypersonic weapons systems.
- Integrated ballistic and cruise missile system.
- Aviation programmes
- Fifth-generation fighter aircraft.
- Transport aircraft (for civil and military requirements).
- Development of gas turbines and engines.
- AI-enabled autonomous systems (land, air and sea).
- Unmanned platforms.
- Development of sensors and seekers for multiple users.
- Metallurgy and composites.

Challenges Ahead

> Victory smiles upon those who anticipate the changes in the character of war, not upon those who wait to adapt themselves after the changes occur.
>
> —Giulio Douhet

Widening of AD Spectrum: In the past, AD had to provide protection from conventional threats i.e. weapons launched from conventional platforms and short-range SAMs. With the proliferation of unmanned and other smaller platforms, sub-conventional threats have been added to the list of AD threats. The vital areas and vital installations need to be protected against these threats. Appropriate detection systems and weapons like CIWS are required to deal with them. On the other end of the spectrum, the ballistic missile threat has increased over the years. Ballistic Missile Defence (BMD) systems with the ability to look and intercept very far are required. The AD threat spectrum has widened on both sides.

Sub-Conventional Threats: The latest challenge faced by the world due to grey zone operations in the aerial domain are the sub-conventional threats posed by aerial platforms like unmanned platforms, drones, swarms, hang gliders and powered gliders, etc. These platforms, besides being used for direct targeting, are also being utilised in roles like Intelligence, Surveillance, Reconnaissance (ISR), smuggling, arms trafficking, etc. In the last few years, the world over, concerted efforts have been made to deal with these threats. They need to be dealt with by the development and employment of detection systems, anti-drone weapons/systems, engagement procedures, and licensing and controlling regulations. AD operations, assets and systems are an essential component in the entire response for mitigation of these threats. A mix of manned-unmanned operations, including unmanned swarms, will be a big challenge in the future.

Hybrid Multi-Sensor Systems: For a clear, accurate, real-time air situation picture, myriad numbers and types of sensors will be required to be integrated. In the domain of sub-conventional platforms, detection and tracking are difficult because the radar, heat, visual, audio, electro-magnetic and noise signatures of these platforms are low. Hybrid systems with multiple sensors would be required. These systems would need Artificial Intelligence (AI) to analyse and compile the piecemeal information obtained from various sensors.

Grey Zone Warfare Effects: Grey zone warfare would not be restricted to war-time. Even in peace-time, these hostile activities may create frequent tense situations. AD, being the first responder, will be put on alert frequently and, may be, for extended periods. This challenge will have to be managed without any dilution in alertness and, at the same time, avoiding burnout.

Network-Centric Warfare: AD operations would be highly network-centric. The real-time flow of information to numerous stakeholders would be very important. Integrated networks with a good architecture, supported by suitable applications, will assist in building situational awareness, planning, communicating, and monitoring the situations in real-time. The information flow would have the need-to-know basis to avoid paralysis due to information overload. The networks would require redundancies and protection measures in terms of firewalls and anti-virus systems. Alternate standby nodes will have to be built in with plug and play or power up and play options.

AI Necessity: In the networked environment, with the integration of thousands of systems, the volume of data would be very large. Further, there will be duplication of data. AI will become a necessity to analyse the data and make it available on a need-to-know basis to avoid information overload. AI assistance would also be required for the decision support feature and what-if options.

Cyber Security: The cyber domain has the maximum potential for grey zone operations and cyber attacks even in peace-time.Unlike a physical attack, a cyber attack can be launched instantaneously from anywhere, at any time and, with little evidence, it is hard to trace and has a high level of deniability. These characteristics make it the ideal and most favoured tool for grey zone operations. Cyber attacks would be launched by the enemy on military networks (including the AD networks). Denial of these networks could prove to be catastrophic and they have to be protected adequately. The information-rich environment will require integrity and security of data. Procedural back-ups will have to be in place.

Space Defence: Space-based systems and applications are embedded in every aspect of military and civil life. Space has become an important domain and warfare has proliferated in this domain. The term air power has changed to aerospace power with the aerial warfare envelope expanding to the domain of space. The term air defence has also changed to aerospace defence. Defence of own space assets would be a challenge in the future.

Recommendations

> New conditions require new solutions, new weapons and imaginative methods for maximum application. New wars are never won in the past.
>
> —Douglas MacArthur

In the game of warfare, one has to keep pace with the latest developments. Some of the recommendations from an AD perspective are as follows:

- We need to invest in new technology research and development. All the major military powers are researching the military use of new technologies.
- All technologies are dual-use i.e. for civil as well as military use. Research for the military use of new dual-use technologies should progress *ab initio* and in parallel.
- Unmanned platforms and drones of different types with a variety of capabilities are performing numerous tasks in the domain of warfare. They have a large potential for AD operations, including surveillance, reconnaissance, detection, suppression of enemy AD by soft as well as hard kill, etc. These platforms need to be used judiciously along with other platforms and systems.
- The threat posed by unmanned platforms and drones has widened the spectrum of AD threats. The threat from sub-conventional platforms needs to be tackled with multi-sensor, multi-weapon anti-drone systems. There is an urgent need for the development and large scale manufacture of these systems.
- On the other extreme of the spectrum is the threat from long-range ballistic missiles. Multi-layered ballistic missile defence needs to be developed and deployed for the protection of the national capital and other strategic locations. These extended-range systems with appropriate adaptations will also be useful against hypersonic weapons in the future.
- All the existing AD assets (sensors and weapons), as well as the ones operationalised in the future, need to be integrated into an AD network.
- The dependence on the networks is increasing. A cyber attack denying the use of an AD network would prove to be catastrophic. Adequate cyber security measures need to be instituted and redundancy needs to be built in it.
- Artificial Intelligence (AI) has lots of potential for use in AD systems. AI-enabled decision support systems with what-if options are the need of the hour.

- The vast area to be monitored for gap-free coverage requires multiple sensors in adequate numbers. A mix of both high power static and mobile AD systems is required.
- AD systems need to cater for all types of terrain. The most difficult is the hilly terrain, where even the airborne platforms have limitations. Mountain radars are required for these areas along with other systems.
- AWACS and AEW&C aircraft are force multipliers and game changers. Adequate numbers should be available to cover the entire area, round the clock, if required.
- Organisational adaptation is an essential part of the transformation. However, change should not be made for the sake of change. A separate AD Command is not operationally viable and is not recommended.
- Grey zone warfare would warrant a situation of frequent and prolonged alerts in the future. These extended periods of high alert status and operational readiness take a toll on both man and machine. Adequate numbers and time-sharing are required to avoid burnout.
- Protective infrastructure is an essential part of the defensive AD. Adequate numbers are required to safeguard aerial platforms and other systems on the ground. Besides quantity, the protective infrastructure should be capable of providing protection against current and future weapons. Going underground provides enhanced protection.
- Passive Air Defence (PAD) helps in damage control and speedy recovery from damage caused by aerial attacks. New technology equipment and systems need to be introduced in the PAD inventory.
- Knowledge of the enemy AD Order of Battle (ORBAT) is essential for mission planning. Investment in ISR platforms and equipment and carrying out a well-planned ISR campaign would pay high dividends.
- Electronic Warfare (EW) has become an important facet of warfare. The AD platforms and systems are vulnerable to EW warfare and need appropriate counter-measures. EW systems and systems for increasing survivability are required to deal with EW threats.
- The entire gamut of AD operations and campaigns has become very complex. Integrated (live and simulated) training solutions are required. AI-enabled systems with the what-if option would be preferable.

- Most important of all is self-reliance. All major military powers in the world have a well-established defence industry. Besides cost saving, it ensures assured availability.

Conclusion

Air warfare, including AD operations, is highly technology sensitive and dependent. AD has been in a state of continuous transformation. Recently, the high pace of technological advancements has led to its rapid transformation. Over the years, AD has gone well beyond the being a defence concept. It is no longer restricted to being defensive. Its employment philosophy and operational concepts have undergone immense changes from the past. AD now provides a vast, gap-free, multi-layered national security umbrella round the clock. Multi-agency Network-Centric Warfare (NCW) integration of all civil and military AD assets ensures clarity, quicker reaction and a synergetic approach.

The advancement of technology and the changing nature of security challenges are the two drivers of the transformation of warfare. Growing employment of grey zone warfare would increase the burden on first responder AD in the future. The spectrum of threats has widened manifold. It ranges from sub-conventional threats from small platforms, on one end of the spectrum, to long-range vectors (ballistic missiles), on the other. Sub-conventional threats, conventional threats and threats from long-range projectiles need different solutions. Offensive and defensive operations, being deeply enmeshed intrinsically, cannot be segregated and compartmentalised under a separate AD Command.

New technologies are making inroads into warfare at a rapid pace. Being an extremely dynamic facet of air power, AD will continue to evolve with the advances in technology. Induction of new platforms, radars, and networking equipment, with appropriate changes in concepts, strategy and tactics, would make AD operations more efficient and effective in the future.

References

1. https://www.vifindia.org/article/2020/july/24/air-defence-is-everywhere
2. https://airpowerasia.com/2020/06/17/air-defence-of-india-the-big-picture-view/

3. https://airpowerasia.com/2021/08/02/air-space-control-challenges-and-the-way-ahead/
4. http://www.indiandefencereview.com/news/challenges-of-integrated-air-defence
5. https://55nda.com/blogs/anil-khosla/wp-content/uploads/2021/05/Technology-and-Air-Warfare-_-Vivekananda-International-Foundation-2.jpg
6. https://www.globenewswire.com/news-release/2020/11/06/2122004/28124/en/Six-Prominent-Technological-Trends-Influencing-the-Air-Defense-System-Market.html
7. https://airpowerasia.com/2021/02/07/akash-air-defence-missile-indias-formidable-weapon-system/
8. https://www.idsa.in/issuebrief/air-defence-command-kkhera-270120
9. https://www.d8.synergiafoundation.org/insights/analyses-assessments/future-conflict-scenarios
10. https://newsable.asianetnews.com/india/air-defence-command-need-to-hasten-slowly-serving-chiefs-best-to-take-calls-qb1ekn
11. https://55nda.com/blogs/anil-khosla/2021/07/01/drone-threat-the-big-picture/
12. https://salute.co.in/air-defence-command-need-for-a-rethink/
13. https://55nda.com/blogs/anil-khosla/2021/02/07/future-conflict-scenario/
14. https://idsa.in/issuebrief/TransformationoftheIndianAirForceovertheNextDecade_vkapur
15. https://55nda.com/blogs/anil-khosla/2020/09/16/rocking-the-boat-during-the-storm/
16. https://en.wikipedia.org/wiki/Indian_Ballistic_Missile_Defence_Programme
17. https://55nda.com/blogs/anil-khosla/2021/07/14/theatre-command-birds-eye-view/

9. Training the IAF's Air Warriors

TD Joseph

Introduction

The common thread of this book, thus far, is all about how air power, with its sensitivity to ever evolving technologies, is itself undergoing a series of so-called 'Revolutions in Military Affairs' (RMAs) in rather quick succession—in platforms, systems, sensors and weapons. As one of the leading air forces of the world, the Indian Air Force (IAF) also has been subject to this transformation in the recent decades and will continue to be so in the future also. The evidence of how such transformation has played across the world for other major air forces has been visible in all the conflicts in the recent decades, with air power being the lead element in a majority of these. Successful application of this most potent of all forms of present-day warfare has depended largely on the leaders who envisaged air power application and the airmen and women who executed those plans. The ease with which success was achieved through the most efficient and precise application, was predicated on the comfort levels and confidence of the combatants involved in operating these systems and weapons. And this came through the strong foundation of training.

Training and professional military education continue throughout the career of an air warrior, especially officers. Therefore, when we talk of training the IAF's air warriors, we need to look at both basic training as well as in-service training. This chapter shall delve into how training could evolve to stay abreast of technological evolutions that drive the RMA, from selection of the right personnel, their basic as well as platform/system/role-based training through their career, and how simulation and simulators provide the opportunity to enhance real-time experiences by facilitating air warriors to try out all possible situations and solutions.

Selection: The Human Resource Task

Qualification criteria for the various branches of the officer cadre and trades of airmen are unambiguously laid down. With the way that warfare, and in particular air warfare, is changing, one can confidently state that given the state of the education system in the country, the parameters more than meet the task. Considering the prospects of a fixed term (in the case of short service commissioned officers and fixed engagement term for airmen) assured job/career, with the added benefits of a military service, there are more than enough takers for joining the air force. Some reports suggest that there are more than 1,000 aspirants for every successful officer candidate, with the ratio being somewhat similar for airmen's selection too.

Embracing next generation technologies would need to be accelerated by the organisation to meet the emerging challenges. In order to meet this requirement of hi-tech warriors of the future, the IAF would do well to focus on selecting officer cadets and airmen trainees with certain specific qualifications and skill sets in fields like Artificial Intelligence (AI), data science and software development in addition to existing skills requirements. Highlighting these requirements alongside the aerial warfare component where pilots and air defence personnel are more visible, would help in attracting the necessary talent to meet future warfare challenges. The Human Resource (HR) department dealing with recruiting needs to give the necessary push for this through wide publicity of the requirements, selecting candidates with niche capabilities and earmarking them for future warfare requirements. Catching the talent pool early, and upfront investment in augmenting their skill sets to meet air force requirements will help in establishing a group of air warriors who can straightaway start dealing with the emerging nature of threats.

An analysis of the officer cadre intake would highlight that a substantial component of successful candidates across branches have an engineering background, and all ex-National Defence Academy (NDA) cadets now graduate with a B Tech degree. The IAF's HR department must identify people from this pool who have a flair for software development, coding, cyber warfare, etc. to strengthen the force that is needed to fight the modern forms of cyber and information warfare. The need is to have the right mix of air warriors with operational experience as well as technical skills. The latter need not be only those with a pure engineering background, but also who have the requisite flair for the job.

The selection criteria for technical airmen indicate youth graduating from polytechnic colleges also being eligible for selection along with those who qualify in the 10+2 examinations. A cursory perusal of the history of airmen's recruitment would prove that such candidates form less than 5 per cent of technical tradesmen recruited. The IAF will stand to benefit in terms of training time and costs if it can attract this group of youth in much larger numbers, to increase their representation amongst new recruits to a high 20 or 30 per cent. Their specific sets of technical skills include what the IAF needs in the current times as well as in the future. According to the IAF's website for airmen's selection (https://airmenselection.cdac.in/CASB/eligibilityCriteria.html) some of the qualifications sought in prospective airmen candidates are Mechanical Engineering (CAD/CAM Design and Robotics), Mechanical (Advance Manufacturing Technology), Manufacturing Engineering/Technology, Electronics and Communication Engineering, Electronics (Microprocessor), Electronics and Avionics, Electronics (Fibre Optics), Electronics (Robotics), Telecommunication Engineering/Technology, Information Technology, Computer Engineering, Computer Science and Engineering, Computer Science and Technology, etc. to name a few. By recruiting such qualified candidates, the IAF would need to focus only on areas like basic air warrior training, general service knowledge, and other generic areas, thereby saving as much as 48 weeks or more of *ab-initio* training. After the initial air warrior training and further training on specific systems, such trainee air warriors can move directly onto the respective systems and be available to combat units at least a year before the current timelines. Therefore, this is an area that the IAF would benefit from, given the right focus and push.

Selecting the Right Instructors

A good understanding of the fundamentals of the job or systems is the first step in the efficient discharge of any air warrior's day-to-day work commitment. It is essential that the air force selects and appoints the right kind of instructors with the right capability to impart these fundamentals well. People with the right qualifications, knowledge, experience on the systems/job, aptitude to teach, commitment to the task, and integrity are critical to laying a strong foundation for the young officer cadets and airmen trainees. However, providing 100 per cent instructors who meet all these criteria faces across three hurdles. Firstly, the organisation cannot afford to deploy all exceptional air warriors on instructional tenures as they would be needed to supervise and execute the tasks in the field units also; secondly, systemic loopholes in HR management tend to allow air warriors (officers and airmen) who do not meet the laid down Qualifying Requirements (QRs) to be deployed on instructional duties; and thirdly, the air force's HR department may not be able to meet the increased demands for instructors to meet the sudden spikes in recruiting, as has happened in the recent times.

The air force has well laid down QRs to select instructors. Complete adherence to these QRs and supervisory audits within the HR department ought to address the second issue. The first and third issues could be addressed by adopting a systematic approach to find options through which a wider pool of talented prospective instructors could be created. Such an approach should identify potential sources of instructors such as retired qualified experts on systems with an aptitude to teach, contractual instructors for non-core subjects like languages and fundamentals of subjects related to physics and electronics (with relevance to air force systems), adjunct instructors who could be contracted to instruct subjects with limited applicability but considered essential, etc.

Similarly, there would be many highly experienced Qualified Flying Instructors (QFIs), veterans with a passion for flying and teaching flying, the willing ones amongst whom could be employed on a contract-basis (based on hours flown or a minimum annual task) to teach flying at our *ab-initio* flying training establishments, Flying Instructors Schools (FIS), etc; or experts on air power, security and strategy, international affairs, etc who could be contracted to impart knowledge at the College of Air Warfare; engineering subject experts for the Air Force Technical College (AFTC); expert administrators who could be deployed at the Air Force Administrative College (AFAC), etc. This would help tap the vast wealth of experience and knowledge available out there amongst the veterans and free up much needed junior and mid-level leaders for the field units and formation headquarters.

The IAF must endeavour to identify existing barriers to the creation of such a pool, and adopt mitigating strategies by reviewing policies. If it is necessary to test the efficacy of the new policy, run a pilot programme at select training establishments/institutes which usually face instructor shortages.

An instructor pool thus created would provide flexibility to the organisation in permanent as well as temporary deployment of instructors to address critical shortages, to meet the demands of spikes in recruitment and to ensure that quality air warriors in both technical and non-technical fields are retained in the field units. The QRs and terms of engagement laid down for all such staff must be revised from time to time based on the recommendations of the field and Training Command, and analysis done by the training directorate at Air Headquarters (HQ) to ensure that air force training keeps pace with evolving changes.

If technology is considered an enabler, the IAF could review whether introduction of hybrid mode of teaching and learning for the airmen's training could reduce the number of instructors required or not. Increased share of online education through content transfer of training and educational material that can easily be learned could help in reducing the instructor-to-trainee ratios, thus, relieving trained air warriors for field duties.

Another aspect that needs to be looked at is the process of selecting or appointing instructors for most non-flying officer training establishments. A board-based selection process for instructors'/combat leaders' courses is done only in the case of flying and other operations branches like fighter controlling and Air Traffic Control (ATC), but not for technical, administrative, education, logistics functions, etc. Nor is there a specific instructors' course like the Flying Instructors' Course, graduating from which is purely performance-based and not assured. Establishing such a selection and training process for other branches would ensure a better quality instructors' pool amongst all the branches in the IAF.

Effectiveness of planning and management of the IAF's human capital will decide the biggest war-winning factor for the future air force—the man behind the machine. This becomes even more critical as technology-driven transformation of the IAF will demand more technology oriented and technology empowered leaders and workers.

Roles Specific Training

The process of the initial role-specific training based on platforms and systems that the IAF's personnel would be employed on immediately after the *ab-initio* training process is quite comprehensive and well-structured to have reasonably met the requirements of systems that existed in the IAF till recently. The IAF must regularly review whether such pattern and resources would suffice to match the requirements of platforms, systems and weapons based on the revolutionising technologies of today and the future that are being inducted into the force.

Officers Training: Aircrew and Unmanned Aerial Systems Crew

Most air forces across the world have reported a steady reduction in flying hours under the belt for its aircrew. This is evident in the case of the IAF too, with a discernible reduction in the overall flying hours for pilots from all three streams. Reduced flying experience translates into challenges in proficiency levels in combat missions as well as instructional/supervisory role capabilities, as also the opportunity to frequently practise specific roles and in maintaining war-winning proficiency in employment of specialist weapons. Regular practice is essential for pilots to deal with contingencies of unusual in-flight occurrences like system failures, adverse weather phenomena, and in the case of Unmanned Aerial Systems (UAS) crew, for manoeuvring under emerging/imminent threat when on missions.

Training to Operate in the Changing Terrain of Operations: The fledgling Royal Indian Air Force (RIAF) cut its teeth in World War II and flew extensive combat sorties in the tropical jungles of Burma and in the low hilly terrain of the North-West Frontier Provinces. In the 1947-48 conflict over Kashmir with Pakistan and the 1962 War with China, the IAF's transport fleet flew missions over the high Himalayas. Barring these, the IAF's fighter fleet fought almost entirely in the airspace over the plains in both 1965 and 1971 Wars. The 1999 Kargil conflict forced the IAF to rapidly adapt to the requirements of flying over the mountains. The air power elements of the North Atlantic Treaty Organisation (NATO) forces (both manned and unmanned platforms) in almost all recent conflicts in West Asia, Kosovo, etc. have also operated over the plains largely.

With the primary threat to India shifting north and eastward to China, almost all air operations will happen over the Himalayas. All aircrew understand the reduced performance characteristics of both the airframe and engine, as also the change in ballistics of weapons at very high altitudes. Therefore, a regular review of combat and support operations training by the IAF will help it to assess the operational potential and capability of its aircrew, UAS operators and systems to fight at very high altitudes. Being one of the most professional air forces in the world, the IAF would have already taken such steps and implemented the necessary corrective measures. However, the importance of the need to sustain this type of training over long periods is critical to operational success. Besides enhancing individual and systemic combat efficiency and proficiency, lessons arrived at from regular training would help in introducing new types of possible as well as emerging challenges with an aim to develop effective counter-tactics.

Weapons Training at High Altitudes: Accurate targeting is the most critical aspect for success in all offensive air operations; and mountains pose an altogether different challenge when it comes to weapon delivery, as the Kargil conflict demonstrated. While changes in the ballistic characteristics of the weapons themselves pose challenges in understanding the physics of weapon performances, it is the impact of minor errors in tracking and delivering weapons on surface targets in the mountains that pose greater challenges. An inaccuracy in target designation by a mere fraction of metre or degree would result in colossal errors on the ground, thereby missing the target altogether. Despite claims of the best accuracies, the success rates of precision munitions in the most recent air offensives in Afghanistan and Syria have reportedly fallen short of the claimed capabilities of these weapons. And that too in an uncontested environment. Therefore, it is essential for the IAF to revive its high-altitude air-to-ground ranges that were created a few decades ago and establish more such ranges in the Central and Eastern Sectors for the aircrew to have regular high altitude weapons delivery practice.

Train for Low Level and Valley Flying Operations: Aircraft of the US Air Force (USAF)/US Navy (USN), followed by the rest of the North Atlantic Treaty Organisation (NATO) air forces adopted tactics of flying above the kill envelopes of surface-to-air weapons during Gulf War I and subsequent operations. What is significant here is that opposing air power elements were neutralised by the Allied forces in the beginning of the conflict itself, leaving only the Surface-to-Air Missile (SAM) elements as the threat. Hence, operations were conducted in an uncontested environment, with plenty of electronic warfare support systems to provide additional protection. It would be unwise for air forces expected to operate in a contested environment to template the tactics adopted by the NATO air forces.

Therefore, the ability and skills to operate at all heights, especially at low levels, during day and night, must continue to be nurtured. This is especially true for the IAF's fighter, transport and helicopter operations to beat the radar systems of its adversaries, which could have some gaps at low levels. One cannot discount the enemy's aircraft operating at low levels, necessitating air interceptions at low levels, which also must be practised regularly, especially in the night. It is well known that flying through valleys below the crest levels provides added protection to aircraft from detection by the enemy's air defence systems. Such training is bound to pay rich dividends in operations in the mountains—the theatre of operations by the IAF in the foreseeable future. Skills of low level and valley flying, and training for these must not be sacrificed at the altar of flight safety. Sustained regular training in these provides enhanced safety. On the other hand, intermittent and infrequent bursts of training could lead to more unsafe operations. Therefore, it is essential that the IAF refocusses on the criticality of flying training at low levels in the plains as well as in the Himalayan valleys.

Peace-Time Training to Fight Wars: Is the IAF obsessed with adherence to rigid safe Rules of Engagement (ROE) for its combat crew, both in the air and on the ground? Is proficiency in simultaneous multi-level multi-spectrum operations being sacrificed for the sake of such safety adherence? Adherence to ROE to ensure flight safety is essential; but so is building up realistic operational skills. The adversary is not going to fight according to your rules. Excessive training and practice adhering to the same or similar sets of ROE and safety parameters may condition combat crew to follow in conflict by habit what they practise in peace-time. Therefore, it is essential that the IAF's operational training is conducted with rules of engagement that permit operational flexibility while ensuring adequate safety. Violations must not be condoned, but, at the same time, out of the box thinking must be encouraged and not treated as violations upfront. Remember, 'we fight the way we train'.

Soft Kill Capabilities: Electronic Warfare (EW) and Intelligence, Surveillance, Reconnaissance (ISR) capabilities have been two critical war-winning factors in most, if not all, air operations, including sub-conventional ones (Chechnya, anti-terrorist operations by NATO forces, etc.) in the conflicts involving the most advanced air forces. The EW and ISR capabilities of the IAF on both manned and unmanned platforms must not only be built up by several factors of the existing ones, but also mastered through realistic training along with sustained updation of threat libraries. The pool of trained air and ground crew proficient in operating these systems must be built up through regular training to facilitate round-the-clock operations during both peace and war. This being the silent factor, it may not, and should not, attract publicity, unlike the high-profile Public Relations (PR) exercises of landing on highways.

Ground-based Combat Crew: The Air Defence Element

Effects of change in the terrain of operations mentioned earlier impact the combat performance of ground-based air defence systems and crew alike of Surface-to-Air Guided Weapons (SAGW), mobile radars, electronic surveillance systems, communications systems, etc. Challenges of reduced line of sight, impact of low temperatures and adverse climatic conditions on equipment as well as crew, deterioration in physical capacity due to reduced oxygen levels, etc. tend to adversely affect the combat efficiency of the entire air defence and communication systems when deployed in the mountains.

While equipment performance levels in the mountains can be simulated during virtual training in the plains, the only way for the human body to adapt to extreme conditions is through sustained physical presence in the high altitudes. Maintenance crew will face a different set of challenges in equipment performance as compared to those obtained in the plains. Therefore, the IAF would do well to deploy its surface air defence elements in such terrain at regular intervals and operate over sustained periods. Live training to these crew must be provided by operating manned and unmanned aircraft simultaneously. In fact, it becomes a win-win situation for all types of combat crew as live training for all can be combined in the same missions. Simulated training in the plains would prepare the crew on what to expect and how to react, but it is only the physical deployment that would prepare the combat and maintenance crew for the real thing.

Technical Personnel Training

In discussions on preparing the IAF for war, it is natural that the focus remains largely on operational and operations crew training. Success in operations depends as much on the skills of the support cast—the maintenance arm and other support branches. As a professional air force, the IAF has been prompt in establishing technical training facilities whenever new systems are inducted. The question is whether it falls into the trap of continuing with age old practices in teaching and training or not. Are the technical personnel spending too much time in Technical Type Training (TETTRA) schools? While cutaway models of engines, systems and weapons are good for explaining and demonstrating maintenance activities, they are too limited in number to give hands-on practice. Limited numbers of modern systems being acquired, and their cost, may not permit the luxury of having adequate live training facilities at these schools or in the field units. The way forward is a transformation to embedded Augmented Reality/ Virtual Reality (AR/VR) training facilities in TETTRA schools and in the field units. A beginning has been made in a few schools and in the Medical Training Centre for Medical Assistants. It is important that these do not remain as mere demonstration pieces; many more systems need to be procured and made available to facilitate all personnel under training to access and operate on these systems to hone their skills. With the infusion of such new technological aids to training, the IAF should be able to review its training pattern to optimise the duration of the training and make personnel available to the field in faster timeframes.

Simulators and Role of AR/VR in Training

Transformations in Information Technology (IT) and Artificial Intelligence (AI) have revolutionised our capabilities to provide near real experience in training through AR/VR enabled systems. It is time for the IAF to embrace such technologies to enhance training capabilities in flying operations, combat support functions, technical training and medical training. The focus on near-real experience simulators tends to be limited mostly to aircraft, combat systems and fighter controlling as well as air traffic controlling systems. Training of technical personnel, doctors, medical assistants, etc. has relied mostly on cutaway models. The emergence of AR/VR and their introduction will not only facilitate enhancement of training experience on existing simulators, but also in the fields of all technical and medical training. The IAF must invest heavily in this.

As stated earlier, flying hours are at a premium to provide considerable experience to aircrew in basic as well as role-oriented training. The IAF does not have enough resources for providing real-time experience in all roles for its aircrew. Therefore, the stress on utilisation of simulators, which has been rightly given a decent impetus in the recent years, needs to be sustained and such training must be taken to the next levels. Virtual training aids with embedded augmented reality will enable aircrew to compensate for the shortfall in hands-on real-time experience. Aircrew would benefit immensely from AR/VR enabled solutions for practising and experimenting with fly-through programmes in the mountains, valleys as well as deserts, with realistic embedded inputs of target systems, enemy Air Defence (AD) weapon systems, interceptions and many other plausible scenarios that aircrew could encounter during operations. Each operational squadron may be equipped with two or more systems to facilitate adequate training for its aircrew. Alternatively, these could be centrally positioned in all flying bases alongside simulators to provide wider utilisation; but, available in adequate numbers for copious use by all aircrew.

The capabilities of, and the facilities available with, the systems simulators developed or acquired recently for controllers, SAGW crew, etc. must also be enhanced through regular injection of embedded AR/VR proactively. It is essential not to fall into the trap of merely reacting to changes in the enemy's capabilities; instead, anticipating evolutions in threat-enhancing technologies and working on solutions early must be the way.

AR/VR based training systems become even bigger enablers when it comes to technical training—on aircraft, weapons and systems, as well as all other combat and support equipment. Using AR/VR, engineers and technicians could learn the nuances of processes and procedures from the simplest to the most complex maintenance activities. Each person could learn his trade through a three-step process. First, observe and learn from a demonstration by an AI powered character who would complete the entire repair or servicing procedure without any human influence; second, do an assisted activity with inputs and guidance from a real instructor as well as an AI empowered virtual instructor; and, finally, do the entire procedure in person on their own; all without any need for real systems.

For this to be most effective, there should be an adequate number of systems that would help the trainees to practice at their own pace and repeat it, if necessary. Thus, they can fine-tune their maintenance skills on full scale digital models of aircraft or systems and their components and develop muscle memory of the activities to be conducted, before moving onto real systems/aircraft. On gaining enough experience in operating these models, all training establishments, institutes and even sections that conduct continuity training could introduce further applications like system tutorials, quizzes (to enable instructors to monitor progress), practical exercises, task guides, etc.

An advantage of adopting such digital technologies lies in the ability of trainees to learn and practise even after regular classroom hours and from their residences (when networked). Thus, the IAF can enhance training values even during periods like the Wuhan virus pandemic, which would not have been possible with its traditional training methods. Young air warriors and the IAF, in turn, will benefit immensely from this. Augmented reality could make training more effective with better learning retention, ability to train even when real aircraft and equipment are not available, and, finally, better outputs. Trainees can learn by making mistakes, avoiding the embarrassment of the consequences that would have been visible on a real system like injuring themselves, damaging the equipment, making it non-available for others, etc. Essentially, it becomes a confidence builder too and will enable quicker progress by the trainees to real-time hands-on training. However, here too it is critical that experienced and senior instructors work hard on updating and mastering the skills to use these teaching aids to be able to impart training with confidence and the necessary expertise. Being more tech-savvy, the incoming young generation would be much quicker on the uptake.

Conclusion

The review of training methods, curriculum and assistive techniques at regular intervals, along with the introduction of modern instructional aids in line with changes in technology and changing equipment profile are critical for the IAF to stay ahead of other air forces. So is the requirement to look freshly at qualifying requirements and standards, skill sets to meet modern technology requirements, selecting the right people who qualify for these, and updation of knowledge as well as the training skills of instructors. Widening the pool of trainers will provide greater flexibility and free personnel qualified in critical skills for combat units. The IAF must anticipate and prepare for warfare in the future through a regular analysis of evolving technologies, especially those available with the likely adversaries or which are likely to be available to them. This will help the IAF plan its equipment and personnel profile to meet these challenges and plan for proper training. There is also an equally critical need to elevate the importance of science and technology within the IAF to higher levels along with wider education of its leaders in addition to regular training. Focus and transition to modern technologies in training such as a copious increase in the utilisation of AR/VR, simulators, etc. are critical to the IAF's ability to remain the premier war-winning factor for India in future conflicts.

10. India's Self-Reliance in Aerospace Design and Development

RK Narang

Introduction

India is currently passing through the second *Atmanirbhar Bharat* (self-reliant) mission in aviation manufacturing after the lesser known first *Atmanirbhar Bharat* mission in aviation manufacturing in the 1950s and 1960s. The first *Atmanirbhar Bharat* mission had neither a name nor was celebrated, yet it had similar intent, actions and outcomes. Air power being technology sensitive relies heavily on innovations in the aviation industry. Air power played a critical role in the outcomes of most wars globally in the last century, including in the India-Pakistan Wars since 1948. On the other hand, non-employment and underutilisation of air power can have an adverse impact on the outcome of a wars. The non-employment of air power in the India-China War of 1962 and underutilisation of air power in the ongoing Russia-Ukraine War of 2022 have been the subjects of intense debates, as many believe that the results of both these wars could have been different.

Air power itself is in the transformational stage as it getting revitalised with the development of the Uninhabited Aerial System (UAS), UAS swarms, Manned UNmanned Teaming (MUMT), hypersonics, high altitude pseudo-satellites and other emerging aviation technologies. The small slow and low flying UAS operating individually, collaboratively and as swarms, have added a new dimension to air power as well as raised new challenges for air defence planners. The leading defence manufacturers of the world are exploring new solutions to counter the threat posed by emerging Unmanned Aircraft (UA) technologies.

India's security challenges are becoming complex with the rising economic and military power and assertiveness of China on its northern borders, the increasing volatility of Pakistan in the west, the China-Pakistan collusion and the external support to insurgency and terrorism in India.[1] These developments necessitate that India develops or acquires significant niche technologies and capabilities to deter its adversaries from indulging in adventurism, respond decisively when required and have a robust internal security system.

Air power is the sum total of the civil-military aviation assets, manufacturing and Maintenance Repair and Overhaul (MRO) capabilities. Aviation manufacturing has never been declared a priority area by the Indian government since independence. Indian civil aviation manufacturing and MRO were neglected for most part of the last seven and half decades; however, reduction in the Goods and Services Tax (GST) on MRO from 18 percent to 5 percent in 2021 was an important step in building the domestic civil aviation MRO capability; however, more reforms are needed. The Indian military aviation industry, with a number of indigenous development projects at the designs and induction stages, is at the cusp of transformation.

The emerging civil drone industry led by starts-ups and Micro, Small, and Medium Enterprises (MSMEs) has a given new lease of life to the aviation manufacturing industry in India. India launched 'Make-in-India', *Atmanirbhar Bharat* and other Design and Development (D&D) initiatives to stimulate domestic manufacturing and optimally leverage domestic technological capital available in the public sector, private sector, academia, innovators, and others. There is realisation that *atmanirbharta* (self-reliance) is essential for India's survival against emerging threats. The launching of the Innovation for Defence Excellence (iDEX) and Mehar Baba UAS Swarm Competition by the Defence Innovation Organisation (DIO) and the Indian Air Force (IAF) respectively resulted in start-ups and MSMEs providing a number of innovative technological solutions for the Indian defence forces in the last four years, while Make-I and Make-II projects under the new Defence Acquisition Procedure (DAP) provided new opportunities to the Indian industry to get into defence and aeronautics manufacturing. These initiatives are in the evolution stage and may need validation and course correction to optimally leverage the potential of Indian industry and innovators. Therefore, there is a need to ascertain the adequacy of, and gaps in, these initiatives to achieve the objectives of *Atmanirbhar Bharat* (self-reliant India)[2] in aviation technologies. This chapter endeavours to examine the following issues:

(a) What are India's technology acquisition options?
(b) How robust are the pillars of air power in India?
(c) What are the India's manned-unmanned civil-military aviation development initiatives, challenges and contradiction?
(d) What is the way forward to make India *atmanirbhar* in manned and unmanned aviation technologies and a drone hub by 2030?

Technology Acquisition Options for India

Air power thrives on technology, and the technological edge in air power can be the difference between winning and losing a war. The US, Russia and Europe led the development of aviation technologies after World War II. India's indigenous aeronautics manufacturing industry, despite a promising start during the 1950s and 1960s, made a limited contribution in building domestic capability in the past due to various reasons. As a result, it remained dependent on Foreign Original Equipment Manufacturers (FOEMs) for niche civil and defence aviation platforms.

India was able to counter the threat posed by its two principal adversaries, China and Pakistan, by acquiring advanced military aviation technologies from all the three leading defence aviation manufacturers, i.e. Russia, the United States (US) and Europe. However, this balance of air power is changing, with China making technological advances in aviation, UAS, space, cyber, Artificial Intelligence (AI), quantum, and other niche technologies. Russia had been India's reliable ally, and it supplied weapons and came to India's rescue in diplomatic and international fora but it never openly supported India militarily during wars. The global geopolitical landscape is also undergoing a major reshuffle, with Russia's increasing dependence on China. The US-China economic relations are also deepening. Therefore, it would be unrealistic to expect the US or Russia to support India militarily during any India-China War in the future.

China's quest for developing advanced manned and unmanned aeronautics technologies has been deliberated upon in the chapters titled

"Pillars of China's UAV Programme" and "China's Foray into Developing New Age UAVs" of the book *India's Quest for UAVs and Challenges*.[3] The US Department of Defence (DoD) annual reports on China's defence capability since 2001 also indicate the progress made by the Chinese defence and aeronautics industries. China's pursuing the development of fifth generation fighters, bombers, large transport aircraft, helicopters; armed, High Altitude Long Endurance (HALE), Medium Altitude Long Endurance (MALE) UAS, logistics supply, amphibious and rotary UAS; Unmanned Combat Aerial Vehicles (UCAVs), swarm UAVs, hypersonic UAS and many other niche aviation technologies indicates its aspiration for technology leadership, success in which could bring a significant change in the balance of power with India. The reducing technology gap between Chinese manned and unmanned aviation systems vis-à-vis leading aviation manufacturing nations indicates the reducing aviation technology acquisition options for India.

Shrinking Window of Opportunity for India

The current technology differential between China and India is the last window of opportunity for India to develop certain niche capabilities that could deter China from resorting to adventurism against India. The difference between the Chinese and Indian economies is close to five times and a significant differences exist between their military and industrial capabilities. However, the deduction of certain researchers, academicians, and policy experts that indigenous options for India are non-existent, and partnerships with global players are the only options is flawed. Partnerships do matter in areas of convergence and should be optimally leveraged, but, at the same time, partnerships have their own limitations. The partner countries have their constraints due to their own national objectives and goals. Also, such partnerships often mean a price to be paid, in terms of compromises on the political, diplomatic and economic fronts. Such compromises may work for some countries but are difficult to accommodate for a large country like India as they impact its large population. The approach of India has to be different from that of other countries to meet its own national objectives, and at the core of this approach would always be *atmanirbharta* as the first and foremost principle.

China: The key challenge for India is to remain focussed on *atmanirbharta* despite lagging behind in economic and military power vis-à-vis China. India has to ensure its own security today before it achieves *atmanirbharta.* This is an argument given by those who believe that security alliance is the only option for India. The emerging challenge has been created by China and the answer also lies with China. The approach adopted by China from 1950 to 2022 is worth examining. China fought wars with the US in Korea, with India, Russia and again with the US in Vietnam between the 1950s and early 1970s. It fought wars against the hardened and most technologically advanced militaries that had won World War II. It took on the two world powers of the era but pursued its own self-reliance approach since the very beginning, i.e. immediately after the Communist Party of China (CPC) came to power on October 1, 1949, and not since the 1970s, or 1990s or 2000, as some commentators believe. This aspect becomes clear from a scrutiny of the establishment of academic, military, scientific and technological initiatives and their funding by China. These aspects have been deliberated upon in the book *India's Quest for UAVs and Challenges*[4] and in reports of the US government. China was not a great economic and military power between the 1950s and 1970s and yet it fought wars with the great powers. Therefore, India too can counter China. It needs capability and technological differentiation and that would come from its own people, including academicians, scientists, innovators, bureaucrats, policy-makers, military personnel, etc.

Some argue that China is a Communist country in which there is no opposition to the decisions taken by the Party, while democracies like India have diverse and divergent views and approaches, which hamper synergy and reduce the pace of capability development. The limitations of democracies are also their strengths as they help them to do course correction and improve their policies, technologies and approaches.

Democracies thrive on leadership, as good leadership is essential for their success. A good leader can always guide the countrymen towards achieving their larger goals. The US, UK and other democratic countries became great nations due to democracy and great leadership. Also, India has proven its capability in the green revolution, white revolution, space, nuclear, metro trains, AADHAR, Unified Payment Interface (UPI)[5] and many other initiatives. If the Indian leadership and stakeholders place their trust in Indian innovators and capability builders, and empower them, they can deliver at par with the best in the world and, in some cases, ahead of the world leaders. The aviation and defence technology and capability gap between the Chinese and global military powers should be optimally leveraged by the Indian leadership and stakeholders to build indigenous capabilities as India may find no one in its support in the future due to the envisaged technological parity between China and global leaders in the coming decades, if China is able to remain united and focussed on its trajectory.

Pillars of Indian Air Power

Air power is the sum total of all available aviation assets in the country and it comprises civil aviation assets, military aviation assets, civil and military aviation manufacturing, and MRO facilities. These pillars of Indian aviation are discussed in the following section to understand their strengths, limitations and future trajectory.

Civil Aviation Assets and Industry

Indian civil aviation platforms predominantly consist of passenger aircraft acquired from the Boeing Company of the US and Airbus Company of the Europe. In addition, light transport, executive and other aircraft have been acquired from Original Equipment Manufacturers (OEMs) located in different parts of the world. India has neither indigenously developed civil jet passenger aircraft nor has it initiated a programme to develop them. Hindustan Aeronautics Limited (HAL) manufactured the Avro transport aircraft under licence, which is on the verge of retirement from service. HAL, Kanpur division, has upgraded the military version of the Dornier-228 light transport aircraft with a glass cockpit and advanced avionics systems for commercial civil operations. The Dornier being of a small size and having a short take-off and landing distance capability, is expected to provide much needed air connectivity in far-flung areas of India that lack road connectivity. India is also planning to develop the Regional Transport Aircraft-70 (RTA-70), which is moving at a slow pace, with no declared technology milestones and timelines being made public.

The MRO of these aircraft in the past was more or less carried out in other parts of the world due to unfavourable tax structures and policies.

The high rate of GST of 18 per cent (against global competitors charging between 0-5 per cent in taxes), airport royalty, restrictive regulations for maintenance technicians and maintenance engineers made Indian MRO service providers uncompetitive as well as dissuaded Foreign Original Equipment Manufactures (FOEMs) from establishing MRO in India.[6] The Indian government took the first corrective action in February 2021 with the reduction of GST from 18 per cent to 5 per cent to provide a level playing field to the Indian MRO industry. The resolution of other anomalies is essential to make India an aviation MRO hub.

Defence Aviation Assets and Industry

Defence Aviation Assets

The Indian military has diverse aviation platforms like the MiG-21, MiG-27, MiG-29 and Su-30 fighters; Mi-8, Mi-17, Mi25/35 and Mi-26 helicopters; AN-32, IL-76 transport, IL-78 refueller and A-50 Airborne Warning and Control System (AWACS) aircraft from Russia; Jaguar fighter aircraft, Sea King helicopters and Avro (HS-748) transport aircraft from the United Kingdom; Mirage-2000 fighter, and Alouette-III and the Lama light helicopters from France; Dornier-228 light transport aircraft from Germany; and C-130 and C-17 transport aircraft, Apache attack helicopters and Chinook transport helicopters from the US. Such a diverse inventory of defence aviation platforms is due to two reasons: first, the inability of domestic industry to develop such platforms in India; and second, due to the aspirations of the defence forces to possess the best that technology can offer. However, the root causes of the failures and challenges of India's domestic aviation manufacturing industry were rarely addressed in a holistic manner, which allowed this problem to persist.

Defence Aviation Industry

The Indian defence aeronautics manufacturing industry does not have many successful platforms to demonstrate its achievements despite having a rich eight-decade-old history of design, development and manufacturing of aviation platforms. The Hindustan Jet Trainer-16 (HJT-16) or Kiran Jet Trainer aircraft; Advanced Light Helicopter (ALH) and Light Combat

Aircraft (LCA) are the only three indigenously designed and manufactured aviation platforms in the inventory of the IAF. India also has the indigenously manufactured Avro (HS-748) medium transport aircraft and Dornier-228 light transport aircraft in its inventory, whose designs were acquired. India missed several opportunities during the 1960s and 1970s when it failed to transform the indigenously designed Kanpur-I and Kanpur-II light transport aircraft, and Hindustan Fighter-24 (Marut) into successful platforms for future generations.[7] However, the above inventory of indigenously designed and developed aircraft and the past history of missed opportunities do not indicate the future potential of the Indian aviation manufacturing industry.

C-295 Deal: India's Failure to Learn from Avro Deal: The Indian Ministry of Defence signed a Rs 22,000 crore deal with Airbus Defence and Space SA of Spain for the C-295 medium weight transport aircraft to replace the aging Avro aircraft of the Indian Air Force. Of these, 16 aircraft would be received in flyaway condition and the remaining 40 would be manufactured by Tata Advanced Systems Limited (TASL) in India. This was the first time that a military aircraft would be manufactured by a private company in India by developing an entire ecosystem comprising the assembly, test, qualification and maintenance of the complete lifecycle of the aircraft.[8]

The C-295 deal was the second medium lift transport aircraft deal after the Avro deal from the point of view of technology transfer. The IAF, under the leadership of Air Vice Marshal (AVM) Harjinder Singh had negotiated the transfer of technology of Avro aircraft in 1959. The first Avro aircraft was built at the Aircraft Manufacturing Depot of the IAF at Kanpur. The manufacturing of the Avro was later transferred to the HAL, Kanpur. India could not leverage the Avro aircraft to build transport aircraft in India. Therefore, it is important to ensure that the C-295 deal is leveraged to design, develop and manufacture transport aircraft in India.[9]

Bright Future: The Indian defence aviation manufacturing industry is undergoing a major transformation with a number of indigenous projects on the verge of certification and operationalisation. These projects include the indigenously designed and developed Hindustan Turbo-Trainer-40 (HTT-40), Intermediate Jet Trainer (IJT), Light Combat Aircraft (LCA) Mk-II, Advanced Medium Combat Aircraft (AMCA), an upgraded version of the

British Hawk Jet Trainer, i.e. Hawk-I. Also, India has designed, developed and manufactured more than 300 Advanced Light Helicopters (ALHs) with further orders of 50 more helicopters. After an uncertain start, the ALH has evolved into a fine flying machine in its category. The positive impact of the ALH can be seen in the expeditious development of the Light Utility Helicopter (LUH) and Light Combat Helicopter (LCH) with substantial improvements in design, maintenance, service life and product support. The LUH and LCH have certain capabilities that are not available in contemporary helicopters around the world since these helicopters have been designed and developed by India for operation in the extreme conditions in India.

Civil-Military UAS Assets and Industry

UAS Assets

The Indian defence Unmanned Aeriel System (UAS) industry primarily comprises UAS supplied by Israel, which include the Searcher tactical Intelligence, Surveillance and Reconnaissance (ISR) UAS, Heron MALE ISR UAS and Harpy loitering munitions acquired from Israel. The Indian civil UAS industry was non-existent till a decade ago; however, in the last few years, government entities started procuring small drones and drone services for agriculture, surveys, homeland security duties, etc. The private industry was employing Indigenously Designed, Developed and Manufactured (IDDM), imported and assembled UAS for a variety of commercial applications, which are deliberated upon below.

Drone Hub-2030: Civil Drone Industry

Indian start-ups and MSMEs are playing a key role in the development and adoption of small UAS for commercial applications. The small UAS commercial applications in India include agriculture, anti-locust, medicine delivery, Survey of Villages and Mapping with Improvised Technology in Village Areas (SVAMITVA), power line, mines, highways, surveys for smart cities, etc. The emerging manufacturing industry, innovative applications and increasing employability of UAS in multiple sectors motivated the Indian government to set an ambitious target of making

India the Global Drone Hub by 2030. The Indian government introduced several enabling policy provisions including the industry-friendly Drone Rules-2021 on August 25, 2021, released the Airspace Maps on September 24, 2021, Productivity Linked Incentive (PLI) Scheme on September 30, 2021, National Unmanned Aircraft Systems Traffic Management (UTM) policy on October 24, 2021, UAS Certification Scheme on January 26, 2022, and Drone Import Policy on February 2022. These reforms opened up 70 per cent of the Indian airspace up to 400 ft in height as a green zone for drone operations, made it easier for drone manufacturers to obtain type certification, and also imposed a ban on the import of complete drones. The Indian government also introduced provisions in the 2022-23 budget to promote Indian start-ups to facilitate 'Drone Shakti' (Drone Power) through various applications and Drone As A Service (DRAAS) schemes. It also launched the Kisan Drone and UAS technician skilling initiatives to encourage UAS manufacturing and adoption.[10]

Technology Initiatives and Airspace Integration: Missing Spokes of Drone Hub-2030: Union Civil Aviation Minister Shri Jyotiraditya Scindia, speaking on the inauguration of the Drone Studio at the National Institution for Transforming India (NITI) Aayog in the presence of its Chief Executive Officer (CEO) Shri Amitabh Kant on May 10, 2022, spoke about making India a drone hub by 2030 on three wheels comprising the Policy, Production Linked Incentive (PLI) scheme, and generating demand. Shri Amitabh Kant, CEO, NITI Aayog, the Indian government's think-tank, on the launching of the Drone Studio programme said that it would act as an anchor for initiating "proof of concepts and pilots at solving service delivery issues". All these initiatives are aimed at promoting the service industry, which is required for sensitisation, acceptance, and broad base adoption of drone technology. However, two core issues that remained unaddressed were: firstly, the plan for the integration of drones in the Indian national airspace with manned aircraft; and, secondly, technological initiatives to develop technologies and systems that are needed to facilitate safe unmanned-manned aircraft operation.[11] India has remained a low-value industry in aviation due to the absence of civil aviation Research and Development (R&D) programmes. However, what is required is to ensure that India undertakes research, development, and innovation initiatives in the promising Indian drone industry to transform its trajectory into a high-value industry.

The Federal Aviation Authority (FAA) of the USA and the European Union Aviation Safety Agency (EASA) of the European Union have elaborate airspace integration plans. Also, they are developing enabling technologies such as collision avoidance systems, UTM systems, remote tracking, etc. They also undertake regular trials to validate emerging technologies related to UTM, collision avoidance, remote identification, drone infrastructure, drone safety reliability, etc. India, on its part, has carried out Beyond Visual Line of Sight (BVLOS) trials with self-funding by the industry; however, the follow-on technological initiatives have been absent. Therefore, it becomes important to examine the following issues:

(a) Doesn't India need to develop UTM, remote tracking, collision avoidance, and other systems for the safe operation and integration of drones?
(b) How can India lead the technology trajectory of drones to become a Global Drone Hub by 2030 without research, development, and innovation programmes?
(c) Will India allow its UAS industry to become a low-value, high volume service industry like its civil aviation industry or take measures to transform it to become the first high-technology, high-value industry?

Indian stakeholders in the Ministry of Civil Aviation (MoCA), Directorate General of Civil Aviation (DGCA), Ministry of Electronics and Information Technology (MeitY), Technology Development Board[12] and industry bodies must deliberate on these issues, and institute measures to make India an innovation and manufacturing-led high-technology, high-value, drone hub of the world by 2030.

Trajectory of Civil Drone Manufacturing: Before we deliberate on *atmanirbharta* in civil drone manufacturing, let us understand the evolution of drone manufacturing in India, which started with the civil sector, led by the start-ups, and is deliberated upon below:

(a) *Phase-I: Design and Development by Start-ups:* This phase covers the time period from the beginning of drone manufacturing in India till the release of Drone Rules-2021 on August 25, 2021. In this phase, Indian innovators, start-ups and MSMEs led the manufacturing of drones and developed a number of drones and associated technologies- including high altitude drones, swarm drones, and drones for surveillance, agriculture and other applications.

(b) *Phase-II: Civil Drone Manufacturing:* This phase covers the time period commencing from August 25, 2021, till today. In this phase, new drone entrepreneurs entered the drone manufacturing business with most of them focussing on manufacturing in the agriculture sector. They manufactured (assembled) drones from imported components with negligible to minimal value addition, which appears to be having an adverse impact on drone innovation and Indigenously Designed, Developed and Manufactured (IDDM) in the country.

Defence UAS Industry

The emerging domestic UAS industry, with the Defence Research and Development Organisation (DRDO) developing MALE, HALE and UCAVs; HAL poised to undertake production of medium and large UAS and UCAVs, and initiating a development niche Combat Air Teaming System (CATS) project; start-ups and MSMEs producing small UAS; and launching of iDEX, Mehar Baba and Technology Development Fund (TDF) Design and Development (D&D) initiatives are emerging as crucial pillars of India's UAS capability building trajectory. The success of these initiatives would be crucial for changing the trajectory of the Indian aviation industry from assembly and licensed manufacturing, to indigenous design, development, manufacturing and export. The size of the Indian UAS industry was estimated to be US$ 1.21 billion by the end of 2021 and its UAS and Counter-Unmanned Aerial System (CUAS) industry is expected to make a quantum jump to US$ 40 billion (Rs 300,000 crore) by 2030.[13] Out of these, about 50 per cent of the market is expected to comprise UAS and CUAS systems for defence and homeland security agencies.

The Indian public sector entity, Aeronautical Development Establishment (ADE), Bangalore, a laboratory of the DRDO, is developing the Rustom-I (Archer), Rustom-II MALE UAVs, and Ghatak UCAV, which will be produced by HAL. The Rustom-I was initially used as a platform to test enabling technologies for the larger Rustom-II and it was later equipped with an air-to-ground missile; however, no Indian user has shown interest in the Rustom-I. The Rustom-II, with an operating altitude of 28,000 ft and endurance of 18 hours, is expected to provide much-needed ISR coverage after user trials, which are expected to commence in the second half of 2022.[14] The Rustom-II would also be armed with air-to-ground weapons.[15] India's Ghatak flying wing stealth UCAV is in an early stage of development. Its scale model carried out taxi trials in 2021 and flying trials of the scale model are expected to commence in late 2022 or early 2023.[16]

Defence UAS Applications

The indigenous small UAS are also being employed for defence, Humanitarian Assistance and Disaster Relief (HADR) and internal security applications. The Indian Army's (IA's) Rs 140 crore order for the acquisition of the Switch UAV from the Mumbai-based idea Forge Company, after competing against Elbit of Israel, the Tata Group, Dynamatic Technologies and VTOL Aviation of India in January 2021 was the first major defence UAV contract given to a private company.[17] The Indian Army placed an order for additional Switch UAVs in January 2022[18] and 200 more in March 2022 after competing with France, Ukraine, Russia, Israel and other companies from India.[19] The display of the armed UAS swarm developed by New Space Technologies during the Army Day-2021 parade on Army Day on January 15, 2021, indicated private sector companies taking a lead in developing niche UAS for military applications. The New Space Research Technologies signed a contract for supplying armed swarm UAS for Rs 200 crore to the Indian Army later that year. It is also developing Air-Launched Flexible Assets (Swarm) or (ALPHA-S) systems for the CATS project of the HAL. Similarly, the Noida-based company Raphe mPhibr signed a contract for the supply of logistics UAS to the Indian Army in 2021.[20]

India's Capability Development Challenges

The Indian defence industry has struggled to transform promising indigenous designs, innovative systems and prototypes into operational systems since independence due to Research, Development and Acquisition (RD&A) gaps. In the RD&A cycle, R&D is the process of maturing technologies while acquisition is the bureaucratic management of the procurement process. The gaps in the R&D cycle and acquisition process have contributed to the continued dependence of the Indian defence industry on imports.

India's RD&A system worked in isolation in the past as R&D and the acquisition processes were considered as separate activities. The stakeholders in India understand the acquisition process better due to the long history of procurement of defence equipment from FOEMs. However, the same cannot be said about their understanding of leveraging indigenous R&D and innovation for capability building. The FOEMs brought their products to India only after they had matured. The personnel of the Indian defence forces and other ministries rarely joined indigenous projects as members of design teams, while defence personnel of leading defence-manufacturing nations actively participate in the design phase. The participation of the private sector in the high-cost defence R&D was limited in the past as writing off huge costs had an adverse impact on their chances of survival.

India realised the need for course correction, took measures to enhance the participation of the private sector in defence R&D and made the acquisition process transparent and responsive. The ownership and support of stakeholders in overcoming design, development and operational challenges, involvement of users in the design and development stages as equal partners and lack of assured orders continue to be the key challenges for the domestic manned and unmanned aviation industry. Therefore, it faces three critical gaps in its RD&A cycle that hinder the development of innovative and niche technologies, including defence systems:

(a) Gaps within the R&D cycle, also termed as the 'Valley of Death'.
(b) Absence of integration between the R&D and acquisition process.
(c) Lack of involvement of the defence forces personnel in R&D projects.

Valley of Death (Gaps in R&D)

India's RD&A gaps can be better understood by studying the report of the Joint Air Power Competence Centre (JAPCC) of the North Atlantic Treaty Organisation (NATO) on counter-UAS technologies that examined the RD&A approach and gaps.[21] The challenges posed by the emerging capabilities of UAS led to the US Department of Defence (DOD) focussing more on R&D than acquisition with a planned expenditure of US$ 404 million on R&D and US$ 83 million on procurement of counter UAS systems in 2021. The gaps in R&D can be understood by examining the Technology Readiness Levels (TRLs)[22], contribution of stakeholders in R&D and, the funding patterns.

Table 1: Description of Technology Readiness Level (TRLs)

TRL-9	SYSTEM DEPLOYED
TRL-8	SYSTEM COMPLETE AND QUALIFIED
TRL-7	SYSTEM PROTOTYPE
TRL-6	TECHNOLOGY DEMONSTRATION
TRL-5	TECHNOLOGY VALIDATION IN RELEVANT ENVIRONMENT
TRL-4	TECHNOLOGY VALIDATION IN LAB
TRL-3	PROOF OF CONCEPT
TRL-2	TECHNOLOGY CONCEPT
TRL-1	BASIC PRINCIPLES

The R&D process is divided into nine levels (TRLs) with academia contributing to technology development between TRL-1 to TRL-4; and industry between TRL-6 and TRL-8, and the gap between TRL-4 to TRL-6 being described as the 'Valley of Death'. The Valley of Death is considered to be the reason for several potential technologies not becoming products and capabilities.[23]

Fig 1: Bridging the Valley of Death by Government Funded Research

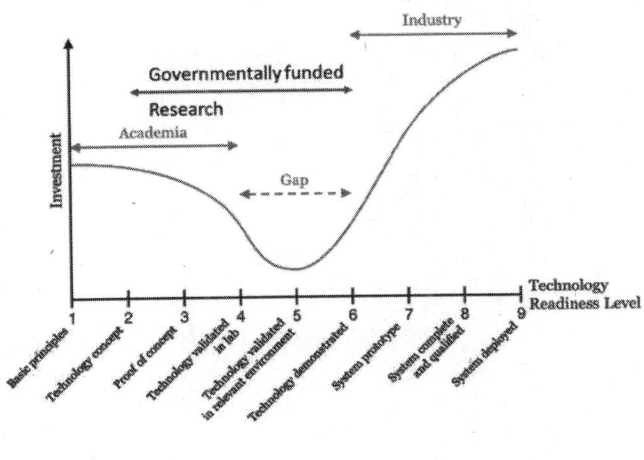

D&D Initiatives, Funding and Procurement Challenges

The R&D funding by the government is essential for filling the gaps created by the Valley of Death in the capability development cycle.[24] India's technology development in the past was led by public sector entities, with limited participation of the private sector companies. The Indian public sector entities, DRDO and Defence Public Sector Units (DPSUs) undertaking high-value technology development projects struggled to transform designs and prototypes into operational products. The Indian government in the last few years started funding private sector companies, start-ups and innovators through D&D initiatives such as the TDF, iDEX and Mehar Baba Competitions to complement the efforts of the DRDO and DPSUs. However, these initiatives partially fill the gaps in R&D (i.e. Valley of Death) since the funding for such initiatives is low and the scope of such initiatives is limited.

The recently launched defence D&D initiatives, i.e. Mehar Baba Competition of the IAF and iDEX of the Department of Defence Production (DDP), Ministry of Defence (MoD), have made a significant contribution to technology development. These initiatives have helped Indian private sector companies, led by start-ups, MSMEs and individual innovators to demonstrate their technological potential in the development of UAS and CUAS systems. The Indian defence forces have acquired indigenously designed small UAS and CUAS systems, which has not only saved precious foreign exchange but also created jobs. However, India's D&D initiatives despite their strengths, have certain limitations, which are deliberated upon in the succeeding sections.

iDEX:[25] iDEX is playing an important role in incentivising innovation among individual innovators, start-ups, MSMEs and academia, while the DRDO and DPSUs do not participate in iDEX. However, iDEX funding is limited to Rs 1.5 crore. The distribution of funding through iDEX from 2018 to 2021 was limited to Rs 10.3 crore to 32 start-ups, while the funding of incubator partners was Rs 4.47 crore.[26] The meagre funding at the rate of Rs 3.4 crore per year is inadequate for leveraging the innovation potential of start-ups, individual innovators and MSMEs for developing high-technology systems

(a) *Absence of Follow-on Competition:* There is no provision for launching the follow-on iDEX or Mehar Baba competitions for the improvement, upgradation or development of high-cost, high-technology systems and this has become a major limitation.

(b) *IP Challenges:* Intellectual Property (IP) of the product developed in the iDEX is jointly shared or owned by the sponsoring entity as per the proposal. The ambiguity or lack of standardisation of IP rights clauses in the iDEX competition becomes unfavourable for the innovator, which deters genuine innovators from participating in iDEX.

iDEX Prime: In a tweet on February 25, 2022, the office of the Indian defence minister declared that the Ministry of Defence would come up with iDEX Prime for which funding would be enhanced to Rs 10 crore; however, the modalities for iDEX Prime are yet to be announced. The enhanced funding would address some of the concerns of the industry.[27]

iDEX for Fauji[28]: iDEX for Fauji has provided a platform for technically competent talented defence forces personnel to develop or contribute to the development of niche technologies and find solutions to the problems faced by the Indian defence forces. However, it remains an individual initiative that lacks institutional support on the lines of the Air Force Research Laboratory (AFRL) of the US Air Force (USAF), Office of Naval Research (ONR) of the US Navy (USN) and Army Innovation Command personnel of the US Army and equivalent organisations of the People's Liberation Army Air Force (PLAAF), which have design, development, testing facilities and laboratories to develop prototypes and transform them into operational products. Therefore, the Indian defence forces would need to create a minimum essential enabling ecosystem in their technical units to provide technical support and guidance. Alternatively, the defence forces may create institutional linkages with the innovation ecosystem such as academic institutions, DPSUs, and industry/incubation partners for optimally harnessing the technological and intellectual potential of the Indian defence forces personnel and transforming their innovations into operational capabilities.

Mehar Baba Competition: The Mehar Baba UAS Swarm competition launched by the IAF on October 8, 2018, was aimed at evolving propriety design, development, manufacturing and production of low cost-high impact solutions for swarm technology. The competition ended in October 2021, with four winners comprising New Space Research Technologies for swarm architecture, Flair Unmanned Systems for communication architecture, Dhaksha Unmanned Systems for UAS architecture and Veda Defence Systems for innovation in design. The Mehar Baba Competition played an important role in advancing UAS swarm technology development in India by almost a decade.[29] The competition has been made an annual event and has enormous potential to contribute in the development of niche technologies.

The Mehar Baba Competition has certain unique features compared to iDEX. It provides larger funding, while iDEX not only provides lesser funding but also requires an equal share of funding by the participants. The Mehar Baba Competition provides an equal opportunity to DRDO, DPSUs, academia, individual innovators, defence personnel and private sector entities to develop niche technologies.

Procurement: The absence of timelines and a defined quantity of product procurement by users are the weak links of the iDEX and Mehar Baba initiatives. Due to the delay in procurement by their only buyer, i.e. the military, the winners are unable to cope with the huge cost of development and the uncertainty of orders.

Funding Challenges: The funding of iDEX and iDEX Prime is not enough to enable the participants to undertake high-technology high-value D&D projects. In addition, iDEX and Mehar Baba participants are expected to produce quality products equivalent to FOEMs like Raytheon, Elbit, etc., which get much higher funding from their respective militaries, the Defence Advanced Research Project Agency (DARPA), Defence Innovation Unit (DIU) and equivalent organisations. Therefore, there is a need to enhance the funding of D&D initiatives.

Technology Development Fund (TDF) and Defence Innovation Challenge (DIC): The TDF is a DRDO, MoD initiative in which up to 90 per cent of the cost of the project undertaken by the private sector and academia, with a maximum limit of Rs 10 crore is funded for a period of two years.[30] However, the scope and extent of funding for this initiative were inadequate to develop high-technology, high value systems. The funding of

TDF is being enhanced to Rs 50 crore, which will enable the participants to undertake high value development projects.

Challenges and Contradictions of *Atmanirbhar Bharat* Mission

Leadership

The most important pillar of Indian policy-making is the Indian political, bureaucratic and stakeholders' leadership. Indian industry looks up to these leaders to take ownership of indigenous projects. The senior functionaries in government funding, financing and auditing entities, and the users play important roles in the success of such initiatives, including the *Atmanirbhar Bharat* mission. The leaders endeavour to deliver results in the shortest possible time while laying down a strong foundation for innovation, technology development and economic prosperity. However, they face the following challenges:

(a) Limited time to deliver.
(b) Limited understanding of aviation and UAS technology development trajectory.
(c) Lack of information about Indian talent and inadequate knowledge of how to leverage it.

Shakespeare's quote in Henry IV Part-2, "Uneasy lies the head that wears the crown" is most appropriate for the higher leadership as they are lonely at the top, and look towards the stakeholders, global players, Indians working for global companies, Indian companies, industry organisations, academia, users, etc. to learn from their experiences and take steps to make India *atmanirbhar*. The plethora of inputs also creates ambiguity and can be leveraged by players with motivated agendas for their own benefits.

Influence of Consultants and Representatives of Global Bodies: The representatives of global consulting companies, Non-Governmental Organisations (NGOs), charity organisations and global bodies such as the World Bank, World Economic Forum, UN, etc. work with the Indian government, DPSUs, think-tanks, industry bodies, etc. and have easy access to policy-makers and policy-making activities and help in formulating roadmaps at the Centre as well as in the states. They become parts of projects or project monitoring or project management of consulting teams, and directly or indirectly, provide consultancy to the senior bureaucracy from the joint secretary rank upward.[31] They become members of policy-making bodies, industry bodies, and studies on sector forecasts, use cases, and manage to influence formulation of policies that appear conforming to the *Atmrnirbhar Bharat* goals but create enough space for foreign companies and subtly dilute the core objective of the *Atmanirbhar Bharat* mission. These global entities have domain experts (including non-resident Indians or Indians working for them) and policy gaps are generated in the absence of equally knowledgeable Indians working for the Indian government. There are such experts available in India but they do not become part of such studies and policy committees, which has an adverse impact on Indian interests.

Ownership

MoCA Ownership in Civil Aviation R&D and Airspace Integration

The Indian Ministry of Civil Aviation (MoCA), unlike its counterparts in other countries (e.g. FAA of the USA) never took the ownership of airspace integration, R&D of civil aviation aircraft, ground systems, and communication and navigation equipment employed in air operations, which contributed in India's continued dependence on the import of such equipment. It also renamed its Research and Development Directorate as the Engineering Directorate in 2009.

Defence Forces Ownership in Defence Aviation R&D Programmes

The defence forces of leading defence-manufacturing nations not only provide funding but also involve their personnel in technology development projects being undertaken in collaboration with industry. The involvement of AFRL, ONR and Army Innovation Command of the US and equivalent organisations of China in the development of aviation, UAS and CUAS technologies shows the enormous benefits of this approach. Design and development work requires a collaborative approach among various stakeholders for overcoming design challenges, e.g. the US adopted a multi-agency RD&A approach in developing CUAS systems with the US Army,

USN, Marine and USAF procuring CUAS, testing them in joint exercises and then giving feedback on their performance for further improvement. However, the Indian defence forces personnel do not become members of the design teams of indigenous projects, which is a limitation in the development and operationalisation of niche defence technologies.

Underleveraging of DFPDS Provisions for R&D. The Delegation of Financial Powers to Defence Services (DFPDS-2021) empowers the three Services Headquarters (HQ) and HQ Integrated Defence Staff (IDS) with a funding up to Rs 27.50 crore for undertaking R&D projects through government/autonomous R&D organisations, in-house defence agencies, professional/technical institutions and the private sector.[32] However, there are no known projects undertaken by the Indian defence services under these provisions to indigenously develop niche, high-technology, high-value systems that can provide a technological edge to them.

Absent Airspace Integration and Aeronautics Technology Development

The year 2021 became the year of civil drone policies after the intervention of Indian Prime Minister (PM) Shri Narendra Modi in mid-2021. The intervention at the highest level had an impact on stakeholders, which resulted in the launching of several enabling policies and policy incentives for the drone sector, intending to make India a Global Drone Hub by 2030.[33] It is an ambitious goal but without the scientific assessment and associated research and development programme for developing enabling technologies for integration and safe operation of UAS along with manned aircraft in the civil airspace. The FAA[34] of the USA and European Union's EASA pursue long-term airspace integration and technology development programmes. The enabling technology development programmes such as the development of UTM, collision avoidance systems and other essential enabling technologies are essential for the development of the drone sector for achieving strategic autonomy in critical technologies.

The absence of an airspace integration technology programme and the lack of ownership of associated R&D programmes are likely to have an adverse impact on the growth of the promising Indian civil drone industry. The Indian drone industry, after a superb start with the number of innovations, is slowly sliding back as import, assemble, and collaboration are increasing, while invention, innovation and creation of niche technologies are gradually declining. This may lead to negligible or little creation of Intellectual Property (IP) in India and a major portion of the revenue may go to foreign countries despite adequate talent and the capability to develop such technologies being available in India. The Indian drone manufacturing industry, like its aviation manufacturing industry, may become a low-value industry with heavy dependence on FOEMs for critical technologies. *Atmanirbhar Bharat* is a great initiative; however, it may not achieve its ultimate objective in the absence of a drone technology development plan, and ownership by, and leadership of, key stakeholders.

Services and Policies are not Substitutes for Technology

India's regional air connectivity initiative *Ude Desh Ka Aam Nagrik*, formulation of the progressive Drone Rules-2021; employment of drones in agriculture, medical delivery and SVAMITVAA schemes, have demonstrated their impact on the common people in a short time. The Services' initiatives cover a large population and their impact is visible in a short time period, while policy reforms provide a foundation but they are no substitute for technology initiatives and cannot bring transformational change.

Aviation Technology Development Roadmap: India is dependent on import for civil aircraft, large military transport aircraft, emerging UAS and associated traffic management technologies, fire-fighting equipment, navigation, communication and other systems and it lacks a technology development plan with funding and ownership by stakeholders.

Testing, Standards, Standardisation and Certification: Testing, standards, standardisation and certification are four important pillars of the aviation manufacturing sector, and the innovation and challenges of aviation and drone manufacturers are deliberated upon below.

(a) **Testing:** In India, aviation testing facilities were available only with DRDO, DPSUs, defence forces and Central Armed Police Forces (CRPFs) in the past. These entities have started allowing the private sector to use their facilities. Their process of approval and their limited numbers makes them inconvenient and inadequate for the private sector, start-ups and innovators to undertake research, frequent iterations during the development and trials, and testing them as and when required, with the least delay. Therefore, there is a need for developing dedicated civil aviation and drone testing sites with the requisite airspace and laboratories. The DGCA is responsible for the airworthiness certification of manned and unmanned aircraft; however, it lacks the manpower to undertake certification and quality assurance of aviation platforms and associated systems.

(b) **Drones and UAS Certification:** In the drone sector, as per Drone Rules-2021, certification of drones up to 500 kg has been delegated to the Quality Council of India (QCI), which, in turn, has further approved three private Certification Bodies (CBs). The certification process commenced recently, but no drone has been certified so far. Also, the policies would need to be formulated and capabilities created to formulate standards, test and certify drones above 500 kg.

(c) **Standards and Standardisation:** India has never focussed on developing India-specific aviation standards and standardisation as civil aviation manufacturing was not its focus area and it depended upon American, European and North Atlantic Treaty Organisation (NATO) standards. India's Bureau of Standards (BIS) has started participating in the formulation of standards for drones, which is at the nascent stage and is inadequate.

Is *Atmanirbhar Bharat* in Aeronautics a National Priority?

> Make in India is "quite ambitious", it has to be ensured that India does not become the low-cost, low-value assembly line of the world. If we go on that path, the growth will come at great price and pain to the people. We need to do original research to design, develop and manufacture in India by using the ideas of the youth, the wisdom of the ages and the vibrancy of democracy.
>
> –Dr APJ Abdul Kalam[35]

India's former President Dr. APJ Abdul Kalam had cautioned in 2015 that the 'Make in India' initiative could make India a low-cost and low-value assembly line of the world. Later on, *Atmanirbhar Bharat Abhiyan* was launched to correct the anomalies of 'Make in India'. The positive impact of the *Atmanirbhar Bharat Abhiyan* has been covered widely; however, its challenge and limitations have not been examined. The initial indications are that after a promising start, the *Atmanirbhar Bharat Abhiyan* appears to be drifting away from its intended trajectory; however, a detailed assessment is needed to ascertain its challenges and initiate measures to make it a success.

India's enormous progress in indigenous aeronautics design, development and manufacturing during the golden period of the 1950s and 1960s was frittered away due to the Indian leadership's lack of understanding of the nuances of aviation technology development trajectory and its challenges. Also, India never declared *atmanirbharta* (self-reliance) in aeronautics manufacturing as a national priority, which added to its unsteady trajectory.

After seven and half decades of struggle, the Indian manned and UAS industry is again at the transformation stages, with a number of indigenous projects in the development and induction stages, with significant scope for export. This is the second moment of reckoning for the Indian leadership as they have to make choices that will decide the future trajectory of the Indian aviation industry. In view of the enormous potential of the Indian aviation manufacturing industry, the first logical step would be to declare the Indian aviation (both manned and unmanned) industry as an area of national priority.

Unsuitability of Global Industry Models

The small European countries follow a collaborative technology development model, as they have less resources and negligible threats from their neighbours. On the other hand, the US does not have any threat from its neighbours and it fights wars away from its homeland. Therefore, such developmental models do not have a critical impact on their sovereignty. Also, some Indian scholars, influenced by European and American defence technology and trade practices, subscribe to their views without understanding the realities and threats faced by India. India is a vast country and has hostile neighbours that have shared interests and leverage with India's arms suppliers, which makes India vulnerable. Therefore, India would need to ensure that *atmarnirbharta* remains its core pillar.

Start Manufacturing by Assembling: A Flawed Approach

Many experts and FOEMs advise Indian policy-makers to follow an incremental approach and start with the assembly of advanced systems. This is a flawed approach for two reasons: one, India seduced by the idea of manufacturing advanced MiG-21 and Jaguar fighter aircraft during the 1970s, discontinued the HF-24 and its upgraded version, the HF-73, which adversely impacted indigenous manufacturing, and took more than four decades to correct; second, Indian start-ups participating in the Mehar Baba and iDEX Competitions have demonstrated that advanced swarm and counter UAS technologies can be developed in India.

Many foreign policy advisors, policy planning experts as well as Indians working for them or having their business in other countries, over a period of time, have been able to convince Indian policy-makers and leaders about the need for hand-holding by global OEMs, and under this pretext, sell their products even in domains in which Indian expertise may be available. Also, many Indian leaders, experts and media personnel, having listened to their views and visited their establishments in foreign countries, start believing that Indian expertise does not exist. These experts from user agencies, the bureaucracy, or finance bodies use their past experiences as a template to apply to all cases, which has an adverse impact on the Indian industry and innovators. These Indian experts often have limited knowledge and have rarely physically owned a start-up, yet they comment on them from a user's or an outside observer's point of view. This is incorrect as they lack understanding of the dynamics and challenges of running a start-up and technology development. These reasons become silent contributors to Indian innovators and start-ups shutting down or selling their stakes to foreign OEMs or migrating to foreign countries and inventing for leading manufacturers of the world. This needs to be changed.

India-Specific Joint Ventures and Collaborations

India has rarely gained from Joint Ventures (JVs) and collaborations with FOEMs. Some FOEMs, lacking the technology or unwilling to share it, create a false impression of technology gaps in India, even though the technologies available with FOEMs may have negligible relevance to India. The acquisition of such technologies adversely impacts business and ultimately the survival of domestic Indian companies that may have toiled hard to develop similar technologies. In the past, the Indian government, while facilitating FOEMs, may have unknowingly placed the domestic industry in a disadvantageous position and created a low-value industry in India. The lack of information about our industry and capabilities with the stakeholders is leveraged by the FOEMs to promote their products. Therefore, there is a need to identify the strengths of the Indian manned and unmanned aviation R&D and manufacturing industry. Thereafter, establish India-specific JVs and collaborations with the FOEMs in identified areas of technology to support and strengthen indigenous design, development and manufacturing.

Contradictions between Atmanirbhar Bharat (IDDM) and Make in India (Assemble in India)

India's *Atmanirbhar Bharat Abhiyan* aims to stimulate indigenous design, development and manufacturing including in defence, aviation, UAS and counter UAS systems. The FOEMs and their Indian counterparts assembling their products under the 'Make in India' scheme are having an adverse impact on the *Atmarnirbhar Bharat* mission. The lack of differentiation between Indigenously Designed, Developed and Manufactured (IDDM) and 'Make in India' (assemble in India) in government procurements and Services' contracts is disincentivising research, innovation and IDDM in the aviation, UAS and drone sectors or rather incentivising assembling and trading. This may prove harmful in the long run. Indian leaders, bureaucrats and users often find it difficult to differentiate between IDDM and 'Make in India' (assembled) products. The presence of Indian leaders at industry events or the launch of their products provides them legitimacy to sell to various users in India. Indian companies assembling foreign aviation, drones and counter-drone systems are able to sell them and gain the Services' contracts from government agencies ahead of IDDM products due to better finances, scale and contacts.

Impact of Drone Policy Contradictions on Self-Reliance in Aviation

Drones are becoming important elements of the aviation manufacturing landscape—drone and aviation manufacturing are interdependent and have several commonalities. The Indian government took several policy initiatives in the last one year to support and promote the drone industry. Out of these, three key initiatives that could have positive impact on aviation and drone manufacturing are 'ban on the import of complete drones', 'Productivity Linked Incentive (PLI) scheme' and 'Kisan Drones scheme'. On the other hand, these scheme did not have adequate safeguards to prevent adverse impact on self-reliance.

India banned the import of complete drones in February 2022; however, it did not ban the import of drone components, as Indian companies were heavily dependent on FOEMs for certain critical components.[36] The launching of the "Kisan Drone" scheme on February 1, 2022[37] and associated subsidies to government entities and kisan bodies provided much needed funding for the procurement and use of drones[38] The Indian government also launched the PLI scheme for drone and drone component manufacturing on September 30, 2021. These initiatives are going to impact not only the drone industry but also the aviation manufacturing industry.

The above drone initiatives, like the aviation manufacturing initiatives of the past, are aimed at supporting the domestic drone manufacturing industry; however, the same initiatives could have an adverse impact on the unmanned and manned aviation industry unless we understand the nuances of the policy contradictions and take corrective measures. These policies could be exploited by motivated companies comprising both Indian companies assembling drones as well as those acting as proxies of FOEMs. Also, data collated by critical components such as closed loop autopilots for drones is vulnerable to exploitation by the FOEMs and adversaries.[39]

The absence of a policy link between procurement of IDDM drones under the Kisan Drone initiative, the lack of incentive for IDDM drones vis-à-vis 'Make in India' (assemble in India) drones under the PLI scheme and the potential of drone manufacturers (assemblers) importing drone components (despite the ban on the import of drones) with little or no value addition, and supplying them in large numbers, could have an adverse impact on IDDM drones; and, thus, on India's goal of developing an innovation-based indigenous aviation manufacturing industry.

Policy on Assessment of Indigenous Content: There is no scientific mechanism for assessing the indigenous content as currently indigenous content assessment is being ascertained on the basis of cost. This allows foreign products to be projected as indigenous ones without significant technological value addition, which adversely impacts India's *Atmanirbhar Bharat* mission.

Indian Human Resource and Its Peculiarities

India struggled to develop aviation and other systems in the past while many Indians around the world continued to lead the development of aviation and defence technologies for the FOEMs, academic institutions and other entities. Many Indians spearheading the R&D organisations of leading countries, including the US, indicates that Indians do not lack capability—the deficiency is in the ecosystem and human resources management. Indian public sector entities faced criticism, and the private sector was viewed as a solution to all the problems. This approach needs to be revisited. Therefore, there is a need to analyse this subject in detail.

DRDO Versus DARPA

DRDO is often criticised for its large number of laboratories, excessive manpower and underperformance versus the lean and productive Defence Advanced Research Projects Agency (DARPA) of the USA. However, the comparison between the two is being done without understanding the challenges and limitations of DRDO versus DARPA. DRDO has been burdened with a number of projects, with only meagre allotment of funds. The lack of ownership by the users, the technology denials, funding limitations, public pressure and organisational efficiency have added to its challenges. Even the creation of a DARPA equivalent organisation in India may face similar challenges if the anomalies and challenges faced by DRDO are not addressed. Therefore, a critical review of its challenges is needed to arrive at a viable solution.

Removing Reservation and Other Reforms in DRDO for Excellence: Despite being India's premier institution, entrusted with the development of niche technologies, DRDO follows reservations in recruitment and promotion of scientists. In addition, DRDO reforms proposed by the Dr. P Rama Rao Committee in 2007, such as establishing a Board of Research for Advanced Defence Studies (BRADS) to function on the lines of DARPA need to be revisited and, where required, adopted, to make India *atmanirbhar* in niche and innovative technologies.[40]

DPSUs Versus Private Sector

DPSUs and the private sector differ in focus on critical and non-critical sectors, work cultures and business practices, and both have their strengths and limitations. China understood the strengths and weaknesses of both institutions, and used the strengths of both to build its defence ecosystem that contributed to reduction in costs, enhanced efficiency and marketing of defence, commercial aviation and UAV systems. It brought a corporate culture to the Aviation Industry Corporation of China (AVIC), sent personnel for higher education in Chinese and international universities to learn management, corporate and production practices and employed them successfully for strategic defence business. In India, the private sector is being seen as a replacement for the public sector, whose ability to replace the DPSUs is yet to be understood and explored. Therefore, a realistic assessment of the capabilities and limitations of the private sector is needed to fully exploit its potential.

Private Sector in R&D: Opportunities and Caution

The Indian DRDO and DPSUs were always under the scanner of the stakeholders, users, and the public due to their inability to design, develop and manufacture defence and aeronautics technologies within a given timeframe, and for exceeding costs. The private sector was considered to be a potential alternative to the DRDO and DPSUs.

Opportunities: The Indian Ministry of Defence took an unprecedented step in March 2022 and earmarked 18 defence platforms for design and development by the private industry, which were proposed to be developed under the following schemes:

(a) Fourteen platforms under the Make-I category in which up to 70 per cent funding would be provided by the government.

(b) Two platforms under the Special Purpose Vehicle (SPV) programme in which industry would be encouraged to take up design and development in collaboration with the DRDO, DPSUs and other government organisations.

(c) One platform under the iDEX programme.
(d) One platform under the Make-II category.

This is a departure from the past as private sector companies were seldom involved in government-funded defence technology development programmes.[41] Out of the 18 platforms, four platforms are related to UAS and CUAS systems comprising HALE UAS, naval shipborne UAS, directed energy and laser weapons, which indicates the significance and priority accorded to the development of UAS and CUAS technologies. In addition, earmarking of 68 per cent of the defence capital budget for procurement from domestic manufacturers is a positive step in supporting domestic industry.[42] Indian companies had demonstrated their capability to develop high performance, globally competitive but small category low-cost UAS and soft kill CUAS systems. The above initiatives involving development of more capable and larger UAS; hard kill and hybrid CUAS systems; and other high-technology systems would require much higher funding to meet the requirements of the Indian defence forces.

Caution: There is a need to exercise caution and ensure that the potential of the private sector is leveraged optimally while maintaining realistic expectations, taking into account their strengths, challenges and limitations. Indian start-ups and MSMEs comprise a powerhouse of innovation as they pursue design and development with significant technology gains; however, for every successful Indian start-up, there are many that fail to convert their designs into successful products due to various reasons. These factors should be examined and remedial measures introduced. On the other hand, big private sector companies prefer going for limited R&D on systems that are already at higher Technology Readiness Levels (TRL-6 to 8) or collaboration with the DRDO, DPSUs and FOEMs for local production, with low to medium technology gains to minimise the risks. The investment of Indian private sector companies in R&D and hand-holding of start-ups is limited, which needs to change.

Lessons from First Aviation *Atmanirbhar Bharat* Programme of 1950s and 1960s

India had pursued the path of *Atmanirbhar Bharat* (self-reliant India) in the aeronautics sector for the first time in the 1950s and 1960s with the development of a number of indigenous aircraft including the HT-2 in 1951, Pushpak in 1958, Krishak (HAOP-27) in 1959, Marut (HF-24) fighter aircraft in 1961, and Kiran Mk-1 in 1964. However, the offer of manufacturing the MiG-21 (assembling) by Russia and the Jaguar by the UK, along with the challenges in indigenous design changed the focus from indigenous development to assembling.[43] The indigenous HF-24 engine and aircraft upgrade in the form of the HF-73 aircraft programme were shelved. These choices had an adverse impact on the domestic industry, which took almost five decades to correct.

India's ongoing Second *Atmanirbhar Bharat* mission in aviation is at similar cross-roads. Indian aviation and the UAV industry have a number of innovative projects and products, as discussed earlier in this chapter. While at the same time, FOEMs and assemblers are inviting Indian leaders to inaugurate their assembled products or are willing to lease their products to Indian users for various applications. The difference between indigenously designed and locally assembled is thinning and, therefore, it would be important to look back at past mistakes and reorientate India's approach to the *Atmanirbhar Bharat Mission*. India must not miss this golden opportunity to become an aviation design, development and manufacturing led high-technology, high-value aeronautics hub that would strengthen India's *atmanirbharta* in the aviation mission and make it an air power to reckon with in the coming decades.

Way Forward

The North Atlantic Treaty Organisation (NATO) countries' failure to provide military protection to Ukraine during the Russian attack in March 2022 has reinforced the fact that indigenous capability is the only way to protect a nation's interests. The Make-I and Make-II provisions in the Defence Acquisition Procedure (DAP), launching of the Mehar Baba, iDEX and TDF D&D programmes, the decision of the Indian government to develop 18 defence platforms in collaboration with private sector, earmarking 25 per cent of the defence R&D budget for the private sector in the 2022-23 budget, and launching the PLI scheme for the manufacturing of UAS and UAS components are opportunities that need be leveraged to fill the R&D gaps (Valley of Death) and develop defence systems such as the AMCA, HALE UAS, CUAS and other technologies.[44] The way forward for some of the issues discussed in this chapter for stimulating the domestic industry and making India *atmanirbhar* in aviation, manned and unmanned technologies, is covered in the succeeding section.

Atmanirbhar Bharat: Realising the Elusive Goal

After the break-up of the Soviet Union, a committee headed by Dr. APJ Abdul Kalam proposed a reduction of defence imports from 70 percent to 30 percent. The Group of Ministers after the Kargil War in 1999, Kelkar Committee in 2005, Rama Rao Committee in 2008, Sisodia Committee in 2009, Naresh Chandra Committee in 2012 and Dhirendra Singh Committee in 2015 made similar recommendations. However, achieving self-reliance in defence and aviation continues to be an elusive goal. Therefore, the following is proposed to build an *atmanirbhar* and future-ready air power in India:

(a) **Leadership Sensitisation Programme:** India's aviation manufacturing industry suffered during the 1960s and 1970s due to the vulnerability and gullibility of the Indian leadership. Therefore, it is proposed that Indian political, bureaucratic, military, and other central and state administration leaders are sensitised about the capabilities of own industry, innovators, and academia, the dangers of lobbying by the FOEMs and world bodies, the challenges faced by Indian entrepreneurs, technology denials to Indian entities, perception and media management, lessons from the past *Atmanirbhar Bharat Abhyiyan* and the desirable approach for the success of the second *Atmanirbhar Bharat Mission* in Aviation.

(b) **Organisational Reforms:** Reorganise the MoCA by establishing an R&D Directorate[45], creating provision for the MoCA taking ownership of indigenous D&D projects and, where required, its personnel becoming members of design teams.

(c) **Policy and Organisational Reforms:** Introduce a core policy, organisational, human resource and other reforms in the Ministry of Civil Aviation, Ministry of Defence, the defence forces, DRDO, DGCA, DPSUs, etc. as elucidated in this chapter.[46]

(d) **Aviation Manufacturing Plans:** Make 10[47] and 20-year aviation development and manufacturing plans, with the requisite funding, stakeholders' involvement and accountability. The MoCA and MoD should lead their respective verticals with the DRDO, DPSUs and industry as partners, as required.

(e) **Airspace Integration Plan:** Make 5 and 10-year plans for manned-unmanned aircraft integration in the Indian national airspace. The MoCA (Airports Authority of India - AAI) and the proposed R&D Directorate should lead the execution of this plan.

(f) **Technological Initiatives:** The MoCA, in collaboration with the MeitY, should launch technological initiatives to develop technologies and systems that are needed to facilitate safe manned-unmanned operations in the civil airspace as well as during combat operations.

(g) **Procurement:** Leverage civil aviation procurements for aviation technology acquisition as per a government-industry joint procurement mechanism, as proposed in the roadmap in India's quest for UAVs and its challenges.[48]

(h) **Export:** Provide diplomatic and policy support and facilitate export of IDDM civil and defence drone, UAS and CUAS systems.

(i) **Introduce the "IDDM Clause" in Aviation, Civil Aviation, UAS and Drone Certification:** Introduce a special IDDM certification clause for certification of civil aircraft, IDDM aircraft components, IDDM drones, IDDM drone components" in aviation, and UAS certification by the DGCA and drone certification by QCI/DGCA.

(j) **Overcoming Policy Incoherence Challenges:** India could take initiatives to overcome policy contradictions and incentivise IDDM. These include:

   (a) Formulate a policy for acquisition of IDDM drones by all ministries.

   (b) Introduce classification of IDDM manned and unmanned aircraft during certification systems, sub-systems, software, components and sensors.

   (c) Carry out realistic assessment of the capability of IDDM manufacturers in scaling up manufacturing and give adequate time to domestic industry to scale up before launching popular aviation platform exploitation schemes.

   (d) Provide incentives to IDDM in procurement of manned and unmanned aircraft and their services by all the ministries.

(k) **Ecosystem:** Establish civil aviation, drone and UAS testing, certification and standards bodies to support India's emerging aviation and UAS industry, as discussed in the book *India's Quest for UAVs and Challenges*.[49]

(l) **India Specific Collaborations:** JVs and collaborations with FOEMs must be India-specific in identified areas of technology sub-technology or sub-system wise to support and strengthen indigenous design, development and manufacturing as discussed earlier. These collaborations must be undertaken only after ascertaining system and sub-system-wise Technology Readiness Levels (TRLs)[50] and Manufacturing Readiness Levels (MRLs)[51] of Indian industry.

Bridging the Valley of Death

India has prestigious academic institutions and a pragmatic industry; however, it has been unable to overcome the R&D gaps (i.e. Valley of Death) in the mid-segment of the R&D cycle due to inadequate funding, lack of the private sector's involvement in R&D, lack of users' participation in D&D initiatives as partners, and the missing connect between R&D and the acquisition process. Some of the initiatives that could help in overcoming the challenges of transforming innovative ideas, designs and prototypes in operational products can be addressed by strengthening India's D&D initiatives are discussed below.

iDEX Prime: The proposed enhancement in funding of iDEX to Rs 10 crore under the proposed iDEX Prime should be made industry-friendly with technical oversight and phase-wise outcome assessments.

Phase-II and III of iDEX and Mehar Baba Competitions: Create a provision for conducting the second and third phases of iDEX and Mehar Baba Competitions with funding up to Rs 50 and Rs 100 crore respectively, to upgrade and operationalise products developed during the first phase as well as undertake new high value niche technology development projects. However, there is a need to create an independent and transparent scientific evaluation mechanisms to obtain optimum gains from these competitions.

2nd edition of Mehar Baba: Indian Defence Minister Shri Rajnath Singh launched the second edition of the IAF Mehar Baba Competition on April 6, 2022, to develop a swarm based system to detect foreign objects on aircraft operating surface.[52] The scope of this competition appears to be limited compared to the first Mehar Baba Competition. However, it would be prudent to:

(a) Take forward this initiative by enhancing the scope and funding of the competition.
(b) Create a provision in the DAP for direct acquisition of products developed by the Mehar Baba Competition winners to harness the innovation potential of Indians.

Mehar Baba Equivalent Competitions for the Indian Army and Indian Navy: The Indian Army and Navy (IA and IN) could launch their own Mehar Baba equivalent competitions to develop advanced and innovative systems.

Innovation Centres for iDEX for Fauji: HQ IDS, IA, IN and IAF may establish/earmark suitable defence innovation centres to support defence personnel participating in iDEX for Fauji. The centres would provide technology, mentoring, funding support and industry connect to selected defence personnel.

Delegation of Financial Powers to Defence Services (DFPDS) Provisions for Funding R&D: The DFPDS-2021 provisions for R&D should be optimally leveraged by the Services HQ and HQ IDS to indigenously develop high technology, high value critical systems that could provide the technological edge. The Department of Military Affairs (DMA) may need to take the lead in encouraging the defence forces to optimally leverage DFPDS provisions to expeditiously adopt capabilities available in the civil sector as well as harness the innovative potential of innovators for the building of niche and innovative defence technologies.

Procurement

D&D Competition Linked Procurement: Introduction of a clause in the DAP for procurement of products developed by the winners of iDEX, Mahar Baba and equivalent D&D competitions is recommended.

Preference to iDEX and Mehar Baba Participants in Procurement: The defence forces and other government agencies should also give preference in procurement to indigenous products designed under the Mehar Baba and iDEX Competitions.

Preference to IDDM in Procurement and Services in Civil-Military Contracts: Companies offering IDDM aviation, UAS and drones or services should be given preference for procurement and Services' contracts by all Ministries.

Positive Indigenisation List for Other Ministries: It is recommended that like the MoD and MeitY, the Ministry of Finance (MoF) may issue a positive indigenisation list that would become applicable to all other ministries. Also, the MoD's positive indigenisation list comprising dual use products or the ones used by other ministries including IDDM UAS and CUAS should be made applicable to all other ministries.

D&D in the Defence Forces

Some of the measures to improve the contribution of the defence forces in D&D projects and enhance synergy with the DRDO, DPSUs and industry are deliberated upon in the succeeding paragraphs. The contribution of the defence forces in D&D projects, undertaken in collaboration with the Indian public sector and private industry may be increased on the lines of the military design organisations of the US, China and other leading nations

Users in D&D Projects: The policies, procedures and other mechanisms are needed for including technical personnel, with the relevant design qualifications from the defence Services in the design teams of D&D projects as partners.

R&D Vertical in HQ IDS: It is recommended to establish an R&D vertical in HQ IDS to bring synergy to D&D programmes, expedite the development of niche defence technologies, and reduce development timelines and costs.

Strengthening of R&D Verticals in the Services: The Army Design Bureau (ADB) of the IA, Directorate of Naval Design (DND) of the IN, and Directorate of Aerospace Design (DAD) of the IAF[53] be strengthened and oriented to lead or steer niche technology projects and their personnel be involved as members of D&D teams of indigenous projects undertaken in collaboration with DRDO, DPSUs and industry.

Assessment of Indigenous Content

Mechanisms such as Systems Development Life Cycle (SDLC) audit or other scientific assessment mechanisms, as deemed appropriate, may be introduced in DAP to scientifically assess indigenous content to prevent the supply of assembled products as IDDM products under the Make-II category, and derailing India's *Atmanirbhar Bharat* mission.

IP Sharing Policy

The MoD and MeitY may standardise the IP sharing policy between the iDEX, Mehar Baba and TDF participants, and the sponsoring government agency, defence forces, DRDO, Public Sector Units (PSUs) to protect the interests of the industry and innovators.

Core Issues

This chapter has examined some of the current opportunities, challenges as well as the way forward. However, it would be prudent to revisit core issues and recommendations made in the chapter "A Roadmap for a Robust Aviation Ecosystem in India" of the book *India's Quest for UAVs and Challenges*, and incorporate the relevant ones while articulating the trajectory of *atmanirbhar* India in air power. A few critical recommendations are given below:[54]

(a) Establishment of a National Aeronautics Commission.[55]
(b) Establishment of a National Aeronautics Innovation Assessment, Certification and Quality Assurance Council (AICQA).[56]
(c) Establishment of a National Aviation Testing Agency.[57]
(d) Establishment of a National Aeronautical University.[58]

Conclusion

The challenges, limitations and vulnerabilities of the ongoing second *Atmarnirbhar Bharat* mission in aviation manufacturing are similar to the ones faced in the first *Atmanirbhar Bharat* mission during the 1950s and 1960s. Therefore, the lessons from the first aviation manufacturing revolution would be useful in correcting the trajectory of the second *Atmanirbhar Bharat* mission. These can be supplemented by in-depth and purposeful research and analysis of the challenges being faced by the aviation, UAS and drone manufacturing industries.

The Indian aviation industry has been at the receiving end for decades due to its flaws and limitations as well as the adverse perceptions created by people with motivated agendas. The delays and failures in the indigenous design and development programmes, especially in the development of the ALH, LCH, LCA and Kaveri jet engine are well known and often criticised; however, challenges faced by the DRDO, DPSUs and the industry in their design and development phases are rarely examined in-depth, understood corrective measures instituted.

The unwillingness to take ownership, lack of in-depth research, lack of understanding of the nuances of aviation technology development and the capabilities of own industry, lack of involvement of stakeholders in technology development projects, working in silos, policy and organisational drawbacks and external influences are some of the key challenges in the *Atmanirbhar Bharat* mission in aviation manufacturing. The biggest challenges to it would come from, firstly, Indian nationals not those involved in familiar with the strengths and weaknesses of Indian policies and ecosystem, and establishing aviation and UAS assembling factories for FOEMs; and, secondly, Indians and non-resident Indians working for FOEMs, world bodies and trying to create space for them in establishing their aviation and drone assembling companies and selling them in India at the cost of domestic manufacturers and innovators. The biggest vulnerability of India would be its leadership which could be incorrectly convinced about the capability in India to carry out the *Atmanirbhar Bharat* mission.

India's two principal adversaries are becoming increasingly hostile, while China's economic and military strength is increasing and the options for India to acquire niche technologies to maintain deterrence are reducing. Therefore, India would need indigenous capability to counter the emerging challenges in a cost-effective manner. Also, it would need to address the technological asymmetry with China by correcting anomalies and filling gaps in its RD&A cycle. The strengthening of D&D programmes, building R&D verticals in the defence forces, involving users (defence forces personnel) in D&D including as members of D&D projects, leveraging of DFPDS provisions by the defence forces, scientific assessment of indigenous content, and linking D&D programmes with procurement are some of the measures that are essential to correct India's RD&A trajectory and become *atmanirbhar* in critical defence and aeronautics technologies.

Indian aviation and the UAS manufacturing industries, with a number of indigenous design and development programmes, are at a crucial phase. They have the ability to transform into manufacturing and innovation-led high-technology, high-value industries of India. Indian policy-makers and stakeholders would have to ensure that their policies, programmes and decisions do not deviate from the core principles of the *Atmanirbhar Bharat* mission. India would need to take the lead in aviation, UAS and CUAS technologies to build robust air power that would not only prepare it for future challenges posed by its adversaries but also deter them from indulging in unwanted adventurism.

Notes

1. Colonel Philip S Mellinger, USAF, "Ten Propositions Regarding Air Power", Air Power History and Museum Programme, 1995. https://media.defense.gov/2010/May/25/2001330281/-1/-1/0/AFD-100525-026.pdf. Accessed on January 1, 2022.
2. "*Atmanirbhar Bharat*" is a Hindi term, which means self-reliant India.
3. R.K. Narang *India's Quest for UAVs and Challenges* (New Delhi: KW Publishers Pvt Ltd. India, 2020), pp. 125 to 202.
4. Ibid., pp. 125 to 202.
5. Unified Payments Interface (UPI) is a system that powers multiple bank accounts into a single mobile application (of any participating bank), merging several banking features, seamless fund routing and merchant payments into one hood. https://www.npci.org.in/what-we-do/upi/product-overview. Accessed on May 23, 2022.
6. "Challenges of Indian MRO Industry", *India Foundation Journal*, Vol.VIII, Issue No. 1, January-February 2020. https://indiafoundation.in/wp-content/uploads/2019/12/9-Gp-Capt-RK-Narang-VM.pdf. Accessed on May 7, 2022.
7. Narang, n. 3.
8. "India Formalises Acquisition of 56 Airbus C295 Aircraft", September 24, 2021. https://www.airbus.com/en/newsroom/press-releases/2021-09-india-formalises-acquisition-of-56-airbus-c295-aircraft. Accessed on May 14, 2022.
9. Narang, n. 3, pp. 302-304.
10. Summary of Union Budget 2022-23, Ministry of Finance, February 1, 2022. https://pib.gov.in/PressReleasePage.aspx?PRID=1794167, accessed on March 12, 2022.
11. "Union Minister Scindia Launches Drone Experience Studio, says India to Become Global Drone Hub by 2030", *The Economic Times, Auto.com*, May 10, 2022. https://auto.economictimes.indiatimes.com/news/industry/union-minister-scindia-

launches-drone-experience-studio-says-india-to-become-global-drone-hub-by-2030/91473336. Accessed on May 15, 2022.

12. Technology Development Board, Department of Science and Technology, Ministry of Science and Technology, http://tdb.gov.in/. Accessed on May 23, 2022.
13. Pia Krishnankutty, "Why India's Drone Market Could Become a Multi-Billion Dollar Industry in Next Decade", *The Print,* July 23, 2021. https://theprint.in/india/governance/why-indias-drone-market-could-become-a-multi-billion-dollar-industry-in-next-decade/700817/. Accessed on January 10, 2022.
14. GAGAN increases the accuracy of the Global Navigation Satellite System (GNSS)
15. Manoj Kumar Jha, "DRDO's Rustom-II UAV Has Reached the Target Altitude of 28,000 ft; No Need To Import ISR Drones: G Satheesh Reddy", *Business World,* April 14, 2022. https://www.businessworld.in/article/DRDO-s-Rustom-II-UAV-Has-Reached-The-Target-Altitude-Of-28-000-ft-No-Need-to-Import-ISR-Drones-G-Satheesh-Reddy/13-03-2022-422723/. Accessed on March 14, 2022.
16. WATCH: TAXI TRIALS OF INDIA'S SWIFT UNMANNED COMBAT AERIAL VEHICLE DEMONSTRATOR, HTTP://WWW.INDIANDEFENSENEWS.IN/2021/10/WATCH-TAXI-TRIALS-OF-INDIAS-SWIFT.HTML. Accessed on April 14, 2022.
17. "Indian Army signs a $20 Million Contract with ideaForge to Procure SWITCH UAV", *UAS News,* January 14, 2021. https://www.suasnews.com/2021/01/indian-army-signs-a-20-million-contract-with-ideaforge-to-procure-switch-uav/. Accessed on January 28, 2022.
18. Snehesh Alex Philip, "As Stand-off with China Continues, Army Orders More India-made Drones for LAC Surveillance", *The Print,* January 24, 2022. https://theprint.in/india/as-stand-off-with-china-continues-army-orders-more-india-made-drones-for-lac-surveillance/811619/. Accessed on January 28, 2022.
19. Huma Siddiqui, "Made in India Drones to do Surveillance for the Indian Army", *Financial Express,* March, 3, 2022. https://www.financialexpress.com/defence/made-in-india-drones-to-do-surveillance-for-the-indian-army/2450401/. Accessed on March 10, 2022.
20. Aksheev Thakur, "IAF Announces List of Winners of Mehar Baba Swarm Drone Competition, *The Indian Express,* October 25, 2021. https://indianexpress.com/article/cities/bangalore/iaf-announces-winners-mehar-baba-swarm-drone-competition-7588658/. Accessed on January 26, 2022.
21. Andre Haider, "A Comprehensive Approach to Countering Unmanned Aircraft Systems", Joint Air Power Competence Centre, August 2019. https://www.japcc.org/c-uas-research-development-and-acquisition-of-counter-uas-technologies/. Accessed on January 14, 2022.
22. Technology Readiness Levels (TRLs) is a commonly used scientific assessment tool to assess the maturity of a given system individually.
23. Muller, et. al., n. 22.
24. Ibid.
25. "Innovation for Defence Excellence (iDEX)". https://idex.gov.in/. Accessed on November 13, 2021.

26. "Self-Reliance in Defence Sector", Ministry of Defence, December 10, 2021. https://pib.gov.in/PressReleseDetailm.aspx?PRID=1780099. Accessed on May 11, 2022.
27. RMO India, @DefenceMinIndia, twitter.com, February 25, 2022. https://twitter.com/DefenceMinIndia/status/1497132924033908739?s=20&t=_sFBL3UWvUvHX7QJfcL5-A. Accessed on February 27, 2022.
28. "iDEX for Fauji", https://idex.gov.in/idex4fauji. Accessed on November 13, 2021.
29. Thakur, n. 21.
30. "Technology Development Fund (TDF)". https://tdf.drdo.gov.in/scheme. Accessed on February 8, 2022.
31. "US Think-Tank RMI's Swift Rise to Become Niti Aayog's go-to Cleantech Advisor", *The Ken,* May 23, 2022. https://the-ken.com/story/us-think-tank-rmis-swift-rise-to-become-niti-aayogs-go-to-cleantech-advisor/. Accessed on May 25, 2022
32. "Schedule-9 of IA, Schedule-13 of Indian Navy and Schedule-9 of AF Act". https://www.mod.gov.in/sites/default/files/DFPDS9721.pdf. Accessed on Februry 15, 2022.
33. "Government of India has Taken Series of Reforms to Make India a Global Drone Hub by 2030", Ministry of Civil Aviation, April 20, 2022. https://pib.gov.in/PressReleaseIframePage.aspx?PRID=1818424. Accessed on May 8, 2022.
34. BEYOND, *FAA.* https://www.faa.gov/uas/programs_partnerships/beyond/. Accessed on May 15, 2022.
35. "Kalam's Word of Caution on Make in India", *Business Standard,* October, 18. 2015, https://www.business-standard.com/article/current-affairs/kalam-s-word-of-caution-on-make-in-india-115101800181_1.html. Accessed on May 13, 2022.
36. "Notification No 54/ 2015-2020 under Notification of ITC (HS), 2022-Schedule-1 (Import Policy), Director General Foreign Trade (DGFT)", Ministry of Commerce and Foreign Trade, dated February 9, 2022. https://content.dgft.gov.in/Website/dgftprod/7d5fd1eb-ad39-4c99-b760-014223657469/Eng-Notification%2054%20dated%209%20Feb%202022%20ITC(HS)%202022%20_with%20Annexures.pdf. Accessed on May 16, 2022.
37. "Budget 2022-2023, Speech of Nirmala Sitaraman, Minister of Finance", February 1, 2022. https://www.indiabudget.gov.in/doc/budget_speech.pdf. Accessed on May 16, 2022.
38. "Samvad with Scindia", Jyotidaritya Madhorao Scindia, May 17, 2022. https://www.youtube.com/watch?v=CftRVNaSx6E. Accessed on May 19, 2022.
39. S E, Mallikarjun Co-Founder Sierra Aerospace. https://www.linkedin.com/feed/update/urn:li:activity: 6931657249283002368?commentUrn=urn%3Ali%3Acomment %3A%28activity% 3A6931657249283002368%2C6931876272465739776%29. Accessed on May 16, 2022.
40. Narang, n. 3, pp. 340-350.
41. "18 Military Platforms including Directed Energy Weapons and Long Range UAVs to be Developed by Domestic Industry: Govt", *Swarajya,* March 12, 2022. https://swarajyamag.com/defence/18-military-platforms-including-directed-

energy-weapons-and-long-range-uav-to-be-developed-by-domestic-industry-govt. Accessed on March 12, 2022.

42. "Summary of Union Budget 2022-23, Ministry of Finance", February 1, 2022. https://pib.gov.in/PressReleasePage.aspx?PRID=1794167. Accessed on March 12, 2022.
43. Narang, n. 3, p. 347.
44. "Para 87-88, Speech of Nirmala Sitharaman, Budget 2022-23", Government of India, February 1, 2022. https://www.indiabudget.gov.in/doc/budget_speech.pdf. Accessed on February 14, 2022.
45. Narang, n. 3, pp. 413-414.
46. Ibid., pp. 340-373.
47. Ibid., pp. 379-380
48. Ibid., pp. 416-417
49. Ibid., pp. 385-390.
50. "Technology Readiness Levels (TRLs)", NASA. https://www.nasa.gov/directorates/heo/scan/engineering/technology/technology_readiness_level. Accessed on May 25, 2022.
51. "Manufacturing Readiness Levels (MRLs)", US Department of Defence, May 2011. https://www.dodmrl.com/MRL_Deskbook_V2.pdf. Accessed on May 25, 2022.
52. "Rajnath Singh Launches Second Edition of Swarm Drone Competiton for Start-ups", *The Hindu,* April 6, 2022. https://www.thehindu.com/news/national/rajnath-singh-launches-second-edition-of-swarm-drone-competition-for-start-ups/article65296709.ece?homepage=true. Accessed on May 16, 2022.
53. "Nowhere In the World is such A Commitment of 450 Aircraft And This Depicts IAF's Plan For Capability Building: IAF Chief VR Chaudhary", *BW Businessworld,* April 11, 2022. https://www.businessworld.in/article/Nowhere-In-The-World-Is-Such-A-Commitment-Of-450-Aircraft-And-This-Depicts-IAF-s-Plan-For-Capability-Building-IAF-Chief-VR-Chaudhari/30-10-2021-410569/. Accessed on April 11, 2022.
54. Narang, n. 3, pp. 281-420.
55. Ibid., pp. 380-384.
56. Ibid., pp. 385-389.
57. Ibid., pp. 389-390.
58. Ibid., pp. 409-411.

Editors and Contributors

EDITORS

Air Vice Marshal **Anil Golani** (Retd) is a Qualified Flying Instructor and an Instrument Rating Instructor and Examiner, commissioned into the Fighter stream of the IAF in December 1982. Fully Ops on the erstwhile Ajeet and Jaguar aircraft. Raised and commanded the first Harpy squadron of the Indian Air Force. Commanded an Air Defence Direction Centre and an operational base. One of the few to have served in senior ranks in both the Joint Services Commands of the country, Andaman & Nicobar Command as the Air Force Component Commander and Strategic Forces Command as the Chief Staff Officer (Air Vector). The other joint services appointments include Air Officer Commanding Maritime Air Operations in Mumbai and Chief Instructor, Air Force, at Defence Services Staff College, Wellington. He has done the Staff Course, Higher Air Command Course and a year's course in International Security & Strategy at the Royal College of Defence Studies, London. Superannuated from service in November 2019.

Presently working as an Additional Director General, Centre for Air Power Studies, New Delhi. Likes to play golf, read and write on issues concerning air power, security and strategy, and national interest.

Group Captain **Vijay Shankar Rana** is a Senior Fellow at the Centre for Air Power Studies. He was commissioned in the fighter stream of Indian Air Force on 13 June 1992. He is an alumnus of Tactics and Air Combat Development Establishment and College of Air Warfare. He has rich experience of operational flying on modern and legacy fighter aircraft of the IAF. During his career, he has held many significant field and staff appointments at Operational Command, HQ IDS and at Air Headquarters.

The appointments include Commanding Officer of a frontline fighter aircraft squadron, Station Commander of an Operational base in Andaman and Nicobar Command, Director of Electronic Intelligence, Director of International Defence Cooperation and Liaison, Director of Doctrine and Head of Strategic and Operational Planning. In recognition of his meritorious service the Officer has been awarded Commendation by the Air Officer Commanding-in-Chief. He is also a recipient of Mention-in-Dispatches.

CONTRIBUTORS

Air Marshal **Anil Chopra,** PVSM, AVSM, VM, VSM (Retd) was a fighter pilot, test pilot, and a pioneer of the Mirage-2000 fleet. He commanded a Mirage-2000 Squadron and the Aircraft and Systems Testing Establishment (ASTE). He was the Team Leader of the MiG-21 Bison upgrade project in Russia. He has commanded operational air bases in both the Western and Eastern Sectors. He was head of the IAF in J&K, and head of the inspections of the IAF. He retired as Air Officer Personnel. He has been a member of the Armed Forces Tribunal, and a member of the Executive Council of Jawaharlal Nehru University (JNU). An avid writer and author. Currently, he is Director General, Centre for Air Power Studies (CAPS), New Delhi.

Air Marshal **TD Joseph** AVSM VM VSM (Retd) is a retired fighter pilot of the IAF. Winner of the coveted "Nawanagar Sword of Honour", he has vast experience in operations, training and leadership positions in the IAF. He is an alumnus of National Defence Academy, Defence Services Staff College, Royal College of Defence Studies and King's College London. He has authored a book titled "Winning India's Next War: The Role of Aerospace Power".

Air Marshal **Anil Khosla,** PVSM, AVSM, VM (Retd) retired as the Vice Chief of the Air Staff in Apr 2019. A fighter pilot, he wields the pen with equal adeptness as he can wield the joystick. He holds two MPhil degrees on defence and strategic studies and is currently pursuing a PhD on China. An ardent blogger (Air Marshal's Perspective) and Sudoku player, he has pursued the latter 10 times up to the national level.

Group Captain (Dr.) **Rajiv Kumar Narang,** Vayu Sena Medal (Retd) is a pilot, author and policy analyst, who took over as Director-Strategic Initiatives at Drone Federation of India in 2021. He is M Sc in Defence & Strategic Studies from Madras University and Ph.D in International Relations from Jawahar Lal Nehru University. He authored a book titled "India's Quest for UAVs and Challenges" and number of research papers on aviation, drones, drone regulations, counter drone systems, Make in India & military history.

Air Vice Marshal **S Bhanoji Rao** AVSM, VSM (Retd) has contributed immensely in the field of air armament. He worked for 14 years in Operations, Plans and Maintenance branches of Air HQ. During his tenures, most of the policies on weapon utilization philosophies and integration of weapons on multiple platforms were formulated. He has also worked as Commanding Officer of Air Armament QA agency of DGAQA and as a Team Leader in Anti-Ballistic Missile Programme. He retired as ACAS (Weapons) on 30 Nov 2019.

Group Captain **TH Anand Rao** is a Senior Fellow at the Centre for Air Power Studies. He has authored a book titled 'India's Space Security Dilemma', released in 2021. He has written many articles on issues concerning 'space security' and has been a panellist on national and international seminars. He has served in many operational and staff appointments in the IAF. He has flown Jaguar and MiG-21 aircraft. He is a Qualified Flying Instructor and has flown various trainer aircraft.

Mr **Abhishek Saxena** is a Research Associate (Nuclear Studies Group) at the Centre for Air Power Studies (CAPS). His research interest focuses on nuclear strategy, nuclear proliferation, and the implications of emerging technologies on national security. Before joining CAPS, he worked as a Research Intern at the Observer Research Foundation (ORF), New Delhi. Abhishek has a Master's degree in Politics and International Studies from the School of International Studies, Jawaharlal Nehru University (JNU), New Delhi and B.Sc. (Hons) in Chemistry from Kirori Mal College, University of Delhi.

Air Marshal **RK Sharma** PVSM AVSM VM (Retd) was commissioned in IAF Fighter stream in 1975. A Qualified flying instructor and an Experimental Test Pilot with extensive experience in testing of prototype airborne weapons and systems. He was Project Director of the LCA flight test programme and has closely worked with DRDO and HAL. He has held appointments of Deputy Chief Of Air Staff at Air HQ, Air Officer Commanding in Chief Eastern Air Command and Vice Chief of Air Staff, before Superannuating in May 2015.

Air Marshal **Daljit Singh** PVSM AVSM VM (Retd) was commissioned in the Fighter stream of the Indian Air Force, in June 1976. He was Director General (Air Operations) at Air HQ, and retired as AOC-in C, SWAC IAF in October 2014. The Air Officer regularly participates in International Air Defence and Electronic Warfare seminars and has written articles on EW and AD in various journals. The Air Marshal has been an active member of Association of Old Crows and has delivered Keynote Addresses during International EW seminars.

Index